GERMAN AIR POWER IN WORLD WAR I

GERMAN AIR POWER
IN WORLD WAR I

John H. Morrow, Jr.

University of Nebraska Press

Lincoln and London

Library of Congress Cataloging in Publication Data
Morrow, John Howard, 1944–
    German air power in World War I.

    Bibliography: p.
    Includes index.
    1. World War, 1914–1918—Aerial operations, German.   2. Aeronautics,
Military—Germany—History—20th century. I. Title.
D604.M64   940.54′4943   81-11588
ISBN 0-8032-3076-1   AACR2

To my parents, Ann Rowena and John, Sr.,
with love and gratitude

Contents

Illustrations

CHARTS

Preface

THIS STUDY, the first scholarly work to examine German heavier-than-air military aviation during and immediately after World War I, is the culmination of an abiding interest in early German air power and the result of dissatisfaction with previous approaches to the subject. Most studies of German military aeronautics have emphasized World War II, while slighting or ignoring developments before 1919. Furthermore, through a romanticized concentration on the heroic exploits of aces, popular aviation and military literature has perpetuated the erroneous image that the air war bore little significance for the more basic events on land. This book, framed from the perspective of military-industrial relations and industrial mobilization, demonstrates a greater importance of aviation in World War I than has hitherto been believed.

Well-written scholarly approaches to World War I aviation history have much to offer, not merely to scholars but also to the wider interested public, but military book clubs and large publishing houses shy away from such offerings, preferring to repackage and reissue the same old anecdotes and exploits. Old wine in new bottles remains old wine. Yet the wine analogy should not be pressed too far, as many wines grow better with age. The same historical anecdotes do not, especially when they perpetuate notions that should have been revised long ago. I hope that this work will enable readers to see the topic of German air power in World War I—its evolution, successes and failures, and the molders of its destiny—in a new light.

I am grateful to a number of organizations and individuals for their assistance. Grants from the Germanistic Society of America, the University of Pennsylvania, and the German Academic Exchange Service enabled me to spend the year 1969–70 in Germany; and summer stipends from the National Endowment for the Humanities in 1972 and the University of Tennessee in 1974 allowed me to complete the research in Vienna. A further grant from the University of Tennessee assisted the publication of this book. Drs. Sandhofer and Fleischer of the Military Archive in Freiburg, Dr. Harald Jäger of the Bavarian War Archive in Munich, and the staffs of the Military History Research Office Library and of the Federal Archive in Koblenz generously made the necessary documents on imperial German aviation available to me, as did Robert Feinfurter of the Austrian War Archive in Vienna with documents on Austro-Hungarian aviation. Peter Grosz most hospitably opened his private collection of documents and photographs. Harold D. Hastings graciously answered my request for pictures, and James Laux my request for offprints of his articles on French aviation. Jan Doyle diligently and expertly typed the original manuscript, and Carmen Lee the revisions. Finally, I should like to thank my parents, Ann Rowena and John, Sr.; my wife, Diane; and my two children, Kieran and Evan. My parents have stood by me through the years, and my dedication of this book to them is a small token of my appreciation for what they have done. My wife, Diane, has served variously and gratuitously as research assistant, proofreader, editor, and general adviser. To Kieran, my six-year-old daughter, and Evan, my three-year-old son, I owe thanks for their "assistance" in typing my drafts of the manuscript and their cooperation, which allowed me to work at home.

GERMAN AIR POWER IN WORLD WAR I

Introduction

THE WAR OF 1914–18 evokes a single image, one of senseless carnage, of a mass of humanity bludgeoning itself to death with modern technology. By 1916 apprehension of a war with a life of its own, beyond man's power to control, characterized the growing despair over a seemingly endless conflict. The war became a monstrous mechanism, the Great Sausage Machine, as British troops so aptly labeled it, because of the capacity of industrial society to mobilize and then pulverize masses of humanity. Perhaps awed by their armies of unparalleled size, generals proceeded to squander them heedlessly, as if bent on destroying those masses that enabled a warfare that they neither understood nor knew how to win. Skill made little difference, in particular on the decisive western front. What mattered were machine guns, artillery, shells, and more shells, to shred and decimate the men caught in five hundred miles of hell from the Swiss frontier to the North Sea. For the soldier consigned to this inferno, death was impersonal, ordinary, capricious.

That image of the war is contradicted by one weapon, the most technologically revolutionary of all. Like a winged steed, the airplane freed the aviator from the sodden, mean, and undefined mass of humanity that struggled rooted to the earth, just as the knight's charger once had. Death in the sunlit realm seemed a personal matter. Individual skill became important once again. The aviator appeared to have control over his destiny. Ironically, the most modern of inventions fostered the preservation of the most atavistic notions of warfare, of chivalry, honor, and of individual courage. It is no wonder that the innumerable accounts of World War I aviation invariably have a heroic air and that the greatest individual heroes of the war are its airmen. The Red Baron, Manfred von

1

Richthofen, is far more familiar than the best known of World War I generals.

Studies of World War I aviation fall essentially into three categories: accounts of individual figures, primarily fighter aces and, to a much lesser extent, other aviators and aviation entrepreneurs; highly detailed technical reference works on warplanes; and military and aviation histories, which recount the progress of the air war at the front.[1] Yet all these approaches present only a partial picture of the significance of aviation to World War I. The heroic accounts and the military histories give the same impression: that the air war was peripheral and thus essentially unimportant. The exploits of individual fighting men logically could have had little consequence in mass warfare, so the air arm is essentially relegated to the role of providing heroes to raise the morale of soldiers and civilians. Military histories concentrate on the ground war and denigrate the importance of industrial production, while aviation historians have focused on the air force's role at the battlefront to the near exclusion of industrial production. Existing official histories of German military aviation are incomplete, as World War II curtailed the efforts of the Military Science Department of the Air Force (Kriegswissenschaftliche Abteilung der Luftwaffe) to complete an official history of the first war. Even those studies that might seem more pertinent to the industry, the popular accounts of aviation entrepreneurs, fail to examine production in the context of industrial mobilization.

Yet industrial mobilization is the dimension that welds all the participants in aviation—the industrialist, the general, and the aviator—into a coherent whole. Every warplane was a product of compromise among frontline requirements, technological ideals, and the realities of production. At the front aviators fought and died in their craft; in the rear the aircraft manufacturers sought to give them more and better ones. At the top, the aviation command set the tasks for the air service, which determined the requirements for industrial production, and its coordination of front and rear, of military and civilian, and of flight units and aircraft industry determined the outcome of the war effort in aviation.

Only the study of industrial mobilization shows the true value of the airplane in the war. The special position accorded to the aircraft industry from 1915 onwards, and particularly during the programs of total mobilization after October 1916, contradicts previous assertions of the peripheral significance of the air weapon in World War I. The armed forces' mobilization of the aircraft industry was a significant aspect of the First World War, because it was the ultimate test of the military's ability to intervene effectively in the industrial and technological spheres. Unlike previous weapons, the air weapon required constant innovation and the rapid expansion of production, and the consequent tension between quality and quantity plagued the military throughout the war. The precondition for the emergence of the airplane as a weapon was the military's energetic action in the industrial sphere; and contrary to previous belief, the German High Command decided in 1915 that the airplane's future significance lay in its use en masse. This decision, and the ensuing mobilization of the aircraft industry, enabled the emergence of the air arm in 1916. Knowledge of this early awareness of the airplane's value in mass warfare refutes the popular conception that the airplane was a weapon of individual, not mass, warfare that was unimportant to the course of the larger war.

Study of the armed forces' mobilization of the aircraft industry in Germany and Austria-Hungary will increase our knowledge of the critical subject of economic and technological mobilization in the first conflict between industrial nations.[2] More specifically, it will show the complex forces—political, bureaucratic, and personal—affecting military-industrial affairs in the Central European empires. Ultimately, this book will explain how Germany mobilized its aircraft industry successfully and thus maintained an effective air arm against great odds, while Austria-Hungary's aviation efforts failed. Then it will conclude with an examination of the effect of the war's outcome on Central European aviation. Defeat in 1918 brought the collapse of the old imperial structures in Central Europe. The disintegration of the Austro-Hungarian Empire effectively curtailed further developments in aviation in southeastern Europe. Monographs on interwar German aviation treat superficially the period from November 1918 to 1920 and concentrate on clandestine aerial rearmament during the 1920s.[3] Yet the preeminent condition in the years immediately after the war was industrial demobilization and contraction, not planning for limited rearmament. Consequently, examination of the contraction of the German aircraft industry and its connections with the military establishment and with the new civilian parliamentary regime in the postwar period to 1921 will bring the story of Central European aviation both to an end and to a new beginning.

The Origins, 1908–14

Military aviation developed under markedly different conditions in

Austria-Hungary and in Germany. The two empires, though allies, contrasted starkly: Germany was the military and industrial colossus of Europe; Austria-Hungary was an agrarian society whose minimal industrial capability was concentrated in Bohemia, lower Austria around Vienna, and embryonically in Budapest. In Germany 40 percent of the population were employed in industry and mining and 35 percent in agriculture and forestry by 1907. In Austria in 1900 only 23.3 percent of the people were employed in industry and mining, against 60.9 percent in agriculture and forestry. These relative levels of industrialization were reflected in military expenditures and ultimately in armed might. In 1914 Germany, with a population of 67 million, spent 37.2 marks per capita on the military, while Austria-Hungary, with a population of 51.3 million, spent 14 crowns (1 crown = 0.85 marks = 0.21 dollars). This disparity in funding was reflected in military strength. The German battle fleet weighed in at over 1 million tons, while the Austro-Hungarian navy, little more than a coastal defense force, was a mere 394,692 tons. The German Army comprised ninety-eight divisions with 4,480 artillery pieces, of which 1,064 were heavy guns, while the Austro-Hungarian Army had sixty divisions with 2,539 field pieces and only 168 heavy guns.[4] The Prussian Army controlled the German military establishment, although the Bavarian Army retained considerable administrative autonomy. The Prussian General Staff formed the nucleus of the Imperial General Staff, and its War Ministry determined the budget of the German Army. The Austro-Hungarian Army was plagued by national divisions and the difficulty of obtaining agreement on defense budgets from the respective Austrian and Hungarian governments. The Prussian Army was consequently the military cornerstone of the dual alliance between Germany and Austria-Hungary, and its relationship with the German aircraft industry was exceedingly important for the evolution of Central European aviation.

The early development of aviation in Central Europe, from the formation of aircraft companies to the construction of airfields, depended upon private initiative, with occasional limited support or subsidies from the military. The first small aircraft companies appeared in Germany in the winter of 1908–1909 and in Austria in the spring of 1909. Successful German firms all began by producing inferior copies of planes invented by French, Americans, and even Austrians; only the Austrian Etrich firm was original in its creation of the birdlike design called the Taube ("dove").

By 1909 civilian interest in the airplane had led to the formation of air fleet leagues and aviation clubs devoted to the promotion of heavier-than-air flight, both civilian and military. The German Air Fleet League (Deutscher Luftflottenverein) had some three thousand members, among them influential businessmen, politicians, and former army officers. The German Aviators Association (Deutscher Luftfahrer-Verband) was the country's largest aviation sport organization and administered pilot licenses and airfield and flight regulations. In Austria-Hungary various aviation organizations banded together to form the Flight Technology Association (Flugtechnischer Verein), which was far smaller and less influential than its German counterpart.[5]

Despite such popular enthusiasm, the armies approached the airplane cautiously. The first German and Austro-Hungarian military airplanes were gifts, in Germany from embryonic aircraft firms which stood to profit directly from military interest in aviation, and in Austria-Hungary from interested civilians. In 1908 the German General Staff established a technical section under Capt. Hermann von der Lieth-Thomsen to observe aviation development and placed it within Capt. Erich Ludendorff's mobilization department. Both became ardent advocates of the airplane. The Austro-Hungarian General Staff, watching intently the interest of the English and French armies in airplanes, was already pressing for aviation forces in 1907. The chiefs of both general staffs, Gen. Helmuth von Moltke in Germany and Gen. Franz Conrad von Hötzendorff in Austria-Hungary, realized that the airplane might be useful for reconnaissance and communications.[6]

While the strategists of the general staffs advocated adoption of the airplane, the German and Austro-Hungarian war ministries, averse to allocating money to untested technical implements that might prove militarily worthless, approached the invention more circumspectly.[7] Aviation historians Capt. Hans Ritter and Maj. Hilmer von Bülow, former German officers who were enthusiastic supporters of the airplane, later accused the German Army of an aversion toward technology that arrested the development of military aviation.[8] Yet such reserve avoided wasting funds and, in Germany's case, diverting them from supposedly superior aeronautical devices like the airship.

The Prusso-German War Ministry initiated contact with airplane inventors and even helped the early manufacturers with airfield subsidies, pilot training contracts, contest awards, and in 1910 a few airplane contracts, but it left airplane development to the industry. When the army, pressured by influential members of the Air Fleet League, attempted to build its own plane in 1909, the dismal failure of the multi-winged abomination confirmed its promotion of private initiative.[9]

Within the German military establishment, the Bavarian agencies, after subsidizing four disastrous construction attempts by one of their officers, took the more reliable course of relying on north German factories. The German Navy found that, despite its interest in seaplanes and an initial allocation of two hundred thousand marks in 1910, aircraft firms were reluctant to accept the challenge and expense of seaplane development.

The first Austrian aircraft companies were the MLG (Motorluftfahrzeuggesellschaft), owned by Camillo Castiglioni, the wealthy director of the Austro-American Rubber Company, and the Jakob Lohner chassis factory's aircraft department, which Castiglioni later acquired. Despite the exhortations of chief of the General Staff von Hötzendorff, the War Ministry withheld its financial support until the firms could produce a successful military airplane.[10] The Lohner firm did provide flying boats to the navy, which had shown an early interest in seaplanes, before the German Navy could acquire seaplanes from the German industry.

By the middle of 1910 the Prussian and Austro-Hungarian transport corps strongly recommended directing the efforts of the industry along military lines in order to avoid falling further behind French aviation. The war ministries remained hesitant and aloof, but the rapid progress of aviation after 1910 rendered this attitude increasingly untenable.[11]

In late 1911 and early 1912, under the pressures of the Moroccan and Balkan crises, the Prussian War Ministry increased its aircraft orders substantially. Through the transport troops it applied more funds, technical standards, and economic controls to the industry in order to focus its production along military lines. The military's virtual monopoly of the consumer market, which remained undiminished throughout the prewar years, enabled it to preserve its grip on the maturing industry. It maintained its economic leverage by preventing the formation of cartels or monopolies within the industry and parlayed this business advantage into the guidance of the industry in technological matters. As the army gained more technological expertise, it established more stringent guidelines and standards in the construction of military airplanes, while the industry tried to meet its demands and to avoid confrontations with the military authorities. The aircraft manufacturers' trade association (Convention deutscher Flugzeugindustrieller) opposed monopoly and cooperated fully with the army. The Prussian Army's pragmatic approach avoided waste before 1912 and afterward channeled the production of the industry toward the development of standard types of reconnaissance and communication airplanes. Its budget for airplanes rose from 36,000 marks in 1909 to 25,920,000 marks in 1914, a reflection of a clear and increasingly firm commitment to military heavier-than-air aeronautics. Furthermore, the German Army used its influential position to help sponsor a National Aviation Fund, which raised more than 7 million marks for military aviation from 1912 to 1914.[12]

The Prussian Army's procurement of increasing numbers of airplanes—28 in 1911, 139 in 1912, and 461 in 1913—fueled the expansion of the aircraft industry. By February 1914 it bought planes from eleven manufacturers—Albatros, Aviatik, LVG (Luftverkehrsgesellschaft), Rumpler, DFW (Deutsche Flugzeugwerke), Euler, Gotha (Gothaer Waggonfabrik), Jeannin, and AEG (Allgemeine Elektrizitäts Gesellschaft). The army's contracts sheltered the industry from the economic recession and capital shortage of the years from 1911 to 1914, and the firms' expansion in anticipation of a future war made their productive potential much higher than the army required in peacetime. Early in 1914 the army estimated that its best eight firms could produce 103–12 aircraft monthly, or one-quarter of its orders for the entire year of 1913.[13]

While most firms were located at Johannisthal airfield, others were situated around Germany—Fokker in Schwerin, Aviatik in Mulhaus, DFW in Leipzig, and Gotha in Gotha. Gotha and AEG were the only large diversified manufacturers in aircraft production. Among the best of the older firms, Albatros and Rumpler had become substantial factories of 745 and 400 employees, respectively. The value of such aircraft plants had risen as they expanded: Rumpler's had grown from fifteen thousand marks in 1908 to 1.4 million marks in 1914; Aviatik's from thirty thousand marks in 1910 to more than 1 million marks in 1914.[14] Their aircraft production was characterized by the reliance on skilled craftsmen, limited serial production, and *Platzarbeit*. Wood and fabric construction placed a premium on woodworkers, while the embryonic aircraft motor industry required large numbers of metal craftsmen. Albatros had introduced limited serial production as early as January 1912, and LVG, Rumpler, Aviatik, Gotha, and AEG followed suit in 1913. In the pattern of work arrangement known as *Platzarbeit*, the "machines were grouped by type . . . and the pieces were moved from one post to another until they were finally brought together for fitting in the assembly shop. . . . The more successful enterprises gave entire floors, or even separate shops, to a single type of tool."[15]

By August 1914 the Prussian Army's technical control over the airplane industry had led to improvement in detailed construction techniques and aircraft safety, but its standardization of monoplane production had caused ossification in monoplane design. Most German designers concentrated on production of the standard Taube monoplane to the exclusion of other types. Only Dutchman Anthony Fokker, an inveterate maverick, constructed light monoplanes. The Taube was approaching obsolescence in 1914, and Maj. Wilhelm Siegert, one of the most dynamic and imaginative of the air arm's officers, concluded that the biplane would become the army's standard type. Its superior speed and rate of climb and shorter takeoff run would make it the mainstay of the Prussian Army's air service.[16] This destiny owed as much to the progress in biplane performance as to stagnation in the evolution of the monoplane.

German biplanes were equal or superior to those in other armies. An Aviatik biplane established a world record for nonstop flight of twenty-four hours and twelve minutes on 11 July 1914 that was not broken until thirteen years later. Only two weeks before the war, on 14 July, a DFW biplane set a world altitude record over twenty-five thousand feet. These achievements are indisputable evidence that the army had succeeded in its aim of developing a rugged, dependable two-seat reconnaissance craft with a reliable water-cooled in-line engine. All of these planes were modified military types powered by the army's standard one-hundred-horsepower Daimler engine, as the Daimler factory nearly monopolized the aircraft motor market.

The General Staff intended to use aircraft primarily for reconnaissance and secondarily for communications and artillery spotting. Siegert expected air-to-air combat and anticipated the use of the plane against troops in the field as a bomber and ground-strafer.[17] At his urging the General Staff was examining the possibility of arming some planes with light machine guns, which had been available since early 1913.

The Prussian Army's embryonic plans for the mobilization of the aircraft industry focused on material procurement and exemptions in 1914. The transport corps command suggested the formulation of delivery quotas, exemption plans, and the accumulation of a supply of finished motors, while its subordinate, the Inspectorate of Flying Troops, would regulate the factories' supplies and production. Exemptions did occasion disagreements: the factories sought as many as possible; the army, as few as possible. Captain Thomsen preferred labor conscription to exemptions. Although these plans were sketchy as of August 1914, the urgency of the international situation prompted the transport inspectorate to order 220 aircraft on 4 July: 42 from Albatros, 40 from LVG, 30 from Aviatik, 36 apiece from AEG and Gotha, and 18 apiece from DWF and Rumpler. The firms in turn immediately placed extensive orders for raw material and parts.[18]

It would take the war for the airplane to realize its potential as a weapon, but the foundations of this potential in north Germany were laid by August 1914. The production companies and designers—Anthony Fokker, Edmund Rumpler, and Robert Thelen of Albatros—were available, as were dynamic army officers knowledgeable about aviation like Siegert, Thomsen, and Ludendorff. Such industrial and military continuity was of the utmost importance, because the development and employment of early aircraft were primarily matters of intuition, experience, and experiment rather than scientific theory translated into reality. Of course, aviation science was increasingly linked to the military in Germany, as the German Research Institute for Aviation (Deutsche Versuchsanstalt für Luftfahrt), a civilian agency for aeronautical research, contracted with the Prussian Army in March 1914 to perform all military trials and research.

The circumstances of military aviation in the rest of the German and Austro-Hungarian military establishments were not so fortunate. The Prussian War Ministry determined the Bavarian Army's aviation budget, the Prussian research unit set procurement guidelines, and the Prussian Army ultimately controlled the mobilization and deployment of the Bavarian air arm. Sensitive about this dependence, the Bavarian Army attempted to buttress its administrative autonomy in aviation after 1911 by procuring aircraft primarily from a Bavarian manufacturer, the Gustav Otto Works of Munich. Although Engineers Inspector Gen. Karl von Brug believed that competition in the Bavarian aircraft industry was essential, even if it meant relying on Prussian firms, the Bavarian War Ministry was convinced that to protect Otto was to safeguard the autonomy of Bavarian aviation. When the Prussian Army excluded the Otto Works from its orders and military competitions, the Bavarian War Ministry retaliated by rejecting the repeated attempts of foreign firms like Albatros, Rumpler, and Gotha to found branches in Bavaria. The price of this particularistic strife was the increasing backwardness of Bavarian military airplanes, as Otto did not keep abreast of aviation progress and gradually was reduced to license production of designs of north German

companies. The Bavarian Army consequently entered the war with only
two aircraft companies—the feeble Otto Works and the embryonic Pfalz
Aircraft Works, which was founded at Speyer in the Bavarian Palatinate
in 1914 to produce light aircraft for military use.[19]

By August 1914 German naval aviation had advanced only slightly
beyond the experimental stage. Numerous technical difficulties, reliance
on the airship, and a small budget slowed the development of a seaplane
force. Although the chief of the Admiralty Staff was requesting airplanes
as defensive weapons against enemy airships and planes and as offensive
weapons for reconnaissance and attack in February 1914,[20] most of the
navy's twenty-four planes in August were not even seaworthy. At least
the navy's list of potential seaplane manufacturers did include two firms
specializing in seaplane production—Friedrichshafen Aircraft Works
(Flugzeugbau Friedrichshafen), which was founded in 1912 on Lake
Constance by Friedrich Kober, Count Ferdinand von Zeppelin's oldest
friend and coworker, and the Hansa-Brandenburg Aircraft Works
(Hansa-Brandenburgische Flugzeugwerke), founded in 1914 by an
Italian magnate from Austria-Hungary, Camillo Castiglioni, who already
owned the MLG in Vienna and the Hungarian Aircraft Works (Ungarische Flugzeugfabrik, or Ufag) in Budapest. Castiglioni persuaded
Ernst Heinkel, a designer with Albatros, to head the firm. This industrial
connection in aviation between the two empires was crucial to the survival
of Austro-Hungarian aviation, which was in dire straits by August 1914.

The Austro-Hungarian Army, lacking a firm commitment to aviation, spent less than 1 million crowns on it in 1914. The Austro-
Hungarian War Ministry set unrealistically high standards for military
aircraft and so awarded few contracts. The Taube, for example, had been
relegated to a training role by 1912 and had to be so severely modified
that it became useless.[21] Yet the Taube saw use in Germany as a first-line
craft through 1914 and even isolated service during the early days of the
war. The Austro-Hungarian War Ministry refused to emulate the German military's policy of direct involvement in civilian affairs to promote
military aviation, despite the exhortations of the chief of the General
Staff. Neither the army nor the civilian government participated in an
Austrian Air Fleet Fund (Österreichischer Luftflottenspende) in 1912
that was clearly intended to be a carbon copy of the German fund, and in
1913 the War Ministry rejected civilian attempts to copy German practices of staging reconnaissance and overland flight competitions with
military and civilian entries.[22]

The feeble funding of aviation and ill-conceived procurement policies left the Austro-Hungarian Army with few reliable aircraft and, more critically, an industry of essentially one firm, the MLG-Lohner combine. In March a fatal crash involving the Lohner Pfeilflieger ("arrow flier"), the army's standard biplane, forced its grounding and left the air arm temporarily without aircraft. In June the Viennese press lambasted the army, censuring it for ruining its domestic producers and causing reliance on foreign producers.[23] The foreign producers were naturally German: DFW's Hungarian Lloyd Aircraft and Motor Factory (Ungarische Lloyd Flugzeug- und Motoren-Fabrik) in Budapest-Aszod, and Albatros's and Aviatik's branches in Vienna.

But the German firms had come too late to prepare the military and industry for the war. By the end of July the army had only forty field airplanes. The War Ministry's mobilization plans entailed no exemptions for the aircraft industry, so on 1 August, at the last minute, it decreed exemptions for workers and managers in the MLG-Lohner company, Aviatik, Lloyd, and Ufag.[24] Austro-Hungarian military aviation forces and the aircraft industry were not prepared for war of any kind, as Conrad von Hötzendorff had feared years before. Although early in 1914 the War Ministry had optimistically promised him eight flying companies by the fall of 1914 and forty companies with 240 planes by early 1916, on 22 July 1914 it reduced the 1916 projection to fifteen companies by 30 June 1916 and confessed that this would only be possible if it drew extensively upon the budget for the following year, 1916–17.[25] Naval aviation, if embryonic, was at least better off than the army, compared to its German counterpart. The navy bought French and American Glenn Curtiss flying boats as models for Austrian firms. By August 1914 the MLG-Lohner concern had delivered 11 flying boats to the navy.

When World War I began in August, German and Austro-Hungarian aviation was inferior to that of the Entente. The Austro-Hungarian and Russian aircraft industries were comparably backward, with the former dependent upon Germany and the latter upon France. French aviation was superior to German, with English aviation third. The French industry of nine companies, for which figures are lacking, had equipped the largest air arm in Europe. The German industry of eleven firms, employing some twenty-five hundred workers by 1914, had delivered more than 450 aircraft in 1913. The English industry, though it comprised twelve companies, employed only one thousand workers and produced 100 planes annually by 1914. The smaller number of firms in Germany and France reflected military policies in both countries to limit the industry to a few proven companies.[26]

A major reason for French ascendancy in aviation was her aeroengine industry's unsurpassed production of small, light engines such as the Gnome rotaries. Germany could boast the Daimler six-cylinder one-hundred-horsepower in-line engine, which, if not as light as the French powerplants, was more reliable and durable. England had no satisfactory engine in August 1914 and was consequently dependent upon the French for engines as well as supplementary aircraft.[27]

The three major powers pursued distinctly different policies toward their service aircraft by August 1914. The French, reluctant to stifle Gallic creativity in aviation, had the greatest variety of types and eschewed standardization. In England the military wing of the Royal Flying Corps preferred a single airplane for mass production and relied on the government's Royal Aircraft Factory at Farnborough to provide it with a standard type.[28] The Germans, like the French, relied solely upon private industry, but directed most of their firms into the production of either a standard biplane or the Taube monoplane. Each firm's aircraft might superficially resemble the product of another company, but were invariably quite different in construction, and parts were not interchangeable. There were disadvantages to all three approaches. The English circumscribed the creativity of private aircraft companies for ease of mass production, supply, and repairs. The French took the opposite course. Ironically, the German industry's standardization procedures limited creativity without providing the advantages of ease of supply, repair, and licensed production.

The German Army's aviation arm was comparable to the best of its opponents. The French could muster approximately 300 frontline planes of a variety of types among its 600 machines, and the English had only some 160 planes. The Germans went to war with 450 airplanes (270 biplanes and 180 monoplanes), of which perhaps 250 were fit for active service. Given the expectations of a short war and of the small role airplanes would play, the German aircraft industry and army were at least as well prepared to commence hostilities as any of their counterparts in other European states.[29]

Yet the longer the war continued, the worse the odds against Germany and Austria would become, because England's industrial might meant that its aviation was a sleeping giant, and the French were quite capable of being the aviation arsenal of the Entente until England could carry its own weight. Ultimately, the length and total nature of the conflict made the speedy evolution of a technological weapon like the airplane both necessary and possible. Four and one-half years of war against the

Entente would be the ultimate challenge for a German Empire whose military and industrial foundations in aviation seemed adequate for the short war expected and for an Austro-Hungarian Empire whose preparations were clearly deficient.

CHAPTER 1

Inauspicious Beginnings, August–December 1914

WHAT IMPRESSES the historian most about the aircraft industry and the flying troops in 1914 is their newness, as both, a mere four years old, responded to their first war, the first major European conflict in a century. The fledgling state of the industry and the military air arm at the beginning of the war was decidedly inopportune, because they faced the herculean task of simultaneously solving the intricacies of their complex relationship and effecting a successful wartime mobilization. But newness was not a problem restricted to the aircraft industry and the flying troops. It soon became apparent that the war itself was unprecedented in several critical aspects. The demands of the fighting front far surpassed anything envisioned by the belligerents, while the conditions of the home front, particularly shortages and inflation, hampered the ability of the army and industry to meet these demands. Furthermore, the first six months of the war, which most contemporaries expected to be its only six months, witnessed two disparate modes of warfare—the war of movement before the battle of the Marne and then the stationary war of the trenches. The success of the flying troops most basically depended upon the ability of the Prussian Army and the north German aircraft industry to provide sufficient airplanes suited for frontline service under such unexpected and widely divergent circumstances. Yet the Prussian Army's development of the aviation arm would be hindered by its own serious logistical problems in the procurement and transport of aviation material and complicated by the existence of separate procurement bureaucracies for the Bavarian Army and the German Navy.

At 1830 hours on 1 August 1914 units of the German Army received their mobilization orders. On 2 August the five battalions of flying troops separated into their mobilization formations—five fliers replacement units (four Prussian and one Bavarian) and eight aircraft staging parks for the supply of equipment and personnel to the fighting units, which comprised ten fortress flight units (nine Prussian and one Bavarian) of four planes apiece and thirty-three field flight units (thirty Prussian and three Bavarian), each with six aircraft. Each of the German Army's twenty-five army corps headquarters received a field unit; each of the eight army headquarters, an aircraft park and a field unit. The fortress units were deployed to the towns of Metz, Strasbourg, and Cologne in the west, and in the east to Posen, Königsberg, Graudenz, and the military bases at Boyen, Breslau, and Glogau.[1]

Although generals initially preferred to employ the cavalry for reconnaissance, by the end of August the airplane had developed from "a supplementary means of information relied upon principally for confirmation" to "the principal means of operational reconnaissance—an important factor in forming army commanders' decisions."[2] On the eastern front aerial reconnaissance was instrumental in preparing the German victory at Tannenberg. In the second week of September, however, the German advance on the western front was halted at the Marne. While aviation reconnaissance reports had been instrumental in preventing a more serious defeat, the end of the war had been postponed indefinitely. Air operations, though not a complete success, had indicated the potential of the flying machine.

The picture on the ground, however, was one of incompetence and inadequacy in the organizational, logistical, and industrial spheres. There was no single authority for all Prussian military aviation that coordinated the frontline units with the Inspectorate of Flying Troops and the War Ministry's aviation section in Berlin. Before the war the Prussian War Ministry held final authority in all matters because of its control of the budget. Now, as financial considerations yielded to wartime necessity, the War Ministry lost some of its authority, which, however, did not devolve upon the inspectorate, because the inspectorate lacked the structure to supervise the aviation units at the front. The inspector of flying troops, Col. Walther von Eberhardt, noted on 12 August in his diary that without aviation staff officers at the various army commands, the flying troops lacked central agencies in the field to collect and evaluate frontline experience for technical and operational use. Eberhardt so lost touch with his frontline units that he had to go into the field on 15 August in an

The Organization of the
Prussian Flying Troops Aircraft Units before March 1915

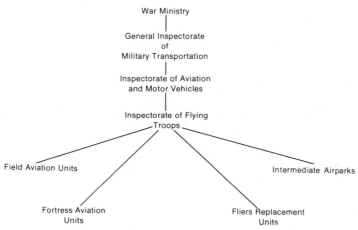

SOURCE: John R. Cuneo, *Winged Mars*, 2:145.

attempt to regain control over his independent troops. The inspectorate in Berlin suffered during his absence, while his temporary presence in the field did not suffice either to control the troops or to gain insights for new aircraft construction. Yet when Eberhardt recommended the creation of a chief of air forces in the field with staff officers at each army headquarters, Minister of War Erich von Falkenhayn, averse to such an extensive measure, demurred.[3] The resulting organizational deficiency—in a military establishment noted for its organization—had dire repercussions on logistical efficiency, resulting in a dearth of materiel reaching the frontline units.

Deficiencies in the military's supply organization threatened to disrupt completely the supply of aircraft to the front.[4] The practice of equipping a unit with different types of aircraft unnecessarily complicated the supply of spare parts. Intermediate air parks often had no liaison with their frontline units. On the right wing of the German Army on the western front, lengthening distances to the depots so ruptured supply that the commander of the air park at Liège, Belgium, let his planes be used for active service. Pilots who had crashed their machines at the front could be found lounging around factories in Germany waiting their turn for new airplanes. Unit leaders zealously sent flying officers in lorries to aircraft factories to commandeer airplanes and drive them to local railway stations for shipment to the front. Frequently the frames arrived broken or crushed; in their haste the officers often forgot that Belgian railway tunnels lacked the clearance of those in Germany. If these incidents were exceptions, they nevertheless cast light upon the organizational and logistical disarray. The flying officers' expeditions home, in flagrant defiance of Eberhardt's orders, impeded the development of new units and the inspectorate's surveillance of available parts and materiel. The factories' adherence to the flying officers' proposals was proof of the inadequacy of the inspectorate's influence on the factories. Eberhardt discovered that the headquarters of the Fourteenth Corps of the Seventh Army actually encouraged the Aviatik factory to equip a wildcat flight unit. The man responsible, Maj. Wilhelm Siegert, commander of Aviation Park No. 7, had attached himself to the headquarters and begun flying at the front in utter disregard of orders. Such enthusiasm, though well intentioned, was clearly not constructive in this instance. Ruthless stopgap measures—requisitioning airplanes from firms, even planes designated for Bavarian and naval units—failed to alleviate the shortage.[5] Ultimately, these logistical problems were solved primarily by the stabilization of the western front during September.

The paucity of aircraft stemmed most basically, not from supply, but from the lack of detailed plans to mobilize the aircraft industry in wartime. Besides the inspectorate's emergency order of 220 aircraft in July 1914, further mobilization plans for the aircraft industry consisted only of a telegram from the inspectorate on 1 August instructing all factories to begin maximum production and to increase their productive capacity.[6] Yet such an order was dysfunctional, as firms seized the opportunity to hoard materials, and thus exacerbated shortages and price increases, for the production of aircraft that had yet to prove their battleworthiness.

The aircraft industry and, to a much greater extent, the aircraft motor industry, simply were not prepared to meet the high loss rate of airplanes. One flight unit was demanding two aircraft daily in August, and the overall loss of airplanes for that month has been estimated at 40 percent of the army's frontline strength.[7] Eberhardt calculated on 4 August that with the factories delivering fifty airframes an only twelve engines weekly (that is, twelve airplanes weekly) to the army, he could not even replace anticipated losses, much less equip new units. Deliveries continued in peacetime quantities, if they were not actually reduced by the induction of essential personnel at the factories. Although an increase in engine production did enable a boost in deliveries from twelve to twenty-four planes weekly by 31 August, field units could still expect to receive less than one airplane weekly.[8]

Various firms attempted to seize the opportunity presented by the war. Count Ferdinand von Zeppelin and his associate Claudius Dornier had often discussed the construction of a giant airplane, so in August they promptly began work on a huge, multi-engined aircraft. At the Siemens-Schuckert Works (SSW), the giant of the German electrical industry, Wilhelm von Siemens, who was interested in building large, twin-engined bombers, had the company reactivate its aircraft department, which had been closed since 1911.[9]

As established aircraft manufacturers prepared to increase production, they encountered difficulties which forced them to request assistance from the army. Within forty-eight hours of mobilization the inspectorate and the test commission had met in the War Ministry with representatives of the aircraft industry, who requested long-term contracts of three months' duration, aid in material procurement, and assurances of exemptions for employees. Companies were already finding raw materials and parts more expensive and difficult to obtain, and some smaller manufacturers, whom the army had not yet paid for their last prewar deliveries, had insufficient liquid assets to purchase materials from subcontractors who were demanding payment in specie. In order to meet the army's demand for shorter delivery times and increased production, the factories would also have to pay higher wages, particularly for night shifts. Consequently, some industrialists requested a corresponding increment in aircraft prices. But the army, while promising assistance with procurement and exemptions, refused to issue long-term contracts and to increase aircraft prices. The inspectorate lacked the information on enemy aviation and the field experience to determine the requisite number of airplanes for the coming campaign. An immediate contractual agreement might thus preclude lowering prices as production increased. The inspectorate and the test commission also anticipated that the industry, facing the prospect of huge wartime contracts, might use the favorable state of the market for its "unjustified enrichment."[10]

The very next day, 5 August, an offer of assistance in overcoming the aircraft shortage was tendered to the army from a most unexpected source—the political arena. Seven members of the Reichstag—Matthias Erzberger and Count Hans Georg von Oppersdorff of the Catholic Center Party, Baron Karl von Gamp-Massaunen and Georg Schultz of the German Imperial Party, Dr. Hermann Paasche of the National Liberal party, Count Cuno von Westarp of the Conservative party, and Dr. Otto Wiemer of the Progressive party—had decided to consult with the military establishment about the aircraft industry. They had convened on their own initiative as representatives of their parties to help the military develop the aircraft industry and a great air fleet to offset English naval superiority. In a preliminary meeting on 5 August in the Imperial Naval Office,[11] officers from the Prussian War Ministry and the Naval Office accepted their offer of consultation, thereby allowing the first direct interference of politicians in their relationship with the aircraft industry.

At 11:00 the next morning, in the parliamentary building, the parliamentary commission hastily convened a meeting of military delegates and the representatives of eight aircraft firms (Aviatik of Freiburg; DFW of Leipzig; and AEG, Albatros, Jeannin, LFG [Luftfahrzeuggesellschaft], LVG, and Rumpler—all of Berlin), three aircraft motor companies (Mercedes Daimler, NAG [Neue Automobil Gesellschaft], and Argus), and five accessories factories. The manufacturers present agreed to deliver some two hundred airplanes monthly after the middle of August: LVG promised forty airplanes; Albatros, thirty-two, then forty-eight after four weeks; DFW and Rumpler, twenty-five; Aviatik, a minimum of twenty; Jeannin, twenty; AEG, a minimum of sixteen; and LFG, four beginning in September. The motor companies committed themselves to 170 engines.

When the conferees reconvened on 7 August,[12] the manufacturers agreed unanimously to allow the military the license-free use of "lesser" patents and to submit patent disputes to the arbitration of the parliamentary commission. Then they accepted the continuation of peacetime aircraft prices until the War Ministry and Naval Office chose to raise them according to increases in workers' wages and raw material prices. The parliamentary deputies recommended that the military's fiscal agencies be empowered to pay a company as much as one-third of the price for series of well-established aircraft types immediately after the initiation of production, with the balance of the payments to come upon final delivery. The commission would arbitrate any disputes arising from these new procedures. Finally, both services announced their intention of resurrecting the prewar system of factory flying schools, of recruiting volunteers (teetotalers were deemed most desirable), and of paying the cost of their training at these establishments.

The motives of the participants in and the outcome of this first encounter of industrialists, politicians, and the military merit close analysis. First, the politicians were all generally interested in industrial affairs.[13] Paasche, a professor of national economy at Rostock, was considered a representative of sugar interests; Wiemer was a syndic in the paper-finishing industry; while Gamp-Massaunen, although an agrarian, tended to defend industrial interests, particularly those of the coal companies. Motivated by patriotism, such men hoped to help the war effort against England. As Fritz Fischer noted, in military, diplomatic, and business circles there was sentiment for "breaking British resistance" through air warfare.[14] In late August the German minister in Stockholm Franz von Reichenau hoped "with all his heart" that Germany "would send airships and aircraft cruising regularly over England dropping bombs" until "the vulgar huckster souls" of those "cowardly assassins" would forget "even how to do sums." Walter Rathenau also advocated "systematically working on the nerves of the English towns through an overwhelming air force," and since he had been instrumental in directing AEG into aircraft production in 1912–13, there is no reason to presume that he was not contemplating the use of the airplane. Although Fischer asserted that most advocates of bombing had the Zeppelin in mind, it is clear from the August meeting that some of them considered the airplane just as important in the assault. Their conception of the use of aviation to offset naval power indicated not only a realistic assessment of the relative naval strengths of England and Germany but also some perception, however vague, of the airplane's potential ability to strike directly at England. They consequently approached the navy first, although the Prussian Army seized the initiative.

The Prussian War Ministry decided to use the willing politicians in its dealings with the industry, and the outcome of the conference reflects its prior planning. The manufacturers, hastily assembled, were persuaded to sacrifice lesser patent rights and price increases in return for the assurance of contracts, exemptions, and pupils for their flying schools. Yet had the industrialists paused to consider the circumstances, they might have realized that they had allowed the abridgment of patent protection in return for concessions that they would have won inevitably. The very fact of the meeting reflected the armed forces' high expectations of the airplane as a useful implement of war; consequently, they would have to guarantee the industry a firmer financial basis to ensure the progress of military aviation. Sizable contracts for aircraft and exemptions, even if the army looked askance at the latter, would thus have been forthcoming. The concession of so-called lesser patent rights had opened a potential Pandora's box of complications. Legally, the resultant breach in patent law might tempt the military to determine what was a lesser patent and to arbitrate in all matters concerning these lesser patents. Practically, the companies were threatening their own position in their rush to assure themselves of contracts: first, they were sacrificing any license fees derived from such patents; second, and more critically, they had inadvertently opened the way for more competition, as eliminating some patents and fees might enable the army to attract more firms to aircraft production.

Apparently the manufacturers simply did not appreciate as quickly as did the military their increased leverage at the opening of hostilities. Perhaps they had grown too accustomed to military dominance. Certainly the rousing patriotism of the moment and the tendency for all to pull together at the beginning of a war were just not conducive to the espousal of an antagonistic stance, especially in the presence of a third and supposedly impartial party of politicians. Whatever the reasons, while the army feared that the industry might use the favorable market for its "unjustified enrichment," the industrialists were so grateful for the favorable market that they neglected to press their advantage.

The army nominally discharged its obligation on exemptions on 9 August, when War Minister Erich von Falkenhayn ordered that firms delivering "arms, munitions, aviation and motor vehicles" to the armed forces should receive prior consideration in exemptions.[15] Yet many men had already been called to the colors, and the army's needs took precedence over those of the industry. The deputy general commands were to grant exemptions only to a few "absolutely indispensable" men for a circumscribed period of time, and officers and men that the army needed badly were not eligible for consideration. This policy affected not only the industry but also other essential aviation organizations. The German Research Institute for Aviation, which performed aircraft stress tests for the army and industry, lost some of its most essential personnel, including the director of its physics section, to mobilization.[16]

By October it was evident that the exemption policy had failed, undoubtedly because of the parsimonious manner in which the deputy general commands had interpreted the term "indispensable personnel." The failure occasioned a memorandum to the deputy general commands on 5 October from Gen. Franz von Wandel, the head of the war department, who explained that the army had to exempt personnel that the aircraft manufacturers considered essential.[17] The interests of national defense made the army's facilitation of the industry's greatest possible expansion imperative. As the special nature of aircraft construction severely circumscribed the pool of suitable skilled labor, Wandel considered it reasonable to presume that the men for whom manufacturers requested exemptions were truly indispensable. The army had promised to exempt such workers, and its denial of the policy or failure to fulfill it would release the firms from any responsibility either for prompt delivery or for the reliable work necessary to ensure the safety of the fliers. After this gentle reprimand to the military bureaucracy, Wandel still insisted that the releases be for a limited duration and that the War Ministry reserve judgment on officers and deputy officers.

By September prices were an additional concern to the industry. In their patriotic fervor in August the manufacturers had agreed to accept prewar prices; by early September the circumstances had become less conducive to such selfless patriotism. Wages, freight charges, material prices, and interest rates had risen. Some factories had paid temporary wage raises of 50 percent in order to meet shorter delivery schedules. The War Ministry learned that subcontractors were demanding price increases of 30 percent and still insisting on payment in cash. With the exception of the price of raw rubber, which had increased 100 percent, raw material prices had risen from 10 to 30 percent (for example, steel, 15 percent; aluminum and steel tubing, 20 percent; copper and tin, 30 percent).[18]

Yet when the parliamentary commission reconvened on 2 September,[19] the War Ministry refused to concede that the expenses of parts and raw material procurement, of wage increases (with the exception of night shifts), or of inducted administrators and workers should significantly influence airplane prices. It would set a specific price increase only when it could ascertain that all manufacturers were cooperating to keep prices low. How it proposed to measure this vague criterion the War Ministry did not volunteer. More substantively, the army resolved to pay its outstanding prewar bills and advances on contracts in order to lessen the firms' need for bank credit. The War Ministry even considered having chambers of commerce encourage subcontractors to accept credit and requesting the help of the Imperial Office of the Interior to prevent raw material profiteering. It would recommend consideration of price ceilings on materials only as a last resort. Finally, the creation of a central agency for the aircraft industry in the military bureaucracy was proposed to ensure the cooperation of the industry in restraining price increases.

In October the War Ministry established the central agency in the aviation department. Staffed by an older flying officer, a parliamentary deputy (Count von Oppersdorff), a manufacturer, and a bureaucrat, it monitored prices and supervised the allocation of labor exemptions in concert with the inspectorate and the deputy general commands.[20]

The army refused to allow the airplane manufacturers price increases and would not intervene directly to arrest the inflation of raw material and parts prices. Despite a stated desire to prevent inflation, the War Ministry never set effective ceilings on material prices, because it lacked direct controls over subcontractors, and its raw materials department, which was established in August 1914 by Walter Rathenau, was directed by the very industrialists who stood to profit most from its operation. Of course, this policy of allowing increases in the prices of the factors of production while freezing the price of the finished product could prevail only temporarily, since the army could not allow aircraft production to become unprofitable. There the situation stood at the battle of the Marne, the industry pressing for higher prices as it sought to increase production, the army promising prompt payment and exemptions yet refusing to raise aircraft prices.

But now the war entered a new phase. As the western front became stationary, problems of supply abated, only to be replaced by others. Trench warfare, which made cavalry reconnaissance impossible, meant that the entire burden of reconnaissance now fell to the airplane. Trench warfare would also necessitate the evolution of specialized aircraft types for duties such as artillery spotting and short and long-range reconnaissance and bombing, while it would make other types in service obsolete.

The stalemate also frustrated temporarily the grandiose designs of bringing England to her knees through aerial bombardment. Driven by the same purpose that had spurred the parliamentary deputies to action in August, Maj. Wilhelm Siegert, who became aviation advisor to the High Command on 19 October, formed the command's flying corps (later given the name Brieftauben Abteilung Ostende, or Carrier Pigeon Unit Ostend) with the aim of bombing England from Calais. Of course, Calais was never captured by the Germans, and since extant aircraft could not reach England from Ostend, the force had to content itself with raids on Dunkirk and French harbors and railroad junctions. Its value was thus much less than intended, and it actually weakened the air service by absorbing many of its most experienced pilots.[21] The lack of suitable airplanes thwarted Siegert's enthusiastic plans, exemplifying the necessity of accepting the limits which aviation technology placed on strategy.

Problems continued to plague the industry and the army. Further increases in parts and material prices occurred. For example, the prices of tin, aluminum, and aircraft fabric rose 35, 50, and 50 percent, respectively, from August to October. Wages in the aircraft industry had risen an average of 6 percent during the same period. Inclement weather in late September delayed the completion of tests on new aircraft. LVG had to interrupt serial deliveries three weeks while it built new machine parts for a light biplane. Motor deliveries, especially of sorely needed rotary engines, fell behind schedule. Under these circumstances the first new aviation unit formed since 3 August did not depart until 28 September for the eastern front. Although the firms at the August conference had agreed to deliver some 200 airplanes monthly, the air service received only 462 new craft between 3 August and 29 November. The aircraft industry was expanding—in September Albatros, LFG, and Jeannin had all received more space from the Johannisthal airfield company—but increasing production took time.[22] Meanwhile, problems arising from the provision and enforcement of performance and construction guidelines and from the prices of aircraft, construction materials, and labor continued to complicate the military-industrial relationship.

With the war stalemated, the army now had time to pay more attention to the quality and performance of its airplanes. In the first months of the war, craft delivered to the front were often defective, while the low ceiling of the Taube, the German air service's standard monoplane, rendered it quickly obsolete.[23] By late fall the inspectorate had regained control of the situation sufficiently to begin enforcing construction standards more stringently and phasing in aircraft that were better suited to the tasks at hand.

Given the special nature of aircraft construction and the absolute necessity of safety, the inspectorate had carefully established construction and delivery requirements. Its construction and delivery guidelines (Bau- und Lieferungsvorschriften) covered all matters from technical construction details and materials for high-stress parts to licensing and flight test procedures, and they were revised annually to keep abreast of progress. Yet the real test was enforcement. Two manufacturers in particular—Anthony Fokker and August Euler—were investigated by the inspectorate between October and the end of the year because of deficient construction.[24] Both factories, though small, had appeared on the War Ministry's list of the top ten German aircraft firms in April 1914.

Anthony Fokker's factory in Schwerin in Mecklenburg in particular was gaining in importance. Fokker, something of a maverick, had been the only German manufacturer to produce light, single-seat airplanes before the war. His small craft were well suited to the new demands of

stationary warfare, and Fokker, demonstrating extraordinary speed of
production, given his small plant and ninety-five workers, delivered his
first production M8 monoplanes in October. Oswald Bölcke, destined to
become one of the great fighter pilots of the war, related on 30 November
that the Fokker's speed, climb, and maneuverability made it the best
aircraft for the air service's major task of artillery spotting.[25] The craft's
poor serviceability, however, prompted the inspectorate to send three of
its civilian engineers, among them the former aircraft manufacturer Hermann Dorner, to inspect the Fokkers at the front and at the factory. The
commission focused on the welding used in Fokker's steel tube fuselages
and components, as the official requirements still did not allow for it. But
Reinhold Platz, Fokker's chief technician, was able to demonstrate that
his fuselages surpassed the safety requirements. This was not the last time
that Fokker's construction techniques and standards would be subject to
investigation. This time, however, the only result of the surveillance was
to show that Platz's use of steel tubing and welding was further advanced
than the inspectorate's guidelines, so the commission allowed the new
technique.

In Euler's case the outcome was not so fortunate, for complaints
from the front in October about the deficient construction and poor
performance of his biplanes led to a lengthy and acrimonious dispute
between him and the inspectorate. The argument centered on one basic
question: Was the manufacturer or the army responsible for aircraft
failure after the craft had been accepted and delivered to the military?
Did the manufacturer's responsibility end with delivery, or, in cases of
apparent negligence, did it include repairs and even substantial
modifications at the manufacturer's expense? The army, naturally believing the latter condition to be the case, supported its claim with the
strongest leverage possible—it issued no more contracts and forced Euler
to the brink of closing his factory. Euler, on the other hand, with much less
leverage, clung to the opposing side—the series had been accepted initially by the army's experts, and there his responsibility ended. Any
repairs or revisions would be paid for, because the army was responsible
for them.

The army decided to use an increase in stress requirements passed in
early December as an excuse to lay the entire matter to rest. Euler would
build under license, thus furthering the standardization of types in the air
service. Yet license construction was anathema to the vanishing breed of
individualistic entrepreneurs to which Euler belonged; it was an insult to
build another's aircraft. Thus Euler went to the length of modifying his

models at his own expense rather than submitting to license production. He consequently obtained no contracts.

The Fokker and Euler cases provide ample evidence that the inspectorate could and did enforce its performance and construction guidelines. Yet its ability to encourage factories to adhere to these standards and new ones as aircraft technology progressed depended as much on aircraft prices as it did on negative sanctions. In order to keep pace with the demands of the front, the inspectorate revised its minimum climb rate from eight hundred meters in fifteen minutes and two thousand meters in one hour to eight hundred meters in ten minutes and two thousand meters in thirty-five minutes in December. When the inspectorate met with the firms about this revision, LVG, Albatros, and Rumpler—the big three of aircraft manufacture, who each produced from seven to ten aircraft weekly—pointed out that they could not meet such demands overnight. Prototype development would take months, and they would first have to exhaust the large amount of material that they had already prepared for their current series. The inspectorate agreed to lower transitional requirements to twelve minutes and forty minutes, but would hear of no more doubts about the firms' ability to meet them.[26] The profitability of serial production was making the companies reluctant to experiment with and build new types. Any conversion of production meant delay and a consequent reduction in profits, which the firms, by implication, were unable to afford because of the army's insufficient prices. After September the army still refused to raise aircraft prices, although this policy was especially hard on small aircraft firms that lacked liquid reserves.

By early December, however, large manufacturers in Berlin had begun to complain vehemently about prices. The parliamentary commission attempted to stifle their requests for increases, emphasizing that the profits from substantial wartime contracts had offset the rise in production costs and enabled LVG, Rumpler, and Albatros to enlarge their plants recently. The larger firms did profit: the cost per biplane was 12,400–15,000 marks and the sale price about 16,000 marks; and the cost per monoplane was 10,500–11,500 marks and the sale price about 14,000 marks. But in January 1915 DFW complained that the saving from serial production no longer compensated for the increased costs of raw materials. In fact, aircraft prices in January were lower than they had been at the war's beginning, having been reduced by some 1,000 marks, while the cost of the factors of production had risen substantially. Average wages for twenty skilled workers at Albatros had risen 14 percent in six months, while prices for materials such as steel, oak, and aluminum had risen from 20 to 100 percent.[27]

In February the army conceded that an increase in aircraft prices was necessary. The extensive induction of skilled workers, exemption orders notwithstanding, and the concomitant use of unskilled hands had lowered per capita output and increased the losses from ruined material. The air service could not afford the deterioration of standards that might result from depressed prices, so the War Ministry decided to apply different standards to the aircraft industry from those it did to older, better-established war industries. Many of the airplane factories—the smaller ones in particular—had entered the war with sizable deficits, and now they faced the expenses of enormous expansion and the continual conversion of production to new types. After the war much of their plant would be useless, so they would have to pay off as much of their wartime investment as possible during the war. Their financial position had to be strengthened sufficiently for them to work undisturbed by financial hindrances. The War Ministry consequently had the inspectorate increase the price of all aircraft delivered after 1 January 1915 by 3 percent.[28]

The announced price increase of February 1915 coincided with and was perhaps occasioned by an early nadir of the fortunes of the German air service on the western front. According to John Cuneo, it had not responded quickly to the demands of static trench warfare for daily artillery cooperation and close detailed reconnaissance flights.[29] The best evidence of this was the paucity of Fokker monoplanes, whose maneuverability made them ideal for such tasks. After winter's limited air activity, a decline in the morale of German aviators was painfully evident in February when the response of the German air service to French attacks in Champagne was at best ineffectual and at worst nonexistent.

If the Prussian Army had experienced great difficulty putting its own house in order, its particularistic and interservice rivalries with the Bavarian Army and the German Navy further impeded the most efficient mobilization of the German aircraft industry.

The Bavarian Army's mobilization of its domestic aircraft manufacturers—the Gustav Otto Works of Munich and the tiny Pfalz Aircraft Works in Speyer—was directly affected by its relationship with Prussia.

The Bavarian Army had contracted with the Otto Works on 14 May 1914 for weekly deliveries of two to three airplanes during a future mobilization, but in August such numbers proved insufficient for replacement and training, much less for the creation of new formations. In recognition of this situation, the Bavarian War Ministry ordered the deputy general commands on 16 August to accord prior consideration to aircraft factories, among other industries, in their allocation of exemptions. One week later the Bavarian flying troops reported nineteen Otto and twenty-four LVG biplanes on its rolls, but prospects were dim for any increase in this complement in the near future. A shortage of aircraft at the fliers replacement unit was delaying pilot training, while the Otto factory's repair duties prevented it from delivering even two airplanes weekly. Otto and Pfalz together, the Bavarian Engineers Inspectorate observed, could not meet the rising demand for training and replacement aircraft. LVG in Johannisthal, though it was training some Bavarian officers, could be relied upon only for limited deliveries of planes. Yet on 29 August the Bavarian War Ministry declined an offer from the Albatros Works in Johannisthal to deliver aircraft to Bavaria; its justification, that Otto and LVG would fulfill Bavaria's needs. Even at the risk of severe shortages, the Bavarian authorities had decided to cling to their prewar policy of restricting the incursions of Prussian factories and of limiting their orders to one or two south German factories. LVG was allowed because the Otto firm built its planes under license.[30]

The attitude of the War Ministry, worried about having too many rather than too few aircraft, contrasts starkly with that of the Prussian Inspectorate of Flying Troops, which was frantically seizing every available airplane in north Germany. While such complacency in Bavaria can best be explained as a desire to avoid an overexpansion of production for

Bavarian Military Aviation, Hinterland Organization

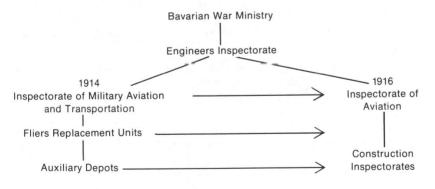

the expected short campaign, it is a first hint that Bavarian parochialism might impede efficient mobilization. Ironically, only the umbrella of Prussian might, however much the Bavarian aviation authorities resented it, enabled them to be so nonchalant about securing more airplanes.

In September further complications impeded aircraft procurement. By mid-month the Prussian inspectorate was sending the Bavarian fliers replacement unit only two Mercedes motors weekly, and no substitutes were available. On 7 September the Prussian inspectorate, which had previously requisitioned all airframes built in north Germany, did allow the weekly delivery of two LVG biplanes to Bavaria. But late in October the inspectorate once again requisitioned all of LVG's production, and only the vehement protest of the Bavarian War Ministry prompted the Prussian War Ministry to order the inspectorate to release the craft to Bavaria. Such pittances, however, would never suffice.[31]

The Otto Works, as Bavaria's oldest and largest aircraft manufacturer, would have to shoulder the burden of production. Otto, however, delivered only fourteen aircraft in nine weeks of war, not twenty-seven as his mobilization contract stipulated. The fault for his factory's inadequate production lay with both the factory and the army. The army was not furnishing Otto regularly with motors, because the Prussian inspectorate, which controlled motor allocation, was not sending them. Munich's Rapp Motor Works was no substitute, as it had yet to produce a working engine. On the other hand, the Otto factory operated inefficiently, taking six days for motor installation.[32]

Despite all these difficulties with aircraft procurement, the Bavarian War Ministry still resisted initiatives from Albatros, which was negotiating with the Machine Factory Augsburg Nürnberg (Maschinenfabrik Augsburg Nürnberg, or MAN) for production of its biplanes. Rejecting the hearty endorsement of the Engineers Inspectorate, which sought competition for Otto, the War Ministry countered that it would scarcely be possible to supply three factories with contracts *after* the war. Two months after the setback on the Marne, the Bavarian War Ministry was more preoccupied with the postwar period and its independence from Prussia than with winning the war.[33]

Ironically, while the War Ministry attempted to protect Otto from Prussian competition, he was accusing the army of favoring Prussian firms and ruining his company to an acquaintance in the Bavarian State Ministry of the Royal House and Foreign Affairs. His accusations, which played on Bavarian patriotism, prompted Bavarian Minister of State Count Georg von Hertling to ask the War Ministry to seek some compromise with Otto in order to avoid injury to Bavarian industry and labor.

Otto's complaint infuriated engineer inspector General von Heinemann, who had already ascertained the factory's inefficiency, and forced War Minister Kress von Kressenstein, who had to justify military policies to Hertling, to consider seriously the benefits of further competition for the Otto factory. While the army might desire the factory's survival, it was beginning to distinguish between the factory and the owner.[34]

At the start of 1915, the Otto and Pfalz works remained Bavaria's main suppliers of aircraft. Otto had delivered some fifty aircraft in the first five months of the war. His monthly deliveries at the turn of the year averaged some twelve planes, which, though unimpressive, showed some stability of production. Pfalz, though it had produced only fourteen planes in the five months and employed only ninety-six workers, had created a successful copy of the French Morane parasol design (a monoplane with wings above the fuselage), which began to replace the Fokker monoplanes in Bavarian artillery spotting units.[35]

The first months of the war had proven difficult for the Bavarian aviation authorities. On 24 January the War Ministry ordered the exemption of workers at Pfalz and Otto, including those who had already been called to the colors,[36] indicating that Bavarian exemption policy, like the Prussian, had suffered in execution. The War Ministry had been unable to obtain sufficient aircraft, yet its extremely circumspect policy towards the formation of new firms in Bavaria was ill designed to correct this inadequacy. Only the Engineers Inspectorate, which continued to encourage MAN and Albatros to form a plant in Bavaria, actively sought a larger and stronger domestic industry. Of course, nothing the Bavarian authorities did, whether attracting new firms or improving the productivity of older ones, could alter the basic fact that Bavaria depended on Prussia for its supplies of the precious Mercedes engine. The Bavarian Army needed to promote a strong south German aviation industry, but to do so the Bavarian War Ministry would have to be less concerned with postwar conditions and more intent on meeting the war's increasing demand for airplanes.

The German Navy faced a struggle not only to develop an aviation force but also to avoid being submerged by the Prussian Army and its demands upon the German aircraft industry. From the beginning of the conflict the army had insisted upon priority of procurement, occasionally with ludicrous consequences, as Anthony Fokker related in his autobiography:

> The very first day that war was officially declared, an army telegram reached me confiscating all planes for its use. The next day an excited navy commander, frothing at the mouth because the army had gotten the jump on

him, dashed up to Schwerin from Berlin in his high-powered automobile and ordered that all my planes must be turned over to the navy. Price was no object. The point was that the navy must have them. It seemed to make no difference whether the airplanes would be of any use to the navy once they got them. . . .

My mood was to say yes to everyone, and sell to the first buyer who planked down his money on the barrel head.

Army and navy officials visited my plant daily, warring with each other, until I thought that Schwerin itself would be turned into a battlefield.[37]

It took a personal visit from Inspector von Eberhardt, who warned the Dutchman that his production was inadequate to cover the orders he was taking, to persuade Fokker to grant priority to the army's contracts. Once again the lack of coordination, this time between the services, was making itself felt. Discipline, orders, even common sense were thrown to the winds in the interservice rivalry for available airplanes, and the picture of the shrewd Dutchman playing both referee and auctioneer to the services was one more indication of the many problems besetting the military in the early days of the war.

Then the General Staff stopped all landplane deliveries to the navy, thus forcing the Naval Office to acquire any landplanes through the Inspectorate of Flying Troops. Capitalizing upon the priority of military aviation, the inspectorate further commandeered all landplane and aircraft motor production. Once it controlled motor production, it dictated the distribution of aircraft production. As of the middle of October the army's insatiable demands impeded the navy's procurement of motors, forcing the Imperial Naval Office to negotiate with the Pussian War Ministry for an allotment of motors for seaplane construction and landplanes. In essence, naval aviation was from the beginning, as Rear Admiral Starke would note in Reichstag hearings in 1918, "only a part of army aviation."[38]

German naval aviation was quite unprepared for war in August 1914, as its rudimentary organization and paucity of aircraft indicated. Although a zeppelin and an aircraft unit antedated the war, a chief of naval flying units (Befehlshaber der Marine-Flieger-Abteilungen), Rear Admiral Philipp, was appointed only on 29 August 1914 at Wilhelmshaven. Within the Imperial Naval Office's dockyard department, an aviation section was formed under Starke for the development and procurement of aviation material. The zeppelin's superior range and reliability continued to make it the navy's choice for reconnaissance, but the navy intended to use its few serviceable airplanes as short-range reconnaissance craft to assist with coastal defense. Aviation historian John Cuneo estimated that the navy had twelve seaplanes and twenty landplanes dispersed at six stations on the North and Baltic seas at the war's beginning.[39] But his figures may be inaccurate, as the naval budget commission reported in 1915 that the navy had twenty seaplanes but no landplanes in August 1914,[40] and few of those planes were suitable for wartime service.

The firm upon which the navy relied for its early patrol planes was Flugzeugbau Friedrichshafen. The navy ordered sixty-seven of Friedrichshafen's twin float craft from August through December 1914, during which time the firm delivered twenty-one.[41] Though slow (a top speed of approximately seventy-five miles per hour) and cumbersome compared to many landplanes, it was eminently reliable and seaworthy. The other companies that supplied seaplanes to the navy in 1914 were all primarily landplane producers—Albatros (seven deliveries), Gotha (three), and Rumpler (twelve)—with the exception of the Berlin yacht firm Örtz, which delivered two flying boats, and the Hansa-Brandenburg Aircraft Works, which delivered one floatplane. None of the firms could produce more than half the planes ordered, with production times ranging anywhere from one week to three months per plane, depending upon the firm. In order to supplement these meager supplies of material, the imperial dockyards at Wilhelmshaven and Danzig received orders in December to undertake aircraft construction, but the dockyards learned that experienced aircraft designers and skilled workers were impossible to obtain.[42] The navy had no choice but to rely primarily on private industry.

Despite its straitened circumstances and the primitive state of naval aviation, the navy conceived in 1914 the need for a torpedo plane, for which it began negotiations with Albatros. Certainly part of the attraction of the torpedo plane concept was its purely naval nature, and by the end of 1914 Albatros, Brandenburg, Friedrichshafen, and Gotha had shown interest in T-plane construction.[43]

The first six months of the war ended rather dismally for German aviation: the Prussian Army air service's performance at the front was inferior; the Bavarian Army's mobilization of its aircraft industry, inadequate; the state of German naval aviation, marginal; and coordination among the three forces in aviation, nonexistent. The absence of a superior agency coordinating all the branches of the German military establishment was felt in aviation from the beginning of the war. The Prussian Army, if the dominant member of the German armed forces, was not sufficiently dominant to direct an efficient aviation mobilization for the entire German state. Furthermore, it had serious difficulty managing its own mobilization of the aircraft industry.

Despite a commanding position in political bargaining with the industry and assistance from the politicians, the army appeared singularly inept in its absence of detailed mobilization plans for the industry, inability to ease the severe dislocation of supply, inadequate execution of exemption policy, and slowness to adjust to stationary warfare. The army sought to control aircraft prices while ignoring wage and material costs, despite its professed awareness of the interrelatedness of all these factors. The military men in the War Ministry were apparently unable to exercise any control over raw material prices because they were not as knowledgeable in such areas as industrialists like Rathenau and Wichard von Möllendorff, who directed the ministry's raw materials department.[44] Consequently, the army controlled the prices of small industries like the airplane manufacturers when it could, while it was powerless to restrict the prices of large industries and raw material suppliers.

If certain aspects of the army's policies vis-à-vis the industry were ill considered, others were quite sensible. It judiciously enforced its construction guidelines. Its price policy was well intentioned in restricting prices for as long as possible and then in increasing them in February 1915 in order to encourage innovation, productivity, and safety. If the policy worked hardships on small aircraft factories, it was because the army considered them insignificant and lacking in the capital necessary for progress.

The army's preference for dealing with large companies was one reason for its attempt to abridge patent protection in August 1914. It intended to lower the barriers to drawing large industrial enterprises to aircraft production. Such companies would not only possess the capital necessary for experimentation and innovation; they would also assume licensed production more willingly than individualistic entrepreneurs like Euler, for whom profits were not the sole motive for owning an aircraft company. The aircraft departments of large-scale industrial combines like AEG and the Gothaer Waggonfabrik, which the army had drawn to aircraft production in 1912–13, were assumed to have the capital reserves to innovate and survive, as would SSW and Zeppelin. AEG was already developing a twin-engine "battle plane" in 1914. The army's price policy thus meshed well with its preference for large companies in aircraft production.

Yet the army would have to promote the expansion of its aircraft manufacturers with care, lest it create what it had sought so fiercely to avoid before August 1914—monopoly. If through the natural evolution toward large size, an evolution that military policies promoted, industrial power in the aircraft industry came to be wielded by monopoly, the army would have more difficulty preserving its control in wartime.

CHAPTER 2

Year of Decision, 1915

THE YEAR 1915 presented the German Army with the challenge of molding the air service into an efficient fighting machine. Limited aerial activity during the winter, declining morale, rapid expansion and the influx of inexperienced fliers hurt aerial efficiency at the front, while the dysfunctional organization of German aviation and its difficulties with the aircraft industry were evident in the rear. Appropriate action was necessary in a number of areas: adjustments to the Prussian Army's own aviation bureaucracy to accord with the growth of the air service and its assumption of a larger role in the affairs of the aircraft industry to improve productivity and aircraft quality and more efficient coordination of the Prussian, Bavarian, and German naval aviation bureaucracies.

Maj. Wilhelm Siegert, the High Command's aviation adviser, discerned, as had Inspector of Flying Troops Eberhardt, that the very structure of the air arm—the absence of one overarching authority and of staff officers at army headquarters—was partially responsible for its mediocre performance. Siegert suggested the formation of a unified aviation command to the High Command, which recommended to the Prussian War Ministry on 9 February 1915 that a chief of field aviation (Feldflugchef) be established to direct all aviation affairs, including industrial production. Although the War Ministry initially refused to have the inspectorate removed from its direct authority, after discussions with the High Command it conceded control over the inspectorate to the chief of field aviation on 26 April with the explanation that it recognized the overweening need "to organize a systematic mobilization of the aviation industry."[1] The entire German flying troops organization was now subordinate to the chief, and the army commands, which directed the operations of the field units, now employed a staff officer of fliers as their liaison with the front.

Col. Hermann von der Lieth-Thomsen, who had served on the prewar General Staff in charge of aviation, became the new chief, and Wilhelm Siegert his deputy. With a small staff of ten officers and twenty-eight men at general headquarters in Charleville, they became responsible for the German air service. One enormous task they faced was replacing the unplanned day-to-day efforts of the individual factories with a coordinated, long-range industrial effort to supply sufficient numbers of aircraft for reconnaissance, artillery observation, bombardment, and the incipient air fighting.

Preparations for this undertaking had begun even before the chief assumed his office. By March, three intermediate staging area aircraft parks had been redesignated army air parks, factorylike enterprises equipped with substantial stocks of material and capable of undertaking major improvements on aircraft. On 1 April the Inspectorate of Flying Troops was separated from the Inspectorate of Aviation and Motor Vehicles, the first step in the removal of aviation from transportation in the military bureaucracy since the creation of the War Ministry's department A7L for aviation in June 1914.

Then on 16 April, some ten days before the chief assumed command, the inspectorate recommended the creation of its own permanent aircraft acceptance commission.[2] The fliers replacement units (*Flieger-Ersatz-Abteilungen,* FEAs,) which were located near factories, had previously supervised aircraft acceptance and trained personnel, but they had experienced a destabilizing turnover of personnel as new flying units were created. Training had conflicted with procurement, and the latter had suffered severely. Now, in the inspectorate's proposal, a Central Acceptance Commission (Zentral-Abnahme-Kommission) would collect, evaluate, and disseminate front and factory experience to four subcommissions, which would deal directly with the widely dispersed factories. Col. Paul Oschmann, the head of the War Ministry's aviation department, approved the formation of the commissions on 3 May 1915.[3]

As of May 1915 the inspectorate was a small, compact organization comprising a test center under Capt. Felix Wagenführ, the new Central Aircraft Acceptance Commission, which traveled to factories checking construction procedures, and eleven FEA's which were still responsible for daily surveillance of construction procedures. The acceptance subcommissions did not appear in final form until the winter of 1915–16, for

The Organization of the
Prussian Flying Troops Aircraft Units, May 1915

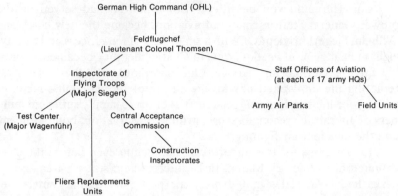

SOURCE: Heinz J. Nowarra, *Fünfzig Jahre deutsche Luftwaffe, 1910–1960*, 1:106.

even in late 1915 the replacement units still performed aircraft acceptance. Most sources ignore the orders of April and May 1915 and simply place the formation of the commission apparatus in the winter of 1915–16.[4] In reality its evolution took some eight months from ratification to full establishment of the new acceptance hierarchy.

The shortage of technically trained men and the inspectorate's difficulty in retaining its technical experts were probably responsible for the long gestation period. One of the best, Hermann Dorner, a prewar aircraft manufacturer who had worked for the test institute since 4 August 1914 and had compiled the first instructions for construction and delivery of military aircraft, resigned to become technical director of DFW in September 1915.[5] The paucity of men with education and experience in aircraft construction and technology not only delayed the formation of the acceptance bureaucracy, it also undoubtedly affected the quality of aircraft acceptance. A. R. Weyl observed that unscrupulous manufacturers resorted to a number of tricks—from altering performance figures to installing inflated bladders in fuel tanks to reduce aircraft weight and increase climb—to obtain acceptance of inferior aircraft. When the frontline units complained, the inspectorate would reply defensively that the acceptance procedure was sound and the inspecting officers honest and competent. Weyl also claimed that inspectorate officials often looked the other way when they inspected Fokker's airplanes and factory.[6] Yet the inability of acceptance officials to detect all the

substandard craft and dishonest techniques did not necessarily mean that
the army intentionally shut its eyes to these violations. To do so would
have wantonly risked the fliers' loss of confidence in the military acceptance bureaucracy. The evidence—the investigations of and restrictions on Euler craft in later 1914 and those on Fokker planes in late 1914
and mid-1915—shows that the inspectorate monitored aircraft production to the best of its ability, given the primitive conditions of early
aviation, the air arm's lack of experience with light aircraft, and the
shortage of technically trained men in aviation.

The aircraft manufacturers, stimulated by wartime opportunity,
were producing designs that taxed to the utmost the army's abilities to
assess aircraft. The giant planes at SSW and Zeppelin, a new all-metal
airplane at Junkers, and the armed single-seat fighter were developed at
this time.

The Zeppelin factory built a multi-engined aircraft at the Gotha
aircraft construction company. The inspectorate initially felt the plane
was too large, but changed its mind after a first successful test flight.
Count von Zeppelin himself flew in the giant on 1 August 1915 and
encouraged its development; consequently, a further factory was erected
in Friedrichshafen in 1915 to build giant airplanes.[7]

SSW forged ahead with two giant airplane projects—one designed
by SSW engineer Forssman and the other by two brothers, Bruno and
Franz Steffen. The Steffens, working independently, had designed a craft
which interested the inspectorate. The inspectorate consequently arranged for them to join SSW and then promptly awarded SSW a contract
to build the bomber. The Forssman giant underwent several
modifications during 1915 which delayed its acceptance. The Steffens'
craft, however, passed company tests in April 1915 and military tests at
Döberitz in June, at which time the inspectorate ordered six more. In
November the army designated these craft R-planes (*Riesenflugzeuge,* or
"giant planes") and stipulated that their engines be repairable in flight.
Despite the complication of meeting the new requirement and prolonged
engine troubles with the craft, SSW delivered all six to the army between
the end of 1915 and June 1917. These craft, the first R-planes to see
service, were used only on the Russian front; in 1915 full utilization of the
R-plane lay some two years in the future.[8]

Another craft of the future had its origins in 1915 in a bath heater
factory. Hugo Junkers, inventor of everything from ship motors to flying
wings, had been interested in the airplane as a means of transportation
since 1909. In 1914 Junkers turned his efforts to the development of an

all-metal airplane for military purposes. When the armed forces took no interest, Junkers began to invest about twenty thousand marks monthly of the 2.5 million marks annual profit from the bath heater factory in Dessau into aviation research in his Aachen test institute. At the beginning of 1915 he built a test institute in Dessau, and in February he offered to develop a metal airplane for the War Ministry. After a visit to his plant in May a War Ministry commission was sufficiently impressed to issue Junkers his first contract for a prototype. He finished the J-1 in December 1915, but encountered difficulties in testing and continued work into 1916.[9]

The army was acting as assessor and cautious promoter of the early metal and giant airplanes, and both types had to undergo further modification before seeing service. In 1915 the inspectorate had just begun to set stipulations for the R-plane and was not yet faced with the metal airplane. But the appearance of the fighter plane, created by a French pilot in a daring stroke of genius, required the inspectorate's immediate attention, lest the German flying troops be driven from the skies. The development of Germany's first fighter aircraft consequently became the most critical test of the military-industrial relationship in construction and technology during 1915.

In the early spring of 1915 the French flier Roland Garros attached a forward firing machine gun to the fuselage of his Morane monoplane and metal wedges to his propeller blades to deflect bullets. Thus armed, he downed a handful of German planes, but on 18 April Garros was forced to land in German territory. His craft, seized before he could destroy it, was shipped to Berlin, where the Prussian authorities promptly summoned Anthony Fokker from his factory at Schwerin to adapt Garros's system for German use.[10] Fokker's adaptation—a mechanical interrupter gear enabling a machine gun fixed to the fuselage of an airplane to fire through the arc of the revolving propeller in the direction of flight—revolutionized air warfare.

The army probably selected Fokker because of his concentration and expertise in the construction of light aircraft. Garros flew a light single-seat monoplane (a Morane parasol type L) powered by a Gnome rotary engine; Fokker was building a modified copy of the Morane powered by an Oberursel rotary, which was a copy of the French Gnome; hence he was the inspectorate's logical choice for the task. In his biography Fokker related that he conceived the gear in a brilliant flash of inspiration while on the train from Berlin to Schwerin.[11] Yet it is more likely, in light of later patent disputes over the gear, that the aviation authorities may have given

Fokker the details of a synchronizing gear patented by LVG engineer Franz Schneider in 1913 and promised to protect him from any suits for breach of patent that LVG might bring. This interpretation would account for the Fokker team's apparent knowledge of Schneider's gear and its ability to develop another mechanism so quickly.

After May the E-plane (*Eindecker,* or monoplane) began to appear at the front in driblets—two by June, only eleven by mid-July. Experienced pilots trained on it at the front; novices, at the factory in Schwerin. Although the plane was not problem-free—it occasionally shot off its own propeller—it rapidly made Fokker a legend, as he demonstrated the airplane to the frontline units.[12] His flying talents made him unique among the great German manufacturers and certainly gave him some advantage over his competitors. He enjoyed close rapport with the great pilots of the German air force from Oswald Bölcke and Max Immelmann to Manfred von Richthofen. Ironically, the inspectorate had taken great pains after the creation of the acceptance commission to sever all ties between the front and the factories in order to avoid the confusion of August 1914. Now, the importance of Fokker and his factory in training pilots on the new plane enabled him to circumvent the bureaucratic prohibition. The inspectorate might direct the formal transmission of information from the front to the factories; the informal lines of communication remained open and would prove valuable to pilots and manufacturers alike.

Despite the enthusiasm of pilots like Bölcke and Immelmann for the new craft, the Fokker monoplane experienced delays in deployment. The Oberursel rotary presented problems while German pilots, who were used to heavy, stable airplanes, had difficulty flying the light, maneuverable monoplane. After three fatal crashes in July and August, the inspectorate disbanded its Fokker training unit at Döberitz, returned the monoplanes to the factory, and forbade their use. Only the intrepidity of the frontline pilots saved Fokker. Immelmann, Bölcke, and others used the machines more offensively than instructions allowed, as they roamed over the front lines in search of prey. Immelmann had gained his first victory in the Fokker on 1 August; others followed, and their success led to demands for more Fokkers. The inspectorate relented and resumed training pilots on the monoplane in October, but now entirely at Schwerin. The inspectorate's ban was usual procedure in the case of a series of fatal crashes; the influence of the frontline pilots in lifting the restriction was new.

All manufacturers began to establish contact with the fighter pilots and seek their suggestions. In the rather uncomplicated circumstances of early wartime aviation, their orders would depend on the pilots' reception of the craft. Ties between the front pilots and factories were reestablished, but now in an extravagant fashion. On leave in Berlin the fliers could bask in the luxury of the best hotels, their every whim catered to by aircraft manufacturers who rented the facilities. Immelmann, the first great Fokker ace, the Eagle of Lille, shunned the Berlin frivolities and spent his leave in November as Fokker's guest in Schwerin, where they discussed the development of a more heavily armed E-plane built especially for Immelmann.[13] The suggestions of the great pilots were valuable, as long as the construction of personal mounts for them did not interfere with regular production of the armed monoplane.

Yet regular production was distressingly meager, as the following monthly totals of Fokker E-planes supplied and accepted show: June—eighteen and eighteen; July—thirty-two and twenty-six; August—thirty-one and thirty-six; October—twenty-three and twenty-nine; November—twenty-five and thirty-two; and December—thirty and eighteen.[14] In late fall he introduced the best of the E-series, the improved, stronger E-3, powered by a one-hundred-horsepower Oberursel rotary. Given the high rate of wartime attrition, the relatively small number of Fokker fighters produced explains why there were never more than fifty in service at any given time, even in early 1916. Limited production consequently restricted the impact of the Fokker E series on the air war,[15] and the Fokker factory was incapable of producing more.

The Steffens brothers at SSW did design a single-seat E-plane that resembled the Fokker, and the inspectorate ordered twenty for construction at the SSW transformer works in Nürnberg during early 1916. The Bavarian firm Pfalz, which had copied the Morane parasol for production before the war, also introduced its own armed monoplane. Neither craft was produced in quantity, and the performance of the Fokker exceeded both.[16] Production of the armed monoplane consequently remained small-scale, essentially for two reasons. The first was the limited production capacity of the three firms involved; the second was the inspectorate's failure to have the craft produced under license by larger firms, which is best explained by the air service's need for the standard two-seat biplane, now armed with a synchronized machine gun and a ring mounted machine gun for the observer. These craft, or C-planes (single-engined armed biplanes), remained the mainstay of the German air service (and all other air forces) during the entire war as they performed their indispensable tasks of reconnaissance and bombing—duties that directly affected the ground war.

The army's relationship with the aircraft industry in technological and construction matters during 1915 shows that while much change occurred in the first year of the war, the effect of the army's prewar policies lingered on. Early standardization on a single aircraft type—the large, stable two-seat airplane powered by a one-hundred-horsepower in-line engine—had served it well as a vehicle with which to develop the German aircraft industry, but it had also hampered the development of other models. Consequently, the industry and the flying troops in general lacked experience in dealing with a variety of aircraft. Now both were faced with the construction, testing, and mass production of many aircraft types, from the very large to the very small, employing new types of construction methods, entailing new aeronautical principles and problems. Further, wartime conditions placed severe temporal restrictions on the development of the airplanes and tested them far more rigorously than the simulated conditions of prewar maneuvers. The industry, on its own initiative and with the aid of the army, was struggling to meet the test; the inspectorate's contribution to this effort included expansion of its bureaucracy to monitor the factories more closely.

The surveillance of plant processes served not only the inspectorate's technological and construction goals but also its formulation of price policy. After the decision to grant a price increase in February, the War Ministry and the inspectorate began to examine the factories regularly in order to set aircraft prices more stringently. Although some firms initially refused to surrender their books, most cooperated, and after several conferences between the inspectorate and the aircraft manufacturers the War Ministry concluded that the rise in wages and raw material prices did not warrant an increase in aircraft prices. Consequently, it did not honor the February price increase of 3 percent. The army's refusal to raise prices was based on the conviction that the profits from larger serial orders of fifty to one hundred aircraft offset the increased costs of production at the major firms, despite their protestations to the contrary during the winter.[17]

The army forestalled price increases in February, but events in Berlin in the spring of 1915 conspired to undermine this decision. Average wages in the Berlin aircraft factories had risen at twice the rate of those paid in all German aircraft factories.[18] Berlin—the center of the German aircraft industry, where the largest firms clustered in proximity to the

Prussian military authorities—was ripe for a management-labor confrontation in the industry. Wage agreements in effect since 1913, when
the factories employed only some five hundred workers, expired at the
end of March. A new agreement on wages and working conditions between the Berlin manufacturers and the German metal and woodworkers
unions would apply to more than four thousand workers in the most
important aircraft factories in Germany.

After several meetings, labor and management sought the mediation
of the Prussian War Ministry. The ministry pressured the manufacturers
toward collective bargaining and the acceptance of a broad agreement, so
further negotiations resulted on 9 May in the following agreement between the Berlin aircraft industrialists and the German metal and woodworkers unions: a normal work week of fifty-one hours, or, if double
shifts became necessary, nine-hour shifts six days a week and six hours on
Sunday; and increased minimum hourly and piecework wages with
additional stipends for heavy work and night shifts. The manufacturers
also committed themselves to use the contracted labor organizations as
much as possible when hiring additional workers. Finally, a new grievance
procedure was established, according to which workers' committees first,
then mediatory commissions of six representatives—three from the
workers organization and three from the association of Berlin aircraft
industrialists—would resolve future problems. The agreement, a mile-
stone for labor-management relations in the aircraft industry, was signed
on 9 May and would remain in effect for one year or until an official
peace, whichever came first.[19]

The War Ministry's role in these negotiations accorded with a policy
memorandum disseminated in May by Gen. Ernst von Wrisberg, head of
the War Ministry's war department. Wrisberg considered wage raises
justified in light of the increasing cost of living and compared them to the
employers' increased war profits. His "Guidelines for Handling Labor
Matters in War Industries" consequently instructed the military authorities to give equal weight to the wishes of employers and employees in
their decisions.[20]

Only four months later, on 16 September, the War Ministry once
again assumed the role of advocate for wage increases for the Johannisthal workers, as it engineered an accord setting hourly wage increases for
single men and women and married workers and heads of households.
Now the metal and woodworkers in the Berlin aircraft industry were
among the highest paid workers in Germany. The industry paid wages
comparable to those in the Berlin metal industry, and wages were one of

the best barometers of an industry's importance in wartime Germany. Although real wages in the aircraft industry declined in 1915, real wages in other war industries declined even further.[21] Yet this promotion of higher wages for aircraft workers, while a positive step to maintain labor productivity in the face of inflation, had a pernicious effect on aircraft prices. Initially, the War Ministry obtained the industrialists' agreement without extending a price increase for aircraft and aircraft repairs. Later, however, the manufacturers persuaded the ministry to make the wage increases, which were retroactive from 1 September, conditional on an increase in aircraft prices, which the War Ministry granted in early October. The War Ministry had two essential goals—to meet the demands of the front and to keep its prices as reasonable as possible. In a sense, however, the attainment of the first, which entailed maintaining productivity through sufficient profits and wages, undercut the second, especially in an inflationary wartime market in which the army exerted no control over raw material prices. The army's support of wage increases therefore enabled the manufacturers to squeeze higher aircraft prices from it, although the War Ministry merely granted the price increase it had promised in February 1915.

The Johannisthal wage movement had other significant repercussions within the industry. In September 1915 the Berlin aircraft industrialists, under pressure from labor and the military to yield on the wage agreements, decided to form a Berlin Association of Aircraft Factories.[22] Some of the largest aircraft manufacturers, like Rumpler, Albatros, and LVG, were making a bid to be independent of the industry's trade association, the Convention of Aircraft Industrialists, which still comprised many small firms. The transitional state of the industry, with some firms well on the way to large-scale industrial enterprises and others little larger than workshops, had caused strains in the convention before the war and had led some factories, particularly LVG, to remain outside the organization. Now that some of the staunchest prewar members of the convention like Rumpler and Albatros had become large producers, they threatened to desert. The War Ministry did nothing to arrest this fragmentation, as it had preferred to deal with the large Berlin firms since the beginning of the war.

Curt Sperling, the general secretary of the convention, prevented the Berlin factories from forming a separate association, but he had to make two concessions to Berlin in order to avoid a breach. He consented first to establish a liaison with the Association of Berlin Metal Industrialists and then to have the convention submit wage rates by city—rather than an average wage for all factories—in future attempts to secure price increases from the army. The second concession also benefited the army, because it prevented factories in other cities from using the convention to obtain disproportionately high wages and accorded with the army's cost accounting procedures, which took into account regional variations. Had the convention had its way, aircraft prices would have been based upon the Berlin market, the highest in Germany.

Yet the convention did not come away empty-handed, because Sperling parlayed the granting of higher wages in Berlin into a price increase for the entire industry. The most logical reason for the War Ministry's change of heart between September, when it would not link prices to the wage increase, and October, when it granted the price increase, was an effective pressure campaign by the entire industry, orchestrated by an astute and experienced negotiator. Furthermore, in mid-October the inspectorate informed Sperling that the industry would be placed on the same level of importance as the Krupp armaments and Zeiss optic firms (that is, the highest level); consequently, those workers that the industry deemed indispensable would be exempted from military service. This achievement, and the War Ministry's role in setting higher wages, prove that the army considered the aircraft industry extremely important to the war effort by the middle of 1915.

The workers wage movement in the Berlin aircraft factories thus culminated in higher wages and prices and in a rift within the industry that was healed only by the acknowledgment that Berlin held a special position. What had given such a far-reaching effect to the initial wage demands was the army's intervention in management-labor relations. Under prewar circumstances the army acted only as buyer, not arbiter of the industry's internal matters. Now, in its dual role of consumer and arbiter of management-labor disputes, the army assumed the responsibility for a wider range of industrial affairs. Consequently, both labor and management, especially the former because of its underdog status, began to look increasingly to the army to solve their problems. The army, determined to maintain industrial productivity, responded in a manner satisfactory to both parties. The emergence of labor as a third party to the military-industrial relationship enabled the army to remain the arbiter in its dealings with the aircraft industry, but in a very different way from prewar, when it had controlled the situation. Now it had to balance precariously between the industrialists and the labor unions, as each pressed for its own advantage.

Spurred by the increasing wartime contracts from the army, the aircraft factories rapidly expanded their plant size and production, as the following table shows:

The Expansion of Five Major Aircraft Companies, 1914–15[23]

Firm	Date	Plant (m²)	Work Force	Production
Albatros	1914	12,824	745	336
(Johannisthal)	1915	19,932	1,235	851
Aviatik	1914	10,000	220	165
	1915	——	330	316
Fokker	1914	10,000	110	32
	1915	——	480	260
LVG	1914	24,229	450	300
	1915	25,542	920	1,020
Rumpler	1914	6,000	630	108
	1915	14,000	835	210

As these figures indicate, firms expanded their production from two to eight times, their labor force from one-half to three times, and overall aircraft deliveries to the army from 1,348 in 1914 to 4,532 in 1915. Expansion peaked during the warm months, but declined significantly in the winter. Albatros's labor force, for example, rose from 430 in January 1914 to 980 in November, then declined to 860 in January 1915, but rose again to 1,460 in November 1915. Albatros also opened a plant in Schneidemühl in east Germany, which delivered 3 planes in 1914 but 322 in 1915. By mid-August 1915 Albatros was delivering 12 planes weekly from its Johannisthal plant and an additional 8 from Schneidemühl.[24]

These production increases enabled the expansion of the flying troops. In March 1915 there were seventy-two field flying units, two fortress units, a high command aviation corps, and sixteen air parks—a strength which, though more than double that of August 1914, was judged inadequate to meet the increased demands of the front. By October there were eighty field and eight artillery flying units, two combat flights for home defense, two aviation corps of the supreme command and eighteen aviation parks. At the end of the year there were eighty-two field and fourteen artillery flying units, and six combat squadrons, approximately 764 aircraft, plus 40 single-seat fighter aircraft. Yet this force remained inadequate; the French air arm alone had the same number of aircraft. Fortunately for the German flying troops, British aircraft production lagged far behind both France and Germany (1,700 as compared to 4,900 and 4,532, respectively) and a Russian air force was practically nonexistent.[25]

This basic inadequacy of production hampered the German flying troops' performance of their duties during 1915. The troops were just recovering from their winter doldrums when the French attacked in the Artois sector in May 1915. The introduction of the armed two-seater C-plane helped restore German morale during the middle of the year. Yet, after a lull in July and August, the German service found itself outnumbered when the French attacked again in Champagne and Artois. Forced on the defensive, the German aerial arm resorted to the tactics of aerial blockade, using all of its aircraft, regardless of suitability, as combat planes in defensive patrols to protect German air space. When the Fokkers arrived, they were dispersed among other types in the blockade, an act that nullified the effect that they might have had as a unit.[26] The Fokker, tied to larger and slower planes, was simply not suited to such tactics, as Immelmann and Bölcke soon noticed. Yet here production clearly affected frontline tactics, because the very lack of Fokker monoplanes and the overall numerical inferiority of the German air service on the western front had caused this blockade mentality. The German air service could hope to achieve, at the very best, only a temporary aerial superiority over a circumscribed area of the front.

The industry had grown fast; the front's demands had grown faster. By the summer of 1915 army air chief Thomsen had realized that drastic measures were necessary to increase productivity in the aircraft industry. In an important memorandum of 2 June he proclaimed that the state of aircraft production, which he considered the most crucial aspect of aviation armament, served neither the interests of the military nor the progress of aviation technology:

> Military aviation must presently rely upon a few factories whose capabilities are thoroughly inadequate to meet the great demands of the present and the near future. Given their completely insignificant financial basis, high profits through serial deliveries are of the greatest importance to them. Costly experiments are avoided, progress is thus retarded, achievement stands still. Without fail, our large industrial enterprises must be induced to undertake aircraft construction . . . , whether they themselves build new plants or, preferably, buy and transform the most proven present small factories into great plants.[27]

He rejected the use of state factories, which he deemed useful only for the mass production of established war materiel. He also suggested the elimination of private flying schools at the factories and the buildup of military pilot training schools as well as the creation of a research, test, and training institute directly subordinate to the War Ministry. All of

these recommendations had as their one basic aim the end of all dependence of the air service on the private initiative of the industry as it then
existed. By drawing heavy industry to aircraft manufacture Thomsen
sought to place production on a firmer financial basis, enable greater
experimentation, and increase competition to the point that the original
aircraft firms would produce or be crushed.

In one area—pilot training—Thomsen's proposals were unrealistic.
It would have been prohibitively expensive in money and personnel for
the army to create and staff sufficient training schools to replace the
factory schools and meet the increased demand for fliers. The number of
factory schools under military supervision actually increased in 1915,
from eleven in March to twenty by the end of the year. The Fokker
factory's essential role as the training agency for its own single-seat
fighter was indicative of the army's overall reliance on the industry for
basic flight training.

Although this relatively minor aspect of Thomsen's program was
impossible to execute, the prospects of success for his major concern—the
enlargement of the aircraft industry—were good. In order to carry out the
chief's plans, the inspectorate formulated a policy of gradually phasing in
new firms by issuing them small initial orders, which, if fulfilled successfully, would be increased. The most important firm it drew to aircraft
production in this manner was the Hannoversche Waggonfabrik AG
(Hawa). As aviation historian Peter Grosz has pointed out, rolling-stock
manufacturers had skilled labor forces, excellent woodworking capacity,
and large stocks of seasoned timber, "a very scarce commodity in wartime
Germany, particularly since forced kiln drying was unknown." In the
summer of 1915 it began to manufacture propellers and shortly thereafter
to assist Fliers Replacement Unit No. 5 in Hannover with aircraft repairs.
The unit trained Hawa's workers in aircraft construction and then had a
Hawa engineer, Albrecht Nuss, released from active duty to become
technical director of the firm's new aircraft department. Soon afterward
the factory won contracts for the licensed production of 24 Aviatik C-1
machines. Production began in November, the first craft passed its flight
and static tests in February, and Hawa would produce 146 Aviatiks
before it continued on to the successful production of its own designs.[28]

The inspectorate also engineered the Benz motor company's acquisition of the Aviatik factory in Leipzig in order to give it a firmer financial
base. The Daimler motor company in Stuttgart Unterturkheim, which
already nearly monopolized the production of aircraft motors, was persuaded to undertake aircraft production, while the Waggonfabrik Linke

Hoffmann in Breslau began the construction of R-planes. As a last measure, the War Ministry loaned the Rumpler and LVG factories substantial funds for expansion.[29] On 20 November Thomsen informed the High Command that the air arm would need one thousand airplanes of all types in service during the coming year. He therefore sought ratification of the inspectorate's measures to increase production during the year and requested exemptions for the aircraft industry's essential workers.[30]

Although the Prussian Army directed its relationship with the north German aircraft industry rather efficiently in 1915, the resistance of the Bavarian Army and the German Navy to any infringement on their autonomy prevented more effective coordination among the three forces.

The Bavarian Army preserved its autonomy in administration and exemptions in 1915, but its independence of procurement was being steadily eroded, as wartime circumstances forced the Prussian Army to rely more on the Bavarian aircraft industry. The Bavarian Army rejected a suggestion of the Prussian inspectorate that it establish an aircraft acceptance commission, instead preferring to have the Engineers Inspectorate form a labor commission to monitor exemptions in the aircraft industry. The creation of a special labor commission, yet no aircraft acceptance commission, differs from the Prussian Army's decision to regulate exemptions within its existing bureaucracy while forming a special aircraft acceptance commission. The Bavarian aircraft industry was too small to require an aircraft commission, yet its more embryonic state and greater use of handicraft methods and skilled workers made a labor commission sensible.[31]

The lack of coordination between the two armies was most evident in the case of the Otto C-plane. Aviation chief Thomsen, whose office gave him control over the operations of Bavarian aviation units in the field but not the agencies in the hinterland, proposed in mid-April that Otto's production of his pusher biplane as an armed reconnaissance craft would alleviate the shortage of C-planes. Subsequently both the Prussian inspectorate and Bavarian agencies ordered battle planes from Otto until Thomsen ended this confusion by suggesting that since Prussia distributed the motors, it should order the planes. The Bavarian fliers replacement unit retaliated in early July by forcing Otto to request material for the C-plane from Prussia. After all, if the Prussians were ordering the plane and supplying its engines, they might as well supply construction materials. This imbroglio was resolved by the failure of the Otto C-plane, which in any case would have been only an interim solution to the shortage of armed planes, as its pusher configuration was less efficient than tractor craft.[32]

The Bavarian Army's relationship with Otto was complicated further by inadequate engine deliveries from Prussia and the example set by the Prussian War Ministry in its dealings with its own aircraft manufacturers. In mid-July, after Otto had succeeded in raising monthly deliveries in 1915 from thirteen to twenty-one, the Bavarian Army reduced and then halted contracts because of its inability to obtain suitable engines from Prussia. The abrupt cessation of contracts in turn caused the company problems with its labor force. In August Otto stopped payment of his cost-of-living raises. In September the metalworkers union requested that the Bavarian War Ministry intercede on behalf of the workers as the Prussian War Ministry had done in the recent Johannisthal wage disputes. The investigation of the army's labor commission, which relied strongly on statistics from the Association of Bavarian Metal Industrialists (Verband Bayerischer Metall-Industrieller, or VBMI), concluded that Otto's wages were significantly higher than those paid in other Munich factories and that the firm's precarious financial condition justified Otto's refusal to reinstate the pay increments. The War Ministry, despite a good record of labor mediation during the war, did not intervene to restore the cost-of-living raise, and the dispute was settled only in late November by a wage increase. By that time, only army subsidies totaling 750,000 marks from September through November were keeping the factory afloat.[33] By December the army had ceased to rely upon the Otto Works, as the following statement from the Bavarian Inspectorate of Aviation and Motor Vehicles indicated:

> The increased need for airplanes through spring 1916 makes a stronger claim on the Bavarian aircraft industry likely, and while the Pfalz Works should meet these demands, the Otto Works, given its plant and organization, is not likely to do the same.[34]

It based this assessment upon a labor commission report of October comparing the two plants, which, though impeded by the Otto factory's failure to record precise work times and Pfalz's refusal to submit its records, concluded that tiny Pfalz with eighty workers was nearly twice as effective as the Otto factory. It could only suggest two solutions to the Otto problem—transfer the works to other hands or place it under military control.[35]

During 1915 the Bavarian military aviation authorities functioned increasingly in the shadow of the Prussian Army, whose distribution of engines and the majority of aircraft contracts enabled it to play a greater role in the Bavarian Army's relationships with its own domestic aircraft manufacturers. By fall the Prussian inspectorate was ordering Pfalz's new monoplane scout directly from the factory and doling Bavaria's share (ten of thirty-five) out to Bavarian field units.[36] The Bavarian Army's ineffectiveness in dealing with its own producers stemmed in part from such circumstances. Pfalz's ability to withhold its books from the labor commission rested upon the fact that Prussia, not Bavaria, gave it both engines and contracts.

The Bavarian Army's inability to make the Otto Works an efficient factory stemmed not only from its lack of control over aircraft contracts but also Otto's personality and the state of the Bavarian aircraft industry. Otto's personality was very similar to August Euler's: both were independently wealthy pioneers; both had fallen behind in aviation technology and had not been able to transform their small shops into large companies; both were rather arrogant and obstreperous; and neither was awed by the military. The highly developed north German aircraft industry enabled the Prussian Army to ignore Euler, but the underdeveloped state of the Bavarian aircraft industry combined with particularism to place the Bavarian Army in the quandary of needing and supporting the Otto Works yet resenting its owner. By the end of 1915, however, the Bavarian agencies' acknowledgement of Prussia's control of the distribution of aircraft contracts brought with it the realization of their inability to maintain the inefficient Otto Works as an independent Bavarian manufacturer.

In 1915 the German Navy developed its small aviation force within the limits set by the Prussian Army's control of engine distribution, but extensive bargaining and arrangements were necessary to avoid overt interservice conflict.

The naval air service expanded from 82 officers and 2,755 men to 225 officers and 3,342 men. In September 1915 the Imperial Naval Office separated the aviation department from the dockyard department and gave it its own business and administrative organization by early March 1916. In September 1915 the first naval landplane unit was also established at the front. In December the seaplane acceptance command (Seeflugzeug-Abnahme-Kommando), which equipped planes from the factories with special naval equipment and then doled them out to the units, was supplemented by a seaplane test command (Seeflugzeug-Versuchs-Kommando), which promptly undertook to rationalize production by reducing the number of service types. Both commands were subordinate to the new aviation department in the Imperial Naval Office.[37] This evolution of the organization of naval aviation paralleled a small but steady growth of its aircraft forces. It maintained a far smaller seaplane force than it desired: in February 1915 it had 59 seaplanes, not the 120 it sought; and in December it had 143, not its desired strength of 236. Seaplane deliveries simply did not suffice for the desired expansion. The small size of this seaplane force, most of whose planes were unarmed, explains why the English reported few encounters with German seaplanes along the Belgian coast in 1915.[38]

During 1915 Friedrichshafen continued its ascendancy as the navy's premier producer, receiving orders for seventy and delivering 84 seaplanes in monthly allotments of three to ten airplanes. Brandenburg had become the second most important seaplane producer, delivering twenty-eight planes in monthly driblets of up to six floatplanes. Albatros, Rumpler, Örtz, and Sablatnig also delivered small numbers of seaplanes, Rumpler simply by mounting its strengthened landplane B-types (single-engined unarmed biplanes) on floats. The navy's contracts, even with firms like Friedrichshafen and Brandenburg, were intermittent, and there were months in which it ordered no planes from individual companies. The delay may have stemmed either from the obvious inability of even the best firms to produce seaplanes at a faster rate than ten per month or from the navy's inability to obtain sufficient motors regularly from the army.[39]

Although naval aviation was sorely under strength, it diverted precious resources to the cautious development of the torpedo plane in 1915. The naval office's dockyard department, torpedo inspectorate, and a flight unit required almost the entire year to probe the concept: modifying a single-engine landplane took until March, and the completion of tests until June, when the navy entertained offers from companies to build serial production T-planes. The tests, however, had indicated that although the basic technical and flight problems of the plane could be solved, a single-engine craft and the small torpedo used were inadequate. It would be necessary to develop a twin-float plane capable of carrying a larger torpedo. In light of the new requirement, two of the firms—Friedrichshafen and Gotha—declined flatly, although they would return to T-plane construction later. Albatros and Brandenburg would attempt to build one T-plane apiece as of September. These craft were only in prototype stages in October, but the Naval Office, expecting one of them

to be ready for testing in the near future, confidently promised the High
Seas Fleet Command that if the tests were successful, it would have five
T-planes ready for the front in eight weeks.[40]

The navy fared better in landplane than in seaplane procurement. Its
force of 64 craft in February 1915 was only 35 under its desired strength,
and by December its force of 115 landplanes *exceeded* its desired strength
by 8. It had received 177 of 194 landplanes ordered since August 1914.
For obvious reasons of simpler construction, landplanes were much easier
to obtain, and this situation was reflected in aircraft prices. For its landplanes the navy paid the same prices as the army. For landplanes with
special equipment it paid more, between 17,800 and 21,550 marks,
depending upon engine size. Seaplane prices were higher—20,800–
26,000 marks—in order to account for floats, stronger construction, and
additional equipment.[41]

The navy no longer complained of difficulties procuring its relatively
small allotment of motors for seaplane production, because the War
Ministry and Naval Office had reached tentative agreement on motor
distribution. Yet friction between the two services threatened disruption
by the end of 1915. An offer on 22 August 1915 from the Naval Office to
exchange naval cannon for sixteen aircraft machine guns required a joint
conference in November to settle the matter. On 15 December the
exchange of a naval officer for the staff of the Feldflugchef and an army
flight officer for the chief of naval aviation was arranged, although it was
not finally accomplished until February 1916.[42]

The Prussian Army's control of procurement from the German
aviation industry enabled it to undermine the bureaucratic autonomy of
the Bavarian Army and the German Navy to some extent, but not
sufficiently to halt unnecessarily wasteful conflicts. Yet its failure in this
area should not obscure the larger significance of the first full year of the
war. The army's measures toward the aircraft industry—the promotion of
the expansion of existing companies, the issuance of more contracts to
neglected ones, and the introduction of firms in other industries to
aircraft production—indicate clearly that 1915 was a very important year
in the development of a German air force. Yet most general histories of
the war begin to devote space to military aviation in 1916 with air combat
over the battles of Verdun and the Somme.[43] This concentration stems
from the tendency of military and aviation historians to concentrate on
developments at the front, to view and periodize aerial developments
according to the great battles of the conflict. While this approach has
merit, it denigrates the importance of long-term preparations, in this case

of an industrial nature. Yet, for a technological implement like the airplane, such preparations were absolutely necessary, and, in Germany, very much in evidence. Whatever the aircraft's performance at the front, important military men and civilians perceived its value, and thus the value of the aircraft industry, from the very beginning of the war. By the summer and fall of 1915, the army had elevated the industry to a position of priority among its war industries. Nothing confirms this better than Thomsen's repeated appeals to transform the industry into a group of giant firms. For those observers who would regard the airplane as nothing more than a glamorous but militarily insignificant development of the war, worthy of mention only because of the aura of individual chivalry and heroism which it brought to the otherwise brutal slaughter of masses of humanity, this evidence of the Prussian Army's appreciation in 1915 of the airplane as an important weapon of war might come as a surprise. The creation of heroes like Immelmann and Bölcke was a serendipitous but secondary benefit of the new arm. The evidence shows indisputably that the proponents of the airplane in the German Army understood that for this invention of the technological age of mass production to realize its full potential as a serious weapon of war, it would have to be mass-produced.

CHAPTER 3

Toward Total War in the Air,
January–October 1916

NINETEEN SIXTEEN, the year of the battles of Verdun and the Somme, found the German flying troops on the western front hard-pressed to hold their own against an enemy always superior in number and often in quality of aircraft. Amid the developments of this critical year, two topics of considerable importance in the military-industrial relationship emerge—limitations of aviation patent protection and the reorganization of the German aviation bureaucracy. The rising importance of aviation necessitated further considerations of patent protection, a topic which had lain dormant since August 1914, when eight major aircraft firms had agreed to allow the military the license-free use of the ill-defined category of lesser patents and to submit patent disputes to the arbitration of a parliamentary commission.

One of the matters at issue was the question of prior patents related to Anthony Fokker's invention of the synchronized machine gun. In 1910 August Euler—Germany's first licensed pilot and aircraft manufacturer—had patented a design for a "destroyer" airplane, a craft with a fixed, forward-firing machine gun (Machine Patent No. 248601, Class 77, Group 2, 24 July 1910). His plane was a pusher machine, one with the engine behind the crew, so he did not conceive of a synchronizing gear. The Prussian authorities, who had no interest in armed aircraft in 1910, had peremptorily dismissed his suggestion, but Euler could claim a prior patent on the use of the airplane as a gun platform for a fixed weapon firing in the direction of flight.[1]

Yet when Euler attempted to secure compensation for infringement of his patent rights, the army first suggested the postponement of claims until the end of the war. When Euler persisted, the War Ministry agreed orally in November to pay him license fees of 750 marks for each of the first one hundred armed planes and 500 marks for each craft thereafter for the duration of the patent until 1925 and to exempt the fees from the war profit taxes. Later, however, it did not confirm the settlement and argued that the parliamentary commission, which had jurisdiction over all patents, considered his patent of limited importance because it could be used only in conjunction with other patents (that is, the synchronizing gear). Euler refused to accept this judgment, and the new year arrived with no resolution of the dispute.[2]

Now, however, the growth of the German air service and the aircraft industry necessitated some clarification of patent guidelines. Consequently, the parliamentary commission called a conference on patents with the military and industry for 20 January 1916.[3] The patent conference proceedings, though no settlement was reached, clearly delineated the positions of the parties involved. The War Ministry felt that it was acting with restraint and within the law in requesting the license-free use of lesser patents, as it could have taken the more drastic step of expropriation by decree. Because of the large military contracts and extensive frontline advice the army provided, it also deemed its request morally correct and considered the release of lesser patents a small price for the industry to pay in return for such benefits. The parliamentary representatives essentially agreed with the army in its attempt to evade patent law, but for different reasons. Baron Karl von Gamp-Massaunen, the most rabid supporter of the army, believed that the national interest, as determined by the government and particularly the military, took precedence over any laws. Albert Südekum, a Socialist relatively new to the commission, felt that the industry was attempting to profit unjustly from the war, so he had no qualms about threatening nationalization of the industry and the induction of the manufacturers, however farfetched these options were. Although Dr. Hermann Paasche sought a cooperative solution, he believed that it should be on the army's terms, as the industry's wartime profits more than compensated it for the forfeiture of license fees. Only Count Hans Georg von Oppersdorff, who worked in the war department's central aviation agency, showed any sympathy for the position of the Convention of German Aircraft Industrialists.

Of all the parties, only the industry found itself internally divided. Euler stood to lose millions of marks if the War Ministry got its way, because it would undoubtedly refuse to make an exception for his patent

even if it was a prewar invention. Consequently, he supported the maintenance of patent laws. Sperling, as general secretary of the motor vehicle
and aircraft industrialists' association, which comprised the industry's
older firms, naturally sided with his colleague Euler. On the other hand,
firms like Linke-Hofmann and Schwade, which built and repaired aircraft
under license, had everything to gain from an abrogation of patent rights
and license fees. The representatives of the industry had divided according to the immediate interests of their firms, thereby preventing the
industry from presenting the united front so vital to the defense of
aviation patent rights.

The day after the meeting, 21 January 1916, Euler received a letter
from Walter Fröbus, the director of LFG, complaining about the attitude
of the parliamentary commission:

> I find it peculiar that the gentlemen of the "voluntary association of the
> members of parliament" . . . seem without exception to be of an opinion that
> is opposed to the interests of the aircraft industry. . . .
> We have worked with this voluntary association from the beginning
> without ever, to my knowledge, inquiring as to its origin. Now, however, this
> seems essential after yesterday's numerous direct and indirect threats of the
> trenches. Even if the legal circumstances have changed, it is still demeaning
> for an industry that is doing its best for the fatherland to receive threats that
> even employers are forbidden to utter to workers.[4]

Ironically, Fröbus, one of the members of the convention who had participated in the August 1914 conference, was partially responsible for the
situation he deplored.

At a meeting requested by Oppersdorff that evening, Sperling,
Euler, and four other aircraft manufacturers resolved that the industry's
position should be to settle all patent matters during the war through
conferences and agreements based on the law. At the army's request they
would disseminate patents and the accompanying technical data to con-
tracting firms for a fee, just as the army would have to pay if it built
aircraft or installed patented parts. At the plenary session of the convention the following day, Saturday, 22 January, the manufacturers adopted
this statement and also agreed that Euler's machine gun patent was one
"of extraordinary importance."[5] The older and more important aircraft
companies had chosen to support the law and August Euler.

Six months of protracted maneuvering ensued, during which Col.
Paul Oschmann of the War Ministry attempted to concentrate authority
in patent matters in the hands of the parliamentary deputies, while Euler
fought to preserve patent law and normal legal processes in the name of

the free market process. Manufacturers, military men, and parliamentary deputies finally reconvened on 20 June, and the outcome of this session was officially confirmed in a War Ministry circular to the aircraft companies on 13 July.[6] Although claims arising from industrial patents were legal, the firms had agreed to waive such claims against the army and navy during the war under three conditions. First, if military workshops built the patented part, the army would negotiate special agreements with the firm. Second, firms that copied patented parts under contract to the military would have to pay for a fabrication right from the original company. Third, the agreement of August 1914 to relinquish lesser patents still applied to the participating manufacturers, and in other cases the license fee could entail no more cost to the army than if the original firm were the deliverer. Business or regular courts would have jurisdiction in disputes over definition of patents and licenses.

The rule of patent law and normal judicial processes had thus been preserved in essence by Euler, Sperling, and those members of the aircraft industry whose interests lay in their preservation. Euler then received 850,000 marks in license fees through November.[7] At the same time, the army had managed to circumvent the law by holding certain firms to their agreement of August 1914 on lesser patents. The army's ambivalence toward the patent laws was apparent. Though reluctant to intervene arbitrarily by decree, it had seized the opportunity to bend the law to its ends where possible without directly confronting opposing interests in the business community. The fragility of law and the importance of economic conditions and interests in determining its preservation or alteration were evident.

By the time the army, industry, and parliamentary deputies had formulated the guidelines for the use of patented materials, the German air service was experiencing trying days. With the opening of the battle of Verdun on 21 February 1916, the air war had begun in earnest. Initially the attacking Germans had secured aerial superiority over the battlefield and in the enemy rear by concentrating their flying units. Yet in late March Capt. Felix Wagenführ of the inspectorate's test institute observed that the German aircraft industry could not keep pace with the huge demand for new aircraft caused by the unexpectedly high rate of attrition during the offensive.[8] Indeed, the French, responding with greater numbers, regained control of the air by May, despite the efforts of Fokker pilots like Max Immelmann and Oswald Bölcke.

The Fokker monoplane had reached the peak of its development by March, and the French and English, if they did not have the synchronized machine gun, had superior aircraft. The British pushers F.E.2b and D.H.2 with their forward-mounted guns were equal to the Fokker, while the French Nieuport biplane, armed with a gun on the top wing and delivered to both French and English units, was equal to the Fokker in climb and superior in speed and maneuverability. To supplement the Fokker, the German units had only its less reliable duplicates, the Pfalz and Siemens-Schuckert monoplanes. After almost falling prey to a Nieuport in March, Bölcke judged the latest Fokker monoplane, the E-4, deficient in climb and suggested the development of modern, light biplane fighters to counter the French biplane. Immelmann, the Fokker monoplane ace, reverted to the E3 after flying the E4, and only some thirty E4s were built.[9]

By June the German air service desperately needed a new fighter plane. That month new Fokker and Halberstadt biplanes began to trickle to the front, but these craft were outclassed from the beginning. Bölcke quickly ascertained that the Fokker biplane was too stable for fighter aerobatics. Furthermore, the quality of Fokker's construction had deteriorated, the result of poor workmanship. On 15 April an inspectorate engineer determined that the quality of Fokker's workmanship and attention to technical details compared poorly to those of the Albatros firm, which was about to come forth with a new twin-gun biplane fighter.[10] In June Albatros received an order for twelve prototypes of its sleek craft, which was powered by the Mercedes 160-horsepower engine, a major reason for its potential. Fokker complained that the army's distribution of the precious Mercedes solely to Albatros constituted preferential treatment,[11] yet the quality of his craft had declined to the extent that the army probably preferred to reserve its limited quantities of the new motor for the promising Albatros fighters.

Then, to add to Fokker's difficulties, on 18 June Max Immelmann fell to his death in an E3. Initial reports stated that the machine fell apart in mid-air. Some believed that his synchronizer had malfunctioned; others, that his propeller had simply broken off and the resultant vibration had torn the plane apart. The factory reputation at stake, Fokker and his assistants examined the wreckage and reported that the control wires had been shot through. Whatever its cause, Immelmann's death damaged Fokker's position and spelled the demise of the monoplane.[12]

Yet worse was to come, and German reconnaissance units detected it in late June. British forces were massing for an attack on the Somme, and when it came on 1 July, the German air service was completely overwhelmed. In the battle area the English and French outnumbered the

Germans by a three-to-one ratio (English, 185 airplanes; French, 201; Germans, 129). By mid-July enemy aerial superiority was unbearable; German aircraft were driven from the skies, and German ground forces cursed the British and the German air service in the same breath. German estimates of 7 August credit the Allies with a two-to-one superiority (500:251), not to mention qualitative ascendancy, and field flight chief Thomsen could not promise much relief.[13] The war was entering a new phase, and the German air service and aircraft industry had begun it poorly.

By the end of August, however, the situation began to improve. On 29 August, Paul von Hindenburg replaced Falkenhayn as chief of the General Staff, and as his chief quartermaster general and éminence grise he brought Erich Ludendorff, long a believer in the airplane. On 31 August the new High Command submitted to the War Ministry an armaments program in which the airplane figured prominently. Industry, Hindenburg declared, would have to compensate for the enemy's numerical superiority; machines would substitute for horses and men. War industries would take complete precedence over other industries; if necessary, a few thousand skilled workers could be withdrawn from the front. Production in all war industries had to increase significantly, and Hindenburg ranked as the first five in order of importance munitions, shells and artillery, machine guns, trench mortars, and airplanes. The New High command regarded industry as a panacea. Hindenburg, believing that infinite increases in production would enable Germany to win the war despite its numerical inferiority, referred to industrial mobilization as "turning an endless screw."[14] Yet to expand the aircraft industry alone to the extent that Ludendorff and he vaguely envisioned would have taken that few thousand workers. There could be no better evidence of their lack of understanding of the industrial home front than this first directive.

At the front the change in leadership was reflected quickly in new aerial policies. The flying troops began to concentrate their strength at the Somme, gradually denuding the Verdun front, although they attempted to maintain some degree of "aerial blockade." In mid-September German aerial resistance stiffened noticeably. After languishing on the inactive list since Immelmann's death, Oswald Bölcke had returned to the front in late August, bringing with him a new fighter group which included Manfred von Richthofen. Fighter Flight (*Jagdstaffel,* or *Jasta)* 2 received new Albatros fighter planes on 16 September and began to score victories the next day. By mid-October, of a total of 885 German aircraft on the western front, the German First and Second armies at the Somme possessed 540 of them.[15] The massing of strength enabled the Germans, though numerically inferior overall, to achieve temporary aerial superiority at the focus of an attack, while the Albatros D-planes (single-engined single-seat armed biplanes) would wrest aerial supremacy from the enemy and hold it through the spring of 1917.

If prospects at the front brightened in September, the picture in the industrial sector remained more uncertain. Although monthly production and delivery figures for aircraft firms are practically nonexistent, they are available for Germany's most important aircraft factory in 1916—the Albatros works.

Albatros Aircraft Works, January–October 1916[16]

Month	Work Force	Aircraft Production	Aircraft Acceptance
January	1,421	73	38
February	1,475	98	99
March	1,580	80	117
April	1,525	50	65
May	1,480	63 + 5 G3[a]	73
June	1,455	28 + 2 G3	30 + 1 W2[b]
July	1,630	90	60
August	1,990	93	94
September	2,006	120	122 + 1 W4
October	2,083	135	162 + 2 G3

[a]G3: twin-engine bomber.
[b]W2 and W4: naval seaplane.

The Albatros work force averaged fifteen hundred employees for seven months and then increased sharply to approximately two thousand in August. Its production of B and C-planes declined drastically in the late spring because of the construction of the seven twin-engine bombers—an exchange of highly debatable value. Then production returned to its former level in July, and in September it rose markedly from some 90 planes monthly to 120. The expansion of the work force in August and production in September are explained by the introduction of the fighter series D-1 and D-2 into production.

Albatros's performance notwithstanding, serious deficiencies remained in the industrial sector. The exemption of skilled aircraft workers from the service was not proceeding well. In late August the navy informed the air arm that in dire need it could surrender 153 skilled aircraft workers, but insisted on replacements for all of them. The fleet also made no effort to conceal its dislike of the measure and observed: "The change is in and of itself completely undesirable. If the matter is to be pursued further, it should be done with the reservation that men of the fleet be considered only as a last resort." Thus the navy, which had 244 skilled workers from the industry, would give up only 153, and these only in extremity.[17] If skilled labor was in short supply, so was quality material. The Bavarian representative at the inspectorate, Lieut. Behl, reported on 1 September that aircraft construction material was steadily deteriorating and becoming more unreliable. The best wood was rapidly being consumed, and complaints about the quality of the remainder were increasing.[18] Accidents compounded these problems: on 6 September the LFG factory was destroyed by fire. Although the inspectorate quickly relocated it, all of its prototypes were destroyed, and production was interrupted.

Faced with such ongoing shortages and temporary disruptions, the inspectorate revised its procurement bureaucracy and production guidelines in September and October to facilitate its supervision of the aircraft industry. These changes had been in process since the summer. As early as May it was apparent that the inspectorate needed modification, and on 31 July the War Ministry appointed a new inspector—Maj. Wilhelm Siegert, deputy acting field flight chief under Thomsen. Siegert's dynamism and his awareness of conditions at the front made him the right man to galvanize the industry to higher production.

On 19 September Siegert issued a directive to the aircraft industry describing the procurement hierarchy, its duties, and its prerogatives.[19] At the top stood the Central Acceptance Commission (Zentral-Abnahme-Kommission), subordinate to the inspectorate's aircraft depot (Flugzeugmeisterei) and composed of a captain as chairman, another officer, a certified engineer, and a staff of ten. The central commission monitored all production, acceptance, and delivery of aircraft, reporting weekly to the aircraft depot and cooperating with the test institute, which was responsible for construction surveillance. It would transmit complaints from the front on production through its subordinate representatives at the firms, the construction inspectorates (Bauaufsichten, or BAs), from which it would receive weekly reports.

While the central commission had been in existence since May 1915, the BAs appear officially for the first time in this memorandum. Comprising an officer, engineer, foreman, test pilot, and three staff members, they were attached to the fliers replacement units and stationed permanently at the aircraft factories. Their tasks were to oversee construction and production in order to ensure careful, uniform work and prompt delivery; to supervise the allocation of raw material and manpower at the plant; to accept airplanes at the firm; to mediate among its management, labor force, and the military; to monitor labor affairs and military person- nel (that is, exempted workers) assigned to the plants; and to take security precautions against fire, espionage, and sabotage. They would protect the army's interests at the aircraft factories "not through the use of police power but as much as possible through cooperation in all matters." They would serve as intermediaries between the firms and the army when the factories sought to secure more raw material or to reclaim indispensable skilled workers through exemptions. A representative of the BA would attend management-labor committee conferences, and the BA would support and protect the factory against "unjust" demands and wage and strike movements from the labor force. With these permanent surveil- lance and acceptance agencies at the firms, the inspectorate had com- pleted its procurement hierarchy. There were nineteen BAs in September 1916, and the number would increase to almost fifty before the end of the war, but there would be no further levels introduced into the chain of command.

The BAs replaced the traveling subcommissions of the Central Ac- ceptance Commission and the fliers replacement units' construction sur- veillance and acceptance commands. Apparently there had been per- manent inspection committees at isolated firms—namely, Fokker—since late 1915, but the September memorandum made the BAs the official organs of aircraft acceptance at all aircraft factories. The guidelines also instituted far-reaching changes in the extent to which the army could interfere in plant affairs. Now the potential for daily interference in all areas of plant life existed, and the directives of "avoidance of police power" and "cooperation where possible" left a large grey area for the BAs' exertion of authority over the firms in their roles as middlemen and monitoring agencies. Through the BAs the inspectorate had secured for itself, in the opinion of the first commanding general of the army air force, a "controlling" influence on construction and production.[20] The official history of Bavarian aviation noted that the powers of the BA "meant an infringement of the rights of private industry that was justified only by the severity of the war."[21] Friction resulted, it acknowledged, but great failures were avoided.

The institutionalization of the BAs involved certain difficulties. The limits of their prerogatives were unclear; interpretations of the guidelines could range justifiably from mere assistance to the factory to ramming change down the throat of a reluctant entrepreneur.[22] According to A. R. Weyl's account of the Fokker factory, Roland Betsch, the engineer of the BA there, actually needed to intervene more effectively to keep Fokker's designer Reinhold Platz abreast of the military construction guidelines.[23] Technical shortcomings reflected the continued shortage of experienced personnel in aircraft construction, although replacement units trained skilled workers to fill the gaps in the BAs' staffs. Several critical problems—the factories' preference for serial construction at the expense of innovation, and steadily increasing raw material shortages—could not be solved by the BAs.

On 6 October the aircraft depot issued a directive ordering "a significant reduction of present aircraft types."[24] The numerical superiority of the western Allies compelled the inspectorate to place heavy demands on the aircraft industry during the coming winter. As it could not rely upon a significant transfer of labor to raise production, it would have to organize available means better. It was no longer practical for firms to produce types that differed little in performance yet necessitated the army's procurement of unwieldy masses of replacement parts. Consequently, the inspectorate would select the best available types for licensed production, and it encouraged further technological progress with the prospect that superior prototypes would win licenses.

Necessity was forcing extensive standardization and licensed production, and the new construction and delivery guidelines for army aircraft took all these new developments into account. In addition to material on construction, delivery, and testing, the guidelines incorporated the agreements on licensing reached at the patent conferences and the role of the BAs in the acceptance procedure.[25]

The procurement apparatus was thus established in the fall of 1916 in an effort to face the specific demands that the chief of field aviation intended to place on the aircraft industry during the coming winter, and in general to meet the ever-increasing needs of the war of attrition. Chief Thomsen had written a memorandum entitled "The Expansion of the Flying Troops in the Winter 1916/17," dated 31 August, although it was not released in its final form until early October.[26] Thomsen, noting such improvements in equipment as more powerful C-planes and the biplane fighter, concluded that the planned expansion of the summer half-year had reached its goals. Yet the western opponents, "summoning all their power and supported by the world raw material market and the American motor and aircraft industry," had been able to increase their aerial numerical superiority and to produce a superior biplane fighter. The

German fliers had been able to endure this "oppressive" superiority only at the expense of severe losses among their best and most proven fliers.

The air service could not rely on sheer weight of numbers to perform essential tasks like tactical reconnaissance, artillery spotting, and aerial fighting; consequently, the organization and equipment of the flying troops had to be improved to the point that they could assert aerial superiority at the decisive point of future battles. Thomsen's technical measures included further development of the C, D, and R-planes. Organizationally, he planned further increases in the number of fighter groups on the western front (7 *Jasta* of fourteen aircraft each were planned in August; in October twenty-four were planned for March 1917). The 81 field flying units of six airplanes apiece and 46 artillery spotting units with four each would all be labeled flying units, and 140 with six aircraft apiece were planned. To coordinate the operations of these units, the staff officers of fliers at the army commands would be redesignated commanders of fliers, with the authority to deploy their formations.

Yet if Thomsen and Siegert might strive successfully to put their own house in order, the ultimate in organization—a unified imperial German air arm—eluded them, thwarted by the opposition of the Bavarian Army and the German Navy.

In 1916 the entire Bavarian aircraft industry became tied to Prussia through contracts or licenses. The Bavarian Army lost complete control of procurement, but clung fiercely to the remnants of its bureaucratic autonomy. In February the Otto Works became the Bavarian Aircraft Works (Bayerische Flugzeugwerke, or BFW), funded by the Bank for Commerce and Industry (Darmstädter Bank), MAN, and Berlin engineer Hermann Bachstein. The War Ministry had refused to lend its support to the attempt of a Bavarian consortium to acquire the Otto Works for two reasons: its financial foundation appeared inadequate, and it planned to include Otto, whom the War Ministry deemed "an unsuitable and unteachable personality." It consequently forced his exclusion from the new factory, which was a subsidiary of the Albatros Works and dependent upon Albatros for its designs and the Prussian Army for its contracts. Peter Eberwein, the former manager of the east German Albatros Works, became manager of BFW, while the board of directors comprised Bachstein, Carl Selzer of the Albatros Works, and representatives of MAN and the Darmstädter Bank.[27]

Pfalz, which was already dependent upon Prussia for contracts, was forced to become a licensed producer of north German firms during the summer of 1916. Its obsolescent E-plane was withdrawn from the front after a series of fatal crashes, and the Prussian inspectorate, dissatisfied with the factory, opposed awarding it new contracts. The Bavarian aviation inspectorate, however, admonished its Prussian counterpart that shutting down a capable firm with excellent workers would be unfortunate when Germany needed every aircraft firm available. The Prussian inspectorate relented, recommending that Pfalz build the LFG Roland D-2 fighter biplane under license so that it would not have to develop a new type of its own immediately.[28] It is unlikely that the Prussian inspectorate intended to close down the factory; rather, it used the threat of shutdown to make the factory a licensed producer of a north German aircraft type.

Despite the complete loss of control over procurement, in late July, when confronted with Prussian initiatives for a unified air force, the Bavarian War Ministry and Engineers Inspectorate remained firmly convinced that the organization of the Bavarian air force must remain separate. Although they acknowledged that its small size made a separate command difficult, they not only opposed air chief Thomsen's strivings for unity, but also were considering the creation of a Bavarian inspectorate of flying troops.[29]

The Bavarian Army's relationship with the Otto Works and with Prussia through 1916 indicates some of the disadvantages of the imperial military bureaucracy's subordination of separate armies to Prussia without their complete integration into the system. The Bavarians' insistence on maintaining, and their resentment at losing, their nominal administrative autonomy from Prussia so preoccupied their thoughts that they neglected the larger aim of winning the war.

In a certain sense the Bavarian Army's relationship with the Otto factory—one of dependence and resentment—was the analogue of its relationship with Prussia. It needed the factory yet resented its dependence on Otto. The Bavarian Army's antagonism toward its omnipotent Prussian counterpart could be requited only indirectly, through petty obstructionism that hindered the entire German war effort; Otto, on the other hand, was eminently accessible and his factory inefficient, so the Bavarian Army unleashed the full force of its resentment on his head. It supported the factory through 1916, but when the opportunity to eliminate Gustav Otto presented itself, it did so firmly and relentlessly.

The subsequent formation of BFW, with the attendant penetration of north German capital, was one aspect of what the *Handbuch der Bayerischen Geschichte* labeled the "internal unification of the national economy of the Bismarck reich," which World War I brought to a conclusion.[30] Thus from a particularistic perspective Bavaria was losing control of some of its domestic firms, but from the imperial perspective this development constituted part of the economic integration of the empire.

The official history of Bavarian military aviation in World War I proudly describes its independence as a virtue which was lost after the Hindenburg Program of fall 1916.[31] The Prussian, or imperial, perspective reproaches Bavaria for its resistance to a unified air arm in 1916 and the deleterious effect of its independence on mobilization through 1916.[32] Certainly, if the standard of judgment is effective mobilization, there can be no doubt that Bavaria's autonomy was disruptive. Yet Prussia was partially responsible for this situation, because the Prussian Army had excluded Bavarian aircraft firms from competition for its contracts before the war. Only in 1915, when the demand for armed aircraft became overwhelming, did Prussia seek more influence in Bavarian aviation. Furthermore, the very autonomy through 1916 that all previous interpretations accept is open to question. Because these interpretations overlook the intricacies of the military-industrial relationship and aircraft procurement, they ignore the gradual erosion of Bavarian autonomy in areas other than bureaucratic purview. As the Prussian Army parlayed its control of engine distribution into a very real control of aircraft procurement, the Bavarian Army was reduced to bureaucratic autonomy and control of personnel in the aircraft factories through monitoring exemptions by its bureaucracy. Yet even autonomy in these areas could be potentially disruptive if the Bavarian Army did not perform these duties with the larger aim in mind of raising total German aircraft production.

Naval aviation was just as determined as the Bavarian Army to preserve its administrative independence. Consequently, the development of naval aviation proceeded calmly compared to its relationship with the Prussian Army. In June the airplane became sufficiently important to warrant an organization independent of the airship. The chief of naval aviation units became chief of flight units (Befehlshaber der Fliegerabteilungen, or BdFlieg) in charge of airplane units, and the new head, Capt. Kranzbühler, moved from Wilhelmshaven to Berlin, subordinate to the naval staff.

Naval aviation continued its gradual expansion during the first half of 1916. By midyear Friedrichshafen's monthly deliveries ranged from figures usually in the low teens to a onetime high of twenty-eight. Brandenburg's monthly deliveries to the German navy never exceeded eight. Gotha, Sablatnig, Albatros, and Rumpler continued intermittent deliveries. The navy had been investigating the possibility of sea G-planes (*Grossflugzeuge,* armed twin-engined biplanes), but by July it was more interested in a new type—the fighter, an armed two-seater floatplane to fend off marauding British flying boats and to protect its reconnaissance machines. The torpedo plane made little progress in 1916, as the firms experienced severe construction problems, and Brandenburg delivered only a handful of the planes for further tests during the year. An abortive interest in shipboard aircraft was stimulated by the Battle of Jutland in May 1916.

In 1916 the most serious conflict naval aviation agencies fought was with the chief of field aviation over the organization of German air forces. On 10 March Thomsen proposed the unification of all aviation agencies in a new independent branch of the armed forces equal to the army and navy. In Thomsen's opinion, the aircraft industry's needs were important reasons for unification: "It cannot be beneficial to the development and most extensive use of the industry, which is still embryonic, if the demands and claims placed upon it come from two independent agencies. Rather, it must be directed according to unified and planned principles."[33] While he perceived that opposition to his plans would stem primarily from administrative sources, he considered it imperative that such measures be quickly undertaken. The imperial constitution, however, had not foreseen the necessity of establishing an agency over the army, navy, and air force. Consequently, in order to avoid a constitutional crisis in wartime, Thomsen reverted to an earlier idea of attaching the new agency to the army.

The navy objected to any bid for unification, ostensibly on technological grounds. Because seaplanes required primarily seaworthiness and long range, while landplanes placed a premium on high speed, climb, and maneuverability, technological development according to unified principles would be impossible. Siegert found this objection groundless, asserting that the difference between giant planes and single-seaters was greater than the difference between land and seaplanes. Furthermore, Siegert argued, the presupposition of unbridgeable differences between land and seaplanes contradicted the fact that the same designers at Rumpler, Albatros, Friedrichshafen, and other companies built both types, indeed that Rumpler even set existing landplanes on floats successfully.[34]

Further friction between the two services lessened the chances of acceptance of Thomsen's proposal. On 26 April the Imperial Naval Office informed the Inspectorate of Flying Troops that it intended to seek legal clarification of its claims on the aircraft industry in the absence of a superior authority. On 12 May the inspectorate objected to the navy's procurement of seaplanes at the LFG factory, which was producing an important C-plane for the army. In response on 14 May the chief of naval aviation units urged the defeat of the inspectorate's attempt to secure control of all naval landplane units on the grounds that the navy should not relinquish two years of coastal work to the Feldflugchef, who knew nothing about the coastal situation. Although the navy had no choice but to concede the army's continued control of supply to these units in August 1916, the landplane force remained under naval control.[35]

In light of this conflict, the Imperial Naval Office declined Thomsen's proposal on 20 June 1916.[36] The chief of naval aviation would not have had sole control over the navy's selection of seaplanes, and if the navy's interests had diverged sharply from the army's, an agency attached to the army would not have considered its interests adequately. Although no final decision had been reached by August, it was obvious the opposition from the navy, as well as from Bavarian aviation agencies, would stymie Thomsen's proposal. In 1921 aviation historian Georg Paul Neumann found it inconceivable that such a pioneering and imperative idea was allowed to be quashed by the "petty" sentiments of naval and state particularism.[37] In reality, more amazing would have been the acquiescence of the Bavarian Army and the German Navy and the consequent surrender of their last vestige of independence—bureaucratic autonomy.

If Thomsen's far-reaching organizational plans had been thwarted, Verdun and the Somme necessitated some change in army aviation. Consequently on 8 October an order of council over the emperor's name was issued from general headquarters stating:

> The increasing importance of the air war requires that all air-fighting and defense forces of the army, in the field and in the hinterland, be united in one agency. To this end I command:
>
> The centralized improvement, preparation, and employment of this means of warfare will be assigned to a "Commanding General of the Air Forces," who will be directly subordinate to the Chief of the General Staff. The "Chief of Field Aviation," with the dissolution of that post, becomes "Chief of Staff to the Commanding General of the Air Forces."[38]

Aviation historian Karl Köhler has correctly labeled this order,

which originated in Thomsen's staff, as the "culmination of the organizational development of the army air forces during the first World War."[39]
Gen. Ernst von Höppner, a cavalry officer who was commanding the
seventy-fifth Infantry Division, became the commanding general of the
air forces, or Kogenluft. His chief of staff was Thomsen; the inspector,
Siegert. Höppner brought to his new office "administrative ability and an
enthusiasm for the airplane,"[40] yet Thomsen and Siegert, who had prepared the groundwork for the new office and the expansion of the air arm,
deserved much of the credit for the past and future evolution of the air
force. Historian John Cuneo noted that historical accounts of German
military aviation after the war often unduly emphasized Höppner's role
and slighted Thomsen's part in developments after October 1916,[41]
probably because Höppner wrote a history of the air force. In reality,
however, it was a triumvirate, Thomsen and Siegert with Höppner commanding, who would be responsible for improving the effectiveness of the
German air force and aircraft industry.

Historians have considered 1916 a watershed in the First World
War, as the battles of Verdun and the Somme dashed both sides' hopes
for imminent victory.[42] These battles also mark the true beginning of
aerial warfare, with both sides' commitment of air arms of increasing size
in their attempt to attain aerial superiority. Yet from the beginning the
German air service found that German aircraft production was insufficient to meet the attrition of total war in the air. Consequently, the army's
measures that year—its attempt to circumvent patent law, the final extension of its procurement apparatus, the introduction of increased standardization and licensed production—all had one basic aim: to increase
the supply of suitable aircraft to the front. The air service's expansion
through the summer of 1916 proceeded according to plan, but the Allies
had surpassed the Germans, both quantitatively and qualitatively. By the
end of the summer chief of field aviation Thomsen had given up all hope
of ever achieving numerical aerial superiority. Although his assessment of
this situation was essentially correct, he based this conclusion on an
overestimation of the American aircraft and aircraft motor industry,
which was practically nonexistent. In the absence of labor and raw material reserves, Thomsen chose to rely on organization and quality of
equipment to give the air service a temporally and spatially limited aerial
superiority. Finally, if Thomsen had failed to obtain an imperial air

ministry, he did secure acknowledgement of the increased significance of the air arm in the appointment of a commanding general and in its new title—air force (Luftstreitkräfte). This recognition of the importance of military aviation coincided with the proclamation of the Hindenburg Program, which decreed total mobilization in an all-out effort to win the war. The new position of the air arm would be reflected in the program's assignment of priorities to the mobilization of the aircraft industry.

CHAPTER 4

Turning the Screw:
The Hindenburg Program,
October 1916–May 1917

CONTEMPORARY OBSERVERS and historians have condemned Germany's total mobilization in the Hindenburg Program, because its uncoordinated measures and unrealistic goals produced near exhaustion in Germany without bringing the war to a successful conclusion. Deputy Chancellor and Secretary of the Interior Karl Helfferich, who opposed the high command's intent to militarize the German economy, remarked, "An army suffers itself to be ordered about, but an economy does not." He considered the Hindenburg Program superfluous, preferring a more un-dramatic and voluntary approach.[1] Historian Gerald Feldman observed that the High Command discarded the Prussian War Ministry's rational premises of husbanding manpower and material and, using purely mili-tary calculations, set weapons and manpower quotas in ad hoc fashion. He consequently labeled the program "a gamble in which the nation's financial resources were recklessly exposed to exhaustion on the basis of unfounded expectations," a venture which "had very little to do either with sound military planning or rational economics."[2]

The Hindenburg Program's effect on the development of German aviation must be judged by the success of the mobilization measures in meeting production goals established at the beginning of the program, in overcoming particularistic and interservice conflicts, and in maintaining German technological parity, particularly in the all-important area of fighter development. The special status of the air force and of aviation procurement was reflected in the structure of the military bureaucracy for

73

total mobilization. At Thomsen's request,[3] Ludendorff opted to keep aircraft procurement separate from the new Weapons and Munitions Procurement Office (Waffen- und Munitions-Beschaffungs-Amt, or Wumba), which was supposed to control all procurement and eliminate fragmentation and conflicts among procurement agencies. This special position complicated overall procurement and impaired Wumba's effectiveness, but it assured the total subordination of aircraft procurement to Höppner and Thomsen and enabled Siegert to function independently of Wumba. This status would facilitate the efforts of the commanding general (Kogenluft) and inspectorate to mobilize the German aircraft industry, but the multitude of problems they would encounter made their likelihood of success uncertain from the start.

The German Air Force Organization for Aircraft, October 1916

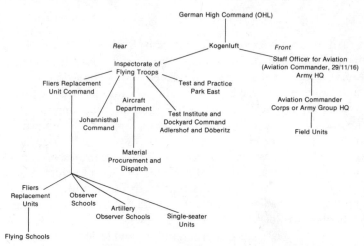

SOURCES: John R. Cuneo, *Winged Mars*, 2:265; stock no. IL 42/14, AM, MA.

   In the fall of 1916 the air force had 1,544 airplanes—910 C-planes, 210 single-seaters, 24 G-planes, and reserves of 400 craft in the air parks. By the spring of 1917 Thomsen planned to expand this force to 2,322 planes in the following array of units: forty-four flight units (264 planes); ninety-eight tactical flight units (588); twenty-seven protective flights units (162); thirty-seven fighter units (518); 120 single-seaters; thirteen battle squadrons (108 G-planes); and nineteen army flight commands or reserves (562 craft). He envisioned the strengthening of the German fighter forces as a major aspect of this expansion. The number of G-planes would be more than quadrupled, indicating plans for future bombing missions, while the number of C-planes, the backbone of the air force for reconnaissance and tactical bombing, would increase by only 100. To furnish this total growth of over 600 airplanes, production was to rise to 1,000 machines monthly by the spring of 1917.[4]

The execution of the production program was the responsibility of the Inspectorate of Flying Troops. In October it standardized production by limiting substantially the number of types under construction and issuing serial contracts for licensed production of the best models. Then it requested the exemption of 3,655 skilled workers for the aircraft and motor firms. In November the War Ministry's aviation department telephoned instructions to the deputy general commands and to the Bavarian and Württemberg war ministries ordering them to assign these workers immediately, if necessary even from the ranks of frontline troops.[5] Extant sources show no other significant activity in the fall, perhaps because the industry was advancing rapidly toward its monthly production goal of one thousand planes—the factories delivered nine hundred in December.[6]

From October through December 1916 the aircraft industry expanded of its own accord, as aircraft manufacturers responded to the opportunities for profit that the Hindenburg Program offered. In October Halberstadt doubled its share capital to 400,000 marks. By the end of 1916 Aviatik, which was owned by Daimler, had not only raised its share capital to 1 million marks but also founded a branch in Bork. In December the Gothaer Waggonfabrik raised its share capital from 1 to 3 million marks to produce G-planes, while AEG bought the Ago aircraft works in Johannisthal and raised its share capital from 360,000 to 1 million marks. AEG also established an R-plane construction department at Hennigsdorff, while SSW expanded its plant in Nürnberg. Industrialist Karl Caspar founded the Hanseatic Aircraft Works in Hamburg with 1.5 million marks capital, while Edmund Rumpler and the Riedinger Balloon Factory (Riedinger Ballonfabrik) of Augsburg formed the Bavarian Rumpler Works in Augsburg on 20 October 1916 with 750,000 marks apiece.[7] The formation of the Rumpler plant, a further example of the penetration of Bavaria by the north German aircraft industry, had been arranged by the Prussian and Bavarian inspectorates, and Siegert had already ordered fifty Rumpler C4s from the factory by the beginning of November.[8]

After such auspicious beginnings, however, deliveries plummeted to four hundred aircraft in January 1917. The reasons were numerous: the coal shortage and transportation crisis, the preoccupation of some factories with the production of parts at the expense of complete aircraft, and the complete failure of others to meet the army's expectations. Repair factories newly assigned to produce training craft, for example, occasionally could not obtain raw materials and failed to make the transition smoothly.[9] These difficulties prompted a flurry of activity from the Inspectorate of Flying Troops in early 1917.

In keeping with the total nature of the Hindenburg Program, the inspectorate attempted to mobilize public opinion through the publication of the magazine *Flug* ("Flight") in January 1917.[10] *Flug* was the official organ of the German Fliers League (Deutscher Flieger-Bund), an organization of fifteen regional associations formed by Wilhelm Siegert to promote military aviation. The association and magazine served not only a propaganda purpose but also an educational and centralizing function. It advertised for aviation inventions and for recruits for the air force, particularly engineers, technicians, skilled workers, and secretaries; it announced courses of instruction in aircraft repairs; and it recommended work in aircraft and motor factories to youth as an apprenticeship to flight training.

The inspectorate simultaneously reorganized its own procurement bureaucracy and the aircraft industry and then took drastic measures to centralize and coordinate procurement. In January 1917 it combined its aircraft depot and test institute into a new aircraft depot under Maj. Felix Wagenführ and also established an R-plane command. The two most noteworthy features of the new depot were its Scientific Information Bureau (Wissenschaftliche Auskunftei für Flugwesen, or WAF) and its department for evaluating captured aircraft.[11]

The WAF was established on 31 January to coordinate all efforts in aviation science and to disseminate aeronautical information to the inspectorate, Imperial Naval Office, research institutes, individual scientists, and aircraft firms. Under the direction of Lt. (reserve) Wilhelm Hoff, an engineer and officer in the aircraft depot, the WAF's nucleus, a small committee composed of Hoff and the representatives of the Naval Office and of German scientific institutes, convened at least every six weeks and then, depending upon the secrecy of the matter under discussion, convened a larger committee which included two representatives of the aircraft industry. After deciding which problems were most important to the industry, the committee assigned them to the most appropriate scientific institute for resolution. Individual firms with a special interest in the matter could also investigate if they informed the WAF.

The WAF compiled and distributed technical reports, a secret journal which published information on captured aircraft and confidential scientific articles pertinent to aircraft construction. The short, concise articles tended to emphasize tables and graphs and presumed academic engineering training. Hoff also kept a secret technical portfolio of statistical data on the industry, aircraft, and materials that circulated only within the inspectorate. He devoted little time to correspondence, but instead traveled to institutes and factories to keep abreast of their progress. His interests determined the WAF's focus of research, and consequently the most serious flaw in its operation was his neglect of aircraft motors, which was not corrected until late in 1917.

The evaluation of enemy aircraft had long aided the inspectorate in its development of German aviation, as Fokker's invention of the synchronization gear in 1915 demonstrated. Now it institutionalized this operation in a special department, which examined captured enemy aircraft minutely and distributed its findings to the German industry and aviation press. The knowledge it gained about French and English construction techniques caused it to praise the latter's methods highly for their scientific basis. The captured aircraft further served a propaganda value as displays in a prize hall in Berlin.

The R-plane command was to propose special construction and delivery guidelines for the increasing number of firms producing R-planes and to enforce them more strictly.[12] The command, like the inspectorate's other new agencies, would enable Siegert to formalize the army's relationship with the aircraft industry more than in the past.

In response to widespread manufacturers' complaints about material procurement, Siegert insisted that they form a War Trade Association of the German Aircraft Industry (Kriegsverband der deutschen Flugzeugindustrie) in January 1917. Siegert had initially proposed the formation of a limited liability company of all the aircraft factories, but after meeting with the manufacturers he contented himself with the creation of a registered association. The association was primarily intended to ease material procurement by securing raw, half-finished, and finished materials for the industry and by advising the inspectorate on the distribution of contracts. By centralizing material procurement in response to growing shortages, however, it ultimately forced the syndication of the aircraft industry. Employers who did not join risked obtaining no materials and thus no contracts; all of the largest companies joined. At the inspectorate's insistence, the association also agreed to place its members' research at the disposal of the WAF and to establish a commission to formulate standards for aircraft parts and the use of ersatz materials in aircraft production. Bendemann, head of the German Research Institute for Aviation and the inspectorate's scientific section, chaired the commission. The industry's war association thus further organized the procurement of materials and airplanes and scientific and technological efforts in aviation. The forced syndication of the aircraft industry was the norm, not the exception, during total mobilization, as producers' trade associations assisted procurement agencies in allocating raw materials and distributing contracts in war industries.[13]

After the formation of the war trade association, the inspectorate's aircraft depot unleashed a barrage of orders intended to coordinate all levels of procurement—the army, aircraft industry, and subcontractors—in its effort to increase aircraft deliveries. In early January the depot contracted with one firm, the New Berlin Brass Works, (Neue Berliner Messingwerke), for the production of sheet brass for the entire aircraft industry. The manufacturers were to inform the inspectorate by mid-January of their brass requirements for the next six months so that the depot could notify the company of the industry's projected needs three months in advance. On 12 January the inspectorate announced its intention to centralize all material procurement for the aircraft industry and further to monitor the transactions between the aircraft factories and their subcontractors in order to prevent an unnecessary splintering of sources. The firms were requested to submit the same information about their needs for parts and materials as they had for brass. Despite the vociferousness of their previous complaints, the factories were lax about complying: at the end of January some firms had not answered, while others had submitted excessive estimates of their brass requirements or incomplete forms.[14]

The depot transmitted a War Office order in mid-February instructing firms to limit their use of tin, with an accompanying dispatch from the inspectorate's raw materials department instructing it to control the distribution of tin to the factories in the future. Drastic increases in the consumption of tin and tin alloy necessitated their allocation only to procurement agencies, not to individual firms. Only the factories' precise surveillance and restriction of their consumption, the depot advised, could ensure undisturbed supplies and production.[15]

The inspectorate continued to match aircraft companies with prospective subcontractors as it had done for brass supplies. In February, for example, it recommended that the piano industry in the town of Eisenberg (pianos did not appear on the High Command's priority list of war material) and the metal firm of Rieck and Haverlander in Berlin contact various members of the aircraft industry's war trade association directly. Yet its coordination was not always successful. In early April the depot advised factories that covered their planes with painted linen to send their linen, unpainted and bleached, to the New Augsburg Cotton Factory for painting. The order was rescinded two weeks later; the overloaded German railways prevented transportation.[16]

Despite difficulties, the inspectorate was determined to rationalize the relationship between the aircraft industry and its subcontractors and the industry's work methods as well, since the very structure and work methods of the factories determined their use of subcontractors. On 24 March Wagenführ, writing on behalf of the Central Acceptance Commission, instructed the BAs in the following manner:

> Every illogical relationship—north German subcontractors delivering to south Germany and vice versa–must be absolutely avoided. Many very capable metalworking factories with equipment for the mass production of stamp, lathe, and milling parts, as well as a number of well-equipped woodworking factories, are presently without contracts, so the time has come for the aircraft industry to employ rational work methods to make its production more profitable and sparing of material. In the aircraft industry, for example, most parts are worked from complete pieces and assembled in a number of complicated work procedures that require special equipment. The same goal can often be achieved as well or better through simpler work methods.[17]

Wagenführ also observed that the use of mass production methods would improve licensed production, because under the current system parts constructed by different licensed producers for the same craft were not interchangeable.

Wagenführ chided the companies on 25 February for luring designers away from competing factories with "exaggeratedly favorable offers." Such practices, he warned, damaged military interests by leading to "unhealthy situations" and delays in aircraft construction. As most employees had been exempted and reclaimed for particular firms, he wanted to be informed of job changes by designers so that he might decide whether they were allowable. Three days later he urged the aircraft manufacturers, as he had repeatedly in the past, to maximize their production of parts and planes for the army. He admonished them, however, not to undertake more contracts than they could actually carry out in order to avoid delays and their accumulation of unnecessary stocks of raw materials.[18]

By April the inspectorate had formulated a list of firms that would receive prior consideration in the allocation of raw materials. It then established an aircraft and motor construction schedule prescribing an optimum production for each factory. If the factory performed well, it was assured of contracts and possible increases in orders; if not, its quota would be reduced and its contracts given to other factories. Difficulties in material procurement would not excuse poor performance, and the inspectorate insisted on smooth transition to the production of new types. In order to prevent delays in motor deliveries from affecting aircraft production, every tenth C and D-plane would be delivered without engines.[19]

Increased standardization, licensed production, and exchanges of vital information encouraged a final crucial aspect of aviation mobilization during the Hindenburg Program—a further increase of military control over patent law. Through 1916 the Prussian Army had circumvented the law without resorting to its powers of decree. According to law the inventor was protected only after publication of his patent and thus had no rights and received no fees for use of his invention until publication. The War Ministry exploited the wartime situation by using its experts in the patent office to prevent the publication of certain patents and then, after having capitalized on the invention, refusing to discuss license fees or indemnities with the inventor on the grounds that he had no rights until the patent was published. If the inventor disagreed with these procedures, he did have recourse to the courts, but this situation gave rise to so many complaints that the withholding of inventions appeared a distinct possibility.

On 8 February 1917, consequently, the Imperial Council (Bundesrat) modified aviation patent law to enable the patent office to distribute unpublished patents to the army and navy if they decided that it was in the interests of national defense. The patent would be placed, unpublished, on the war rolls, where only the military would have access to it. There were now two classifications of patents—those with war worth that could be distributed without publication and without the possibility of investigation, and those without war worth, to be distributed after publication and protection of the inventor's interests. The first category entailed no public notice or claims proceedings and the reduced importance of patent office tests, and it practically ensured the annullment of later claims, although an inventor could apply to the patent office and the imperial court for redress. The War Ministry's power to regulate patent matters had increased, because while the earlier arrangement had granted it no specific prerogatives with the patent office beyond placement of its representative there, the new ruling now enabled it to examine all patents and to decide how it would deal with inventors. The new ruling, instead of giving relief to the inventor, simply legalized arbitrary measures taken by the military regarding patents.[20]

The army's attitude toward patents affecting the synchronization gear after 1916 amply shows the effect of the new law. After the army paid Euler a total of 1 million marks, it ceased payments, although Euler complained that his interpretation of their unwritten agreement called for fee payments for the duration of the patent until 1925.[21] The War Ministry decided to expropriate the patent and pay a lump sum rather than potentially exorbitant license payments. Yet Euler was fortunate, compared to LVG, which brought suit against Fokker and the army for infringing upon Franz Schneider's synchronizing gear. The patent senate of the imperial court judged that although Fokker's gear differed from Schneider's, it still infringed upon the earlier patent.[22] The army never indemnified LVG. In the mobilization of the last two years of the war, the army simply ignored patent law and the civil courts.

The inspectorate's measures and the modification of patent law enabled the army increasingly to interfere in and control the affairs of the aircraft industry. Yet raw material and manpower shortages and the consequent inflationary spiral of raw material prices and wages as well as transportation delays resulting from the steady deterioration of rail service were conditions that the army's policies either exacerbated or could not cure.

In wage disputes in the aircraft industry, the Prussian War Ministry continued to mediate in favor of the workers. Gerald Feldman related a confrontation of the Berlin aircraft industrialists with the unions in the fall of 1916, when, despite the existence of a tentative agreement, Count von Oppersdorff of the War Ministry's aviation department summoned labor and management to his office and insisted upon further concessions to the workers. When the manufacturers protested that such concessions to the seven thousand workers in the industry would lead to similar demands from the sixty thousand similar workers in other Berlin war industries, Oppersdorff replied that he had to have the airplanes, regardless of the repercussions in other industries.[23] By January 1917 wages of the aircraft industry's skilled workers in Berlin had risen 100–69 percent since August 1914 and far surpassed the rise in the cost of living, while the average increase in the war industries over that same period of time was 78.2 percent.[24] The cost of living rose more rapidly after October 1916, but the wages of the workers in the aircraft industry, real wages included, more than kept up with the increase in the cost of living during the Hindenburg

Program. The War Ministry's assistance in ensuring the superior wages of the aircraft workers demonstrates the army's continued appreciation of the importance of the airplane and of the special nature of the aircraft industry, though at the expense of worsening the inflationary spiral.

The army had to meet the wage demands of the aircraft workers, who were in short supply, yet on 9 March the High Command insisted that wage increases be slowed because they caused strikes and were detrimental to troop morale.[25] In fact, workers in the aircraft industry in Berlin played a prominent role in a wave of strikes in April 1917.[26] A Spartacist flier of 17 April, the first day of the strike, proclaimed that over two hundred thousand workers had struck in Berlin, including those at "AEG, . . . in the aircraft industry at Johannisthal, at Argus, Rumpler, and the LVG, etc." Some five thousand workers from AEG Hennigsdorff, where the aircraft works were located, and two thousand at Staaken Luftschiffbau, where R-planes were built, were participating on 18 April. When the Spartacists announced that the workers were returning to work by 21 April, they noted that "only in the aircraft works of AEG in Hennigsdorff was work still completely stopped," and it did not resume until 23 April. Contrary to the High Command's belief, the aircraft workers probably struck in spite of, not because of their wage raises. If their successful struggle with the industrialists gave them a sense of newfound strength, the general conditions of insufficient food rations, rising agitation, and inflation gave them more than sufficient cause to strike.

The Hindenburg Program also exacerbated Germany's raw material shortage. At least the aircraft industry was supposed to receive adequate supplies of raw materials, as the High Command instructed the War Ministry on 16 February 1917 that despite the steel shortage, there should be no hesitation in the production of crucial items like airplanes, machine guns, and locomotives.[27] The inspectorate's measures during the winter and early spring were also designed to alleviate the effect of the raw material shortage on aircraft production. Consequently, the industry would be supplied with essential materials if at all possible, but the price would be high. The average price of sixty-three raw materials essential to aircraft production rose, from August 1914, 98.7 percent to 1 October 1916, 148 percent to 1 December 1916, 184 percent to 1 January 1917, and 232 percent to 1 July 1917. Shortages of raw materials became more severe as the largest metal deliverers could no longer keep delivery dates. Raw material shortages and transportation problems led subcontractors to set prices upon delivery of goods, which might be as long as three to eight months after the original contract. And the contractors refused to guarantee their products because of the worsening quality of raw materials during the winter of 1916–17. If materials in the finished aircraft were questionable, their prices, and those of the airplanes, still rose rapidly. A twin-engined G-plane ordered in October 1916 to be delivered by April 1917 cost 38–41,000 marks upon order; yet because of delays it might be ready in May 1917 at a price of 75,000 marks or after May at 85,000 marks—an increase of more than 100 percent. Delays in aircraft deliveries and rapidly climbing prices were commonplace during the Hindenburg Program.[28]

The new air force bureaucracy removed neither the particularistic nor the interservice conflicts that had previously impaired the efficiency of aviation mobilization. In a history of the German air force during World War I written in 1920, Georg Paul Neumann described some of the absurd effects of particularistic conflicts on the aircraft industry. Because of a relatively high level of industrialization, Württemberg had a surfeit of skilled workers that were sorely needed elsewhere. Yet the Swabian War Ministry was reluctant to release its citizens for industrial service elsewhere in the empire. Instead of sending more workers to Staaken near Berlin where they were needed for R-plane construction, the Swabian War Ministry shipped them to Flugzeugbau Friedrichshafen in Friedrichshafen on Lake Constance in order to keep them in Württemberg. According to Neumann, trained electrical mechanics served as watchmen and janitors with flying units stationed in Württemberg while air stations in less industrial areas used mechanics whose civilian professions had been in agriculture.[29] The inability to properly allocate skilled workmen exacerbated labor shortages and wage inflation in key industrial areas and hurt production in those areas where skilled workmen could only be replaced by untrained workers.

The manner in which particularism affected mobilization was extremely complex, because it could not be separated from other factors, like differing regional levels of industrialization; tensions between the demands of the front and the rear; the relationship among quality of production, exemptions, and female labor; and the problems of establishing branch factories of major Berlin firms in other areas of the empire. The formation of the Bavarian Rumpler Works in Augsburg, for example, necessitated a search for Bavarian subcontractors, because initially the branch factory had to employ the same subcontractors as the Johannisthal firm. The result had been an overburdening of the subcontractors and an inefficient use of the German transportation system, which

Wagenführ's directives to rationalize the relationship between aircraft companies and their subcontractors were intended to halt.

The best example of the complex effect of particularism on industrial mobilization during the Hindenburg Program involved Prussia, Bavaria, and the BFW factory. Neumann devoted little time to this episode, except to lament that the Prussian inspectorate had not acquired the right to monitor Bavarian aircraft production or to intervene in the personnel affairs of the Bavarian BAs when it assumed the responsibility of supplying machines and equipment to Bavarian units. Consequently, the guidelines of the War Office and High Command for exempting workers for work in the aircraft factories were applied in imbalanced fashion in Bavaria and resulted in the failure of BFW's production in early 1917 that damaged supply and caused friction between agencies in the homeland. Neumann concluded that particularism was the sole culprit in the affair. Yet this case merits a more careful examination, because it was in reality far more complex than Neumann indicated.

Late in 1916 BFW reported constant difficulties in obtaining skilled workers, and the factory's paucity of skilled labor was at issue in February 1917 when the aircraft depot transmitted several reports of poor workmanship on BFW craft to the BA with instructions to make certain that the firm improved its work.[30] BFW's director, Carl Selzer, attributed these problems to the excessive induction of male skilled workers and their replacement by untrained female labor. BFW's labor force was 19.9 percent female (296 of 1,491), while the Albatros factories in Johannisthal and Schneidemühl, which had replaced men with women as much as the increased demands for aircraft allowed, employed only 16.7 and 16.2 percent women, respectively. Women's performance of a high proportion of tasks formerly handled by male workers had been accompanied by increasing complaints of incompetent construction of BFW aircraft. "Even with the most careful guidance of all untrained workers and with the surest surveillance of all individual construction processes," Selzer declared, "these disadvantages will obtain as long as production lies to such a far-reaching extent in the hands of untrained female workers." Aircraft construction entailed mainly handicraft, not machine work, and handicraft techniques, which took regulated training and years of practice to learn, simply could not be acquired in a few weeks or months by women presenting themselves for work. They consequently could not replace men in aircraft production as easily as they could in other industries such as shell turning or rifle milling.[31]

Selzer's letter was indicative of the tension between the demands of the front for manpower and of the industry for skilled labor. Replacing inducted skilled labor with untrained workers was not feasible in an industrial enterprise operating on handicraft construction principles. Yet Selzer erred in focusing on women; the real key to the problem was untrained labor, regardless of sex. During the wartime labor shortage numerous openings previously held by skilled workers, who were invariably male, had to be filled with unskilled laborers, who were women and, to a lesser extent, youth. Consequently, women were cited, however unfairly, as examples of how untrained labor might disrupt quality production.

The Bavarian inspectorate accepted Selzer's appraisal of the special nature of aircraft construction, but explained that military demands motivated its directives to release male personnel for service. It suggested that BFW claim that all its positions were temporarily filled in order to avoid having to accept more female workers, and then it would cooperate in securing more exempted workers for the factory.[32]

On 3 March 1917, the commanding general of the air force (Kogenluft) telegraphed the Bavarian War Ministry that frontline units had reported forced landings and fatal crashes of BFW craft. When the Prussian inspectorate had called the factory to account, BFW attributed the problems to faulty construction material and errors caused by the Bavarian aviation inspectorate's constant induction of its skilled workers and insistence that the factory employ untrained and unusable women. Kogenluft proposed two measures to rectify the situation: first, relieve the present BA of its duties and have the Bavarian BAs, like those of other states, assigned by and subordinate to the Prussian inspectorate; and second, insure adherence to guidelines from the War Office and High Command (Oberste Heeresleitung, or OHL) for exemptions to the aircraft industry by having Prussian, not Bavarian, BAs monitor the factories' labor and materials. The telegram insisted on their immediate execution, or the Prussian inspectorate would prohibit BFW aircraft entirely.[33] Kogenluft and the inspectorate were using BFW's faulty construction and its allegations of the Bavarian hierarchy's responsibility for its failure as an excuse to gain complete control over exemptions and the aviation bureaucracy, the last preserve of Bavarian authority.

Yet reports from Bavarian agencies indicated the true complexity of the situation.[34] First, fault for the production problems lay with both the BA and the factory. Within the factory efforts to spur productivity had entailed sacrificing quality construction and safety standards. "Slovenliness" and poor intrafactory relationships had probably resulted from

BFW's assumption of Otto's inefficient work force and the placing of a
north German business director at the head of the Bavarian firm. The BA
suffered most from the lack of a clear definition of its prerogatives.
Caught between its superiors and the firm, it was blamed for shortcomings yet not sufficiently empowered to remedy them. Its acceptance of
aircraft was hindered by the barrage of orders from the Prussian Central
Acceptance Commission to modify planes in production to keep them up
to date for combat. The demands of the front may have necessitated these
changes, but their execution delayed the entire process of production and
acceptance, occasionally to the point where intolerable bottlenecks occurred. Finally, the reports of the Bavarian agencies indicated that the
problems had been corrected by the beginning of January with the installation of a new BA and the increased stability of skilled labor.

Ironically the BFW and BA problem became more incidental as the
dispute between the Prussian and Bavarian authorities intensified. Gen.
Karl von Brug, engineers inspector, was certain that Kogenluft was
simply trying to eliminate Bavarian agencies from aircraft procurement
and using the threat of closing BFW as a threat to get its way. The
Bavarian military plenipotentiary in Prussia visited General Höppner and
Colonel Thomsen at general headquarters to express his displeasure at
the peremptory tone of the telegram.[35] He found Höppner "extremely
astounded" at the "unintended" effect of the missive, and the commanding general apologized profusely for the misunderstanding. Thomsen, however, was not convinced of the telegram's inappropriateness and
attributed its tone to the urgency of the matter. The plenipotentiary
assured Thomsen that the Bavarian war minister, who had two years' field
command experience, was aware of the circumstances at the front and
would be the last person to ignore the urgency of the situation. Judgment
without investigation, however, would be premature. Suggestions, he
allowed, would be welcome, but not in such a dictatorial and categorical
form—one to which the Prussian War Ministry might be accustomed but
one which Bavarian authorities did not appreciate. Thomsen finally ex-
pressed regret at the telegram's tone, promised to edit future missives,
and requested that the plenipotentiary mediate between Kogenluft and
the Bavarian War Ministry in the future. While the plenipotentiary
agreed to intercede, he observed that other independent field agencies
were able to obtain the greatest cooperation from Bavaria without intermediaries. On this acerbic note, the conference ended.

On 17 March the new Bavarian war minister, Gen. Philipp von
Hellingrath, informed Kogenluft that the firm's "poor and frivolous

work" was the major source of the problem, although the BA had certainly failed to bring some problems to the attention of its superiors and had not acted energetically enough to correct the firm's shortcomings. The BA's chairman had consequently been removed, and the War Ministry had formulated new exemption guidelines that corresponded to those of the High Command so that BFW would conform more to the north German factories in the composition of its labor force. Hellingrath refused to subordinate the BA to the Prussian inspectorate and was, in fact, convinced that the Prussian Central Acceptance Commission's constant orders and Albatros's poor structural designs were responsible for the disruption, though he did not say this to Kogenluft.[36]

The Bavarian military aviation authorities had preserved their bureaucratic autonomy from Prussia, however inefficient the Prussian Army and aviation historians like Neumann judged the division. Yet the detailed examination of the BFW case of early 1917 shows that the particularistic division of German military aviation during the Hindenburg Program served to complicate problems of a more fundamental military-industrial nature with time-consuming debates and bureaucratic imbroglios between the Prussian and Bavarian agencies.

Naval aviation agitated the German air force less than did the Bavarian agencies, perhaps because the navy's use of seaplanes could justify some separation on grounds of military efficiency. More critically, the army's prior claim on the aviation industry enabled it to limit indirectly the size of naval aviation and thus interference with its mobilization of the aircraft industry.

The navy's operational demands were essentially determined by the need to respond to the aggressive forays of English naval aviators. In the summer of 1916 marauding English patrol planes drove German machines from the skies over the English Channel and the lower North Sea. By the fall the English were inflicting heavy losses on German dirigible patrols over the North Sea. To counter these assaults the German Navy required not only larger seaplane forces but also new types—a fighter and a multi-engined seaplane.[37] Naval aircraft development consequently focused on the evolution of these two types from mid-1916 until the end of the war.

In July the chief of the Admiralty Staff requested an initial complement of sixty-one single-seat floatplane fighters. Albatros, Hansa-Brandenburg, and Rumpler produced twin-float versions of their previous landplane types in relatively small numbers: Albatros delivered 118 W4s from September 1916 until December 1917; Brandenburg supplied

58 KDW seaplanes through February 1918, although the type was rather difficult to fly; and Rumpler, 88 6B craft to January 1918. Although the single-seaters performed their escort duties well, on 7 September 1917 naval agencies decided that the difficult raw material and industrial situation forced a limitation of aircraft types. They chose to eliminate the single-seat floatplane fighter because of developments that had begun in the fall of 1916.[38]

At that time German seaplane stations had requested a defense fighter, a two-seater which could defend itself when attacked from the rear. Rear Admiral Starke, head of the aviation department in the Imperial Naval Office, discussed such development mandates with the manufacturers in periodic two-hour conferences in Berlin. Hansa-Brandenburg's chief designer, Ernst Heinkel, found the choice of either the 160-horsepower Mercedes or the 150-horsepower Benz engines constraining, yet had a small floatplane built in eight weeks and shipped to Warnemünde for tests. When the firm's chief test pilot discovered that the plane was tail-heavy, Heinkel overnight had a factory crew remove the top wing and set it thirty-five centimeters to the rear of the plane to correct the center of gravity. The result justified Heinkel's belief that construction was best done "über den Daumen gepeilt"—literally, by taking one's bearings over one's thumbs, that is, by guesswork and trial and error. The W12 (W—Wasserflugzeug, or seaplane) proved to be a superior airplane, as fast and maneuverable as a single-seater though larger and heavier. Brandenburg produced 146 of them. In the hands of accomplished pilots such as Lt. Friedrich Christiansen, commander of Seaplane Unit I at Zeebrugge, the W12 broke English aerial superiority and took command of the air over the Flanders coast from Zeebrugge to Ostend in 1917.[39]

The navy met much less success with multi-engined craft. First, naval aviation agencies could not agree on the merits of the various types. In July the chief of the Admiralty Staff suggested the avoidance of twin-engine bomber development, because it could only further delay the production of single-engine armed reconnaissance planes and torpedo planes. Yet Seaplane Unit II, presuming that G-planes could fly safely on one engine, wanted them for reconnaissance over the North Sea in the fall. The chief of naval flight units (later naval flight chief) Kranzbühler was more interested in R-planes.[40] The T and R-planes consequently took precedence over the G-plane.

The torpedo-planes underwent tests in 1917. The first Gotha WD14, delivered to the seaplane test command in June 1916, was accepted in January, and the craft began service in Flanders in March 1917. After the Brandenburg T-plane arrived at the front in May, seaplane units advised the test command that its takeoff and climb characteristics were so abysmal that it took one hour to attain six to seven thousand meters, if it managed to lift off the water at all. In June the use of all T-planes was postponed because even the Gothas needed strengthening.[41]

The R-plane, giant three to five-engined craft, had offered a potential focus of cooperation between military and naval aviation that never materialized, because the same firms attempted to build aircraft for both services. The navy was most interested in the designs of two branches of the Zeppelin concern, VGO (Versuchsbau Gotha Ost, later Staaken) and Claudius Dornier's Zeppelin Lindau. With the support of Feldflugchef Thomsen and Adm. Dick, chief of the Naval Office's dockyard department, Zeppelin and the Robert Bosch firm had financed the formation of the VGO, which moved from Gotha to Staaken on 1 August 1916. In 1917 Staaken was attempting to set its giant designs, the only R-planes to attain serial production during the war, on duraluminum floats. By 1916 Dornier had already designed two metal flying boats at Lindau, and his third design won a naval contract in April 1917.[42] Nevertheless, by the middle of 1917 the navy had no multi-engined airplanes in service.

Fulfillment of the needs of naval aviation detracted little from military aviation procurement during the Hindenburg Program. The seaplane fighter was mandatory for a defensive force and could not be considered a waste of scarce resources, especially since relatively few were built. Furthermore, Hansa-Brandenburg had been designated a naval factory from the beginning by agreement of the inspectorate and naval office. The T and R-seaplanes, on the other hand, were superfluous, particularly because the state of aviation technology made their realization extremely difficult and expensive for the marginal rewards they offered. Particularly in the case of the R-plane, the navy's insistence on complicating an already complex machine through the addition of floats undoubtedly impeded production of army types on order.

Despite innumerable hindrances, from shortages to bureaucratic rivalries, the ultimate success of the Hindenburg Program in aviation would be determined by the progress of the German Army and aircraft industry in two areas, fighter development and overall production. The evolution of the fighter plane during the Hindenburg Program illustrates the benefits and the dangers of standardization and of the use of information gleaned from the seizure and evaluation of enemy aircraft, two techniques that the Inspectorate of Flying Troops emphasized in its effort to mobilize the industry.

The Albatros D1 and D2 fighters became the backbone of the German fighter units in the fall of 1916, and by January 1917, when they reached the peak of their service, they comprised some 67 percent of the fighter craft at the front. The German fighter forces under the leadership of Oswald Bölcke outclassed their opponents, and it was the superiority of the Albatros D2 that enabled the young Manfred von Richthofen to best the British ace Maj. L. G. Hawker on 23 November.[43]

In the fall of 1916 the Inspectorate of Flying Troops acquired some French Nieuports, a sesquiplane design of unusual beauty and superlative maneuverability. Wilhelm Hoff distributed the planes to Albatros, Euler, and SSW and requested an improved copy, as the air force had no immediate prospects of a superior machine. The Euler craft showed no promise. SSW copied the design rather faithfully and produced the D1, which received an initial order of 150 machines on 25 November 1916. Siemens Halske had so much difficulty producing the geared rotary engine for the D1, however, that only 95 craft of the first order were completed, and a later order of 100 craft placed in March 1917 was canceled in mid 1917 because the type was obsolescent.[44]

Albatros designer Robert Thelen produced a sesquiplane version of the D2. Tests of the new D3 in September and October were so successful that Albatros received the largest single production contract—for four hundred machines—for any plane to that time. Yet in service the D3 was plagued by recurrent lower wing failures, and after the lower wing was strengthened in April–May 1917, the deterioration of workmanship and material continued to cause problems.[45] Nevertheless, the D3 enjoyed a long career—some still serving in 1918—because the German air force and aircraft industry were slow to develop a better fighter.

Fokker's construction had deteriorated so that in November and December 1916 his planes were temporarily prohibited from frontline use, while his factory applied its expertise in welded steel tubing construction to the construction of steel parts for AEG G4 craft. Fokker's temporary elimination from fighter production was no great loss, as his biplane series D1-5, which were produced from the summer through the fall of 1916, was quite inferior to the Albatros. Although some 565 of the series were built and some of them saw frontline service, they were relegated to training duties.[46] Other fighter craft in service at the time were the LFG D2, which was built mainly by Pfalz under license, and the

Halberstadt D series, which had formed some of the first flying circus units with the early Fokker biplanes and the Albatros Dls. Yet all these craft were inferior to the Albatros, which was the only one capable of wrestling aerial superiority from the enemy.

Under these circumstances, emphasis on production of the Albatros was most logical and paid great dividends. In January 1917 there were 13 D3s at the front, in March 137, in May 327. The east German Albatros Works at Schneidemühl alone built 840 of them between April and August 1917. In April 1917 the circumstances were most favorable for the Albatros and the German air service. The British attacked at Arras when they possessed a preponderance of obsolete airplanes and before their new fighters like the Sopwith triplanes, SE5s, and Bristol two-seater F2s were available in any number. The German air service, its fighter forces reorganized into *Jastas,* or circuses, equipped with the new Albatros and led by Manfred von Richthofen, took a frightful toll of British airmen, who pressed their offensive patrols regardless of the risk. If the British had more than twice the number of fighters—385 versus 114— and all aircraft—754 versus 264—at the front in April, the Germans equalized the situation somewhat by shooting down 151 British airplanes for losses of 66 of their own. The month became known as Bloody April.[47]

At the end of April, however, the new British fighters began to regain the advantage, and according to one source, Aaron Norman, the German air force was ill prepared to meet the new challenge.[48] Its upper echelons, convinced of the superiority of the Albatros, had undertaken little developmental work in the nine months since the introduction of the Albatros biplanes. Norman's assessment of complacency, although he fails to substantiate it, has much merit. Even before the war standardization on a single type in the German air service had led to a stagnation of aeronautical development, and despite the pressures of wartime, in which no such inertia was permissible, the overwhelming success of the Albatros had undoubtedly fostered a complacent attitude. Albatros did have a successor for the D3 ready and on order in April 1917, yet the overconfidence was obvious: the Albatros D5 was nothing more than a lightened D3 airframe, and, more crucially, the aircraft depot had tested only the fuselage and rudder of the D5. It chose to consider the wings the same, although the fuselage-wing interface differed from the D3 and aileron cables were now run through the upper wing. The omission proved fatal. When the D5 reached the front in May 1917, wing failures began immediately. Nevertheless, with no better aircraft to rely upon, the Inspectorate of Flying Troops ordered 200 D5s in April and 400 in

At the beginning of May it reckoned the monthly loss of D-planes at 540 and held out the prospect of contracts for 1,500 D-planes to Albatros and 600 Ds of a type to be determined to Pfalz over the next six months.[49]

The policy of standardization on the Albatros had initially resulted in a superior craft, but slavish adherence to the design and the consequent failure to foster competitive designs of future promise forced reliance on the Albatros series long after its prime. Consequently, in the late spring of 1917 German fighter pilots faced the prospect of combat on a mount with serious flaws at a time when the British were moving to full-scale production of superior scout aircraft. The policies of the Hindenburg Program in fighter production had thus been a mixed blessing. Successful through April 1917, the time when the program was to climax, they led ultimately to a dead end by May, and German fighter pilots paid for this error in the coming months.

The ultimate criterion for evaluation of the mobilization's success was whether monthly production attained the one thousand mark by the spring and the service was able to increase its complement of craft by five hundred. Previous secondary sources are vague about the subject. Alex Imrie's work on the air service mentions only that as of the summer 1917 the program of fall 1916 had still not been completely carried out.[50] Hilmer von Bülow, writing in the early 1930s, was self-contradictory on the topic of the Hindenburg Program.[51] He stated that Siegert's energy was not equal to the task and that "even an immediate conversion and merger of the German aviation industry in a huge war trade association and the centralization of raw material procurement could not eliminate the accumulating difficulties of supplying the front." He further acknowledged that modification of the air service's frontline organization did not compensate for losses of airplanes. Yet after all these critical qualifications he concluded, with no supporting evidence, that, "on the whole, however, through the requisitioning and coordination of all the powers of the homeland, the great program was successfully carried out almost completely through the early year of 1917." Bülow's conclusion conflicts with Imrie's, and neither supports his contentions, although evidence exists to substantiate a more thorough analysis.

It is impossible to determine with certainty the extent to which the army and industry attained the goal of 2,322 aircraft at the front by the spring of 1917, although one German military history of the war credits the German air arm with 2,271 airplanes early in 1917.[52] Yet if one presumes these figures to be correct, they are quite amazing, because there is rather solid evidence to show that the aircraft industry failed to attain its production goals. In December the factories had delivered 900 craft; in January, only 400. The official history of aircraft motor production during the war by J. A. Gilles asserts that aircraft production declined from 450 to 260 between December 1916 and February 1917, although he acknowledges that his figures are approximate.[53] There are no production figures for March and April available, but official monthly production deliveries for the months from May through September 1917 are 789, 1,012, 731, 927, and 915.[54]

So production, which fluctuated substantially, did not even approach the one thousand aircraft target with any regularity until the late summer of 1917, some four months after the April deadline for the mobilization. Even if the plan had taken into account such drastic declines in production during the winter, and there is no evidence to show that it did, its failure to meet the spring deadline is undeniable. And since production and frontline strength were linked, it is not possible that the air service could have fulfilled the program completely, unless sacrifices were made somewhere. But where? One method used with regularity later in the war was the deployment of units at half strength, but the figures for spring 1917 list numbers of aircraft, not units. There is one further, and very likely, possibility—the production of training and reserve aircraft was sacrificed for that of combat planes during the Hindenburg Program. This expedient would also be used frequently later in the war. If so, the German air force was mortgaging its future for the present, because trained air crews were in increasingly short supply as the war continued.

The overall picture of aviation mobilization during the Hindenburg Program is thus one of partial success. The army's measures did enable the air service to increase its effective strength, but the severe problems of shortages during the winter prevented the aircraft industry, after early strides, from meeting its production goals in April. Organizational measures—revamping of the military procurement bureaucracy, standardization of production, the organization of the industry, the rationalization of its plant operations and of its relationships with subcontractors—could not mitigate the effects of irremediable shortages of skilled manpower and raw materials.

Exemptions of some thirty-five hundred skilled workers for the entire aviation industry were probably insufficient for the production increase, particularly in light of the serious deficiencies in the motor industry. It is also uncertain whether all these workers were assigned, because the Kogenluft staff were reluctant to exempt men for the industry, despite their recognition of the airplane's importance.

The crisis of the winter of 1916–17 caught the air service planners unprepared and prompted a flurry of orders in 1917. Yet some of these orders, such as the shipment of all linen to one factory for painting, failed because they ignored aspects of the overall crisis—here the railroad breakdown—in their attempt at coordination to prevent wasted manpower and materials. Winter had always been a period of downturns in aircraft production, and the planners should have planned for one in advance, although they might not have anticipated its severity.

The air force was unable to organize its own house, as Prussia's Bavarian and Swabian subordinates refused to let their procurement bureaucracy be rationalized out of existence. When Kogenluft sought to incorporate the Bavarian procurement bureaucracy, its heavy-handed method increased the determination of the Bavarian authorities to preserve their autonomy, and the resulting administrative imbroglio wasted time and manpower.

Finally, and most critically, the air force's decision sacrificed the future to the immediate six months of the Hindenburg Program in fighter development and in the production of combat aircraft at the expense of training planes. Yet the army had no plans for winning the war on the western front during that time; the High Command was actually awaiting a British offensive in 1917. When the panacea of the submarine failed to win the war, the air force was doomed to face the Allies at a severe disadvantage numerically and, in the all-important category of fighter planes, qualitatively, during the second half of 1917.

CHAPTER 5

Pressed by a Phantom: The America Program, June 1917–March 1918

In April 1917 the United States entered the war. The Germans were struggling to defend themselves against heavy British and French attacks around Arras, on the Aisne river, and in Champagne, but the High Command reasoned that America could not bring the weight of her forces to bear before the spring of 1918. Ludendorff proceeded to plan a great German offensive to win the war in the spring of 1918 before American might fell upon Germany. An enlarged air force was essential to his attack. Consequently on 3 June—the month in which aircraft deliveries to the army first exceeded one thousand, the goal of the Hindenburg Program—Kogenluft and the Inspectorate of Flying Troops met to discuss a new expansion program aptly entitled the America Program.[1]

They anticipated that while the absence of an American aircraft industry would prevent a rapid buildup of American squadrons, America's great technological potential would enable her to send engineers, businessmen, and even workers to raise the industrial capacity of the Allies, who would in turn send advisers to help develop an American aircraft industry. Kogenluft concluded that by early 1918 Germany would have to reckon with greatly increased aerial opposition over the western front. Kogenluft proposed its expansion plan to the High Command on 18 June, Ludendorff endorsed it and set it before the Prussian War Ministry on 25 June 1917:

> America's entry into the war compels a considerable strengthening of the air force by 1 March 1918. In order to be somewhat equal to the combined English-French-American air fleet, I order the formation of an absolute minimum of forty new fighter groups (*Jagdstaffeln* 41–80) and seventeen new flight units (*Fliegerabteilungen* 184–200).[2]

95

The air force required the following increases: 24,443 men by 1 January 1918; monthly production of approximately two thousand planes and twenty-five hundred motors; monthly deliveries of fifteen hundred aircraft machine guns; and a doubling of the monthly allotment of gasoline from six thousand tons to twelve thousand tons and of aircraft motor oil to twelve hundred tons. Ludendorff believed that the needs for oil and gasoline for all agencies could be met by "wise thriftiness," but he did question whether the increase in aircraft and engine production would be possible without impairing other arms industries. Then he elaborated on the industrial mobilization entailed by the program: the allotment of 2,000 men for the aircraft factories and 5,000 for the motor factories by 1 December 1917; retention of the aviation industry's labor force where possible and the provision of trained replacements for men eligible for the draft; provision of food, heating and production fuels, and machinery for the industry; and the placement of aviation production on raw materials priority lists immediately after submarines, with special consideration in the allotment of aluminum.[3]

In a letter to the War Office, Ludendorff insisted on the complete fulfillment of the program, which he labeled "of extraordinary importance":

> I repeat that an adequate increase of our airplanes in early 1918 is of crucial importance and request that all provisions be made to enable the production of two thousand aircraft and twenty-five hundred motors monthly as soon as the raw material situation improves through the stated measures, or, in case it should become necessary, through use of the last reserves for the task.[4]

The magnitude of these measures indicates that the America Program was to be the climax of the army's mobilization of the aircraft industry. Before the War Office and the War Ministry could submit their assessment of the plan, Inspector Siegert asked for cooperation in labor and food allocation from the deputy general commands and central police agencies. He particularly requested adequate food supplies and physically strong, technically trained personnel. Siegert emphasized that regular materiel supply meant more to the air force than to any other branch of the armed forces. With twenty thousand trucks at the front, for example, the interruption of truck production for a month would leave nineteen thousand. The cessation of aviation production for a month would reduce frontline strength by half and cause the collapse of the air force. He urged maximum secrecy, the protection of the industry from espionage, and, as his last important request, a lessening of correspondence.[5]

Yet, as the Inspectorate of Flying Troops prepared to execute the program, other agencies began to express their doubts about its feasibility. At a fuel conference involving the War Office; the departments of war raw materials, transportation, and aviation in the Prussian War Ministry; and the inspectorates of flying troops, motor vehicles, and airships, the High Command was informed that it had overestimated available fuel and other materials. Instead of twelve thousand tons of fuel, the conference estimated that the air service would receive only eight thousand tons of gasoline and oil through January 1918 and only six thousand tons after January. The Inspectorate of Flying Troops even proposed sending German workers to Romania to obtain the precious oil, but this suggestion was rejected. The War Ministry informed the inspectorate on 19 July that fulfillment of the program to the extent Ludendorff considered possible would seriously impair other armaments production. It consequently proposed that the inspectorate reduce its monthly production goals to sixteen hundred aircraft and eighteen hundred motors. After a further round of meetings, the High Command decided to strive gradually for the original limit, although it allowed the sixteen hundred and eighteen hundred figures to stand and informed Kogenluft on 25 July that "a certainty of fulfilling the America Program completely no longer exists in our economic situation."[6]

Despite such reservations, some observers favorably assessed the prospects of the successful completion of the America Program. Lieutenant Krug, the Bavarian representative at the inspectorate, believed that in spite of problems of raw material procurement and motor production, a "ruthless" use of the factories would enable the program's fulfillment. While he hoped that licensed production of motors would increase the insufficient output of the Daimler and Benz monopolies, he anticipated no difficulty in procuring sufficient airframes.[7]

Lt. Franz Reichelt, emissary of the Austro-Hungarian flight arsenal, reached the same conclusion through detailed calculations.[8] For the Hindenburg Program's one thousand plane and twelve hundred motor monthly production, a labor force of approximately forty thousand in the aircraft industry, thirty thousand in the motor industry, and forty to seventy thousand in subcontracting firms had sufficed. In May 1917 Germany had produced one thousand planes with thirty-one aircraft factories, or an average production per factory of thirty planes. To double this production, Reichelt noted, the War Ministry's aviation department was requesting the "surprisingly small" number of two thousand workers for the aircraft industry and five thousand for the motor factories. Yet such numbers would suffice, because the factories already had the "best" labor force, their plants and machinery were substantial and first-class, and aircraft and motor firms had received priority in material procurement and transportation space.

Reichelt also observed variation within the aircraft industry: LVG, one of the best organized firms, produced one hundred planes monthly with twenty-two hundred workers and little reliance on subcontractors; Rumpler produced only sixty craft monthly with the same number of workers and more subcontractors. Improving the organization of factories like Rumpler would enable the High Command to double production without substantial increases in the industry's labor force. Reichelt estimated that on the average it took fourteen workers in the aircraft industry and eight in the subcontracting firms to produce one plane a month, given prompt delivery from the subcontractors. Now there would be forty-two thousand workers for the minimum of sixteen hundred planes, or twenty-six workers per plane per month, which he considered more than sufficient for Germany. If the motor industry suffered from incorrect organization and the dispersal of production in small factories, then "ruthless" measures could achieve the designated production increases with only five thousand more workers. Certainly Reichelt's optimism stemmed from his awe of Germany's military and industrial prowess, compared to Austria-Hungary's, but the coincidental usage of the term "ruthless" by both Krug and Reichelt describes not only the manner in which they expected the Prussian Army to execute its measures but also the precondition for the success of the America Program.

If the program's success demanded ruthlessness, Maj. Wilhelm Siegert was perfectly suited for the task. On 31 July he issued to the aviation industry a rousing dual challenge—from the American aircraft industry and from the German frontline troops—that showed not only a flair for the dramatic but also a willingness to disregard all but military considerations in the execution of the America Program.[9] Most essentially he recommended the aircraft industry's complete and unquestioning participation in the war trade association. To meet the American challenge, the manufacturers would have to disregard all personal and financial consideration in their effort to supply the front with the best aircraft. He wanted to hear no further complaints about losses of interest or injury to shareholders from belated raw material deliveries and no refusals to allow licenses in order to protect monopolies. It was time, he declared, to forget about peace and remember wartime duties. Everybody at home earned more than those risking their lives at the front, and "the loss lists of the industry," Siegert noted sarcastically, "still showed many empty pages." The execution of the America Program necessitated the subordination of the industry to a single will—his own.

Siegert's stridency stemmed in part from his awareness that there was opposition in the industry to the war association—"dark, mysterious currents seeking to disturb its prosperous workings." The refusal of some factories to enter distressed him, since the disadvantages of entry that they so "irresponsibly" feared were certainly not as great as the advantages to the air force from the industrial union. He reminded the manufacturers that their complaints of spotty raw material delivery had prompted him to form the association to help supply materials to members for inspectorate contracts. He was now determined to strengthen the association's authority. On 16 June he had empowered it to conclude contracts for delivery by 1 April 1918 and had promised financial coverage for all such contracts until 1 May or beyond if necessary. His commissar to the association would work closely with the air force representative in the War Office and the inspectorate's raw materials department to support it. In his opinion, the association had functioned well during its short existence: its procurement of wood, steel tube, brass, and carbide had certainly helped the industry, and its role as an industrial committee of the inspectorate relieved him of the daily burden of hearing hundreds of complaints and requests.

Siegert attacked the source of defiance to his wishes—refusal to join the association—as one where "pretension and achievement were least in accord." The object of Siegert's wrath was none other than August Euler. Euler had not kept pace with aviation progress, and his small factory of 180–200 workers had been relgated to the role of subcontractor for LVG trainers. Euler had not entered the association, because he felt that it violated the principles of free enterprise. Siegert's assault unleashed a vitriolic exchange of letters over a five-month period between him and Euler,[10] a correspondence which indicated that the forced syndication of the industry was no panacea. Faced with the failure to centralize and regiment procurement completely, Siegert intended to close all the loopholes in the association's regulations and silence all opposition, even if it came from a firm as insignificant as the Euler works. But Euler refused to be silenced, and Siegert the militarist found himself confronted with an individualist laissez faire entrepreneur.

If Siegert was openly contemptuous of the industry, Euler, one of the first German manufacturers to be aware of the airplane's military potential, had come to oppose the military's aviation policies even before the war as detrimental to the full development of the airplane and ultimately even the military's interests. The war association marked a further step in his disenchantment with the army's meddling in the affairs of the aircraft industry. He particularly resented the proliferation of the military bureaucracy and mediative agencies, its disregard of the law, the resort to secrecy to silence opposition—exactly the measures that Siegert regarded as necessary to mobilize the industry to its fullest potential. Euler was certainly correct in his assertion that the military plans could do nothing about basic and irremediable shortages of material.

Yet Siegert's argument cannot be ignored. These same shortages, and the controls evolved rather haphazardly over time to alleviate them, meant that a system of rationing and allocation was absolutely necessary for Germany to continue the struggle. The army could not abandon them, because then the war machine would collapse. So the army proceeded on its course, ignoring Euler's assertions and interfering increasingly in the affairs of the aircraft industry as the America Program continued. The army could not organize away the problems it faced, and its unwieldy bureaucracy might even exacerbate them. Furthermore, its heavy-handed regimentation might elicit opposition from the firms that had joined the war trade association.

The absence of a single agency efficiently coordinating procurement within the army and between the army, navy, and the various imperial states caused wasteful conflicts. On 11 November Ludendorff complained of the incoherence of procurement, as manufacturers set procurement agencies against each other, selected contracts on the basis of profit, not priority schedules, and took every opportunity to increase their labor force and coal supplies excessively.[11] On 18 December Wumba advised the independent procurement agencies to distribute new contracts only with the participation of the War Office, which would settle any interagency conflicts.[12]

Yet the War Office's huge bureaucracy could not force these agencies to relinquish their independence. It remained at best a coordinator. Consequently, no office had sufficient control to introduce a coherent price policy, as was indicated by the system for setting wood prices in 1917. It took a conference of the War Office; the inspectorate; the war trade association; the Prussian Ministry of Agriculture, Domains, and Forestry; and representatives of the owners of certain private forests to establish the prices. Still, there were difficulties enforcing adherence to them, because the aircraft industry found that it could acquire birch wood only at exorbitant prices through middlemen who completely ignored the decision of the authorities.[13] Furthermore, as Euler had predicted, without price controls the price of raw materials continued its rapid rise as new procurement programs made additional demands on already limited reserves.[14]

There were no laws to force the firms to abide by those military regulations that existed, such as, for example, the submission of company ledgers to procurement agencies for profit and price checks. While the major aircraft manufacturers consented to submit detailed information of their costs, the aircraft motor companies had declined, submitting only summary information, and they were protected under the law.[15] The military bureaucracy's power of enforcement lay in its ability to stop contracts to recalcitrant manufacturers, yet such action could not be taken against firms, like the aircraft motor companies, that were indispensable to war production. Price regulation and stringent policing of raw materials and war material suppliers were impossible with a huge, poorly coordinated, and inefficient bureaucracy that defied rational and economic considerations.

Another impediment to mobilization was the industry's resistance to rationing. In November 1917 the aircraft depot reported that the industry was "naturally" fighting the rationing of raw materials because of "a lack of trust" and the "compulsion" related to rationing.[16] This resistance had assumed significant proportions by the late fall of 1917. In November one firm which was urgently demanding two thousand kilograms of fuselage varnish was caught with eleven months supply already on hand. The firms' demands for gasoline in particular often exceeded their consumption. One firm requested fifteen thousand kilograms and used ten thousand; another, twelve thousand and used four thousand; a third eighty-five hundred and used three thousand; and another thirty thousand for a consumption of four thousand kilograms. One aircraft factory was discovered hoarding ninety crates of urgently needed Mercedes motor spare parts. Firms used flight fuel for motor vehicles.[17] Such instances suggest that the factories responded to the shortages and the controls by circumventing the controls and hoarding precious goods, possibly to trade them for other materials in a black market. The inspectorate's frequent admonitions to the BAs to monitor the factories closely also suggest that evasion of the regulations was widespread.

Such hoarding compounded raw material shortages. In the fall of 1917 the allotment of fuel to the air service was to be doubled to twelve thousand tons. In July it received eleven thousand tons, but in September its allotment dropped drastically to four thousand and in November to one thousand tons. Available quantities of raw materials did not suffice for the aircraft industry to receive its demands for rubber, aluminum, copper, nickel, tin, and coal without severely damaging the rest of the armaments industry. New adjustments were constantly sought in laborious negotiations. The High Command decreased the allotment of rubber to the communications and motor vehicle troops, had the construction of shell fuses altered to save aluminum, and further reduced allotments to other industries. Yet these were mere palliatives.[18]

By January it was difficult to secure most metals, although steel tubing was available in sufficient quantities and Wumba had obtained enough machine tools for the industry. Cement and iron shortages prevented the firms from constructing permanent buildings. Textiles and fabric were more difficult to obtain; the demand for electrical machines was increasing at a time when there were fewer available. In February the shortages of electrical machinery and construction iron remained severe. The coal shortage had worsened with no prospects for improvement, although major aviation firms in southwest Germany, with the exception of Daimler's aircraft factory, received sufficient coal. The imperial commissar was generally limiting supplies of gas and electricity, but was expected to make an exception for the industry given its importance. The inspectorate's supply of tin had been reduced fifty percent. Although the aircraft industry now had five wire subcontractors, they could not compensate for lost time and earlier shortages. The industry was attempting to use substitute metals in aircraft production—for example, using aluminum coolers on training aircraft. Overall, the situation during the winter of 1917–18 was grim as shortages wrought havoc with production.[19]

The collapse of the German railroads during the winter and spring impeded delivery of raw materials and finished aircraft. In late March the continued railway stoppages prevented SSW and LVG from shipping their G-planes and placed SSW in particular in a quandary, because the factory could not bring finished airplanes in out of the harsh weather, nor could it afford to delay production until the finished craft had been shipped. In general the raw material shortage and transportation crisis consumed a considerable amount of Siegert's time and strength.[20]

The aircraft industry did not receive its designated allocation of exempted skilled workers. As the motor industry received only twenty-four hundred of the five thousand it was promised, it is quite likely that the aircraft industry did not even receive half of its allotted two thousand workers. The workers that the industry did obtain were often of inferior quality, and bad food and long hours of overwork in night shifts reduced their productivity further. To make matters worse, the factories were not always able to retain the skilled labor force that they already possessed.[21]

The long hours and inadequate food made the workers ripe for strike unrest. In mid-January some five hundred workers at the Hanseatic Aircraft Works struck because of unequal and insufficient food distribution. In the major German strike of 28 January in which four hundred thousand workers in Berlin alone stopped work, aircraft workers participated prominently. Factories such as Gotha, DFW and Aviatik in Leipzig, Halberstadt, Junkers, and Fokker continued production "aside from the usual insignificant stoppages" because they were located in cities that were unaffected by the strike. The entire aircraft and aircraft motor industry in Berlin stopped, as did BFW and Pfalz in Bavaria.[22] One of the strike's leaders, Spartacus supporter Fritz Ulm, worked in the Rumpler Works and described the origins of the strike there. He sought out the shop steward of his department, who, although no "comrade," was at least a "reliable" fellow, and they agreed that the department would go out on strike together. Immediately after starting work on 28 January, he easily convinced his colleagues to strike. The waverers took heart when the shop steward arrived with the news that other departments had already resolved to strike. After the breakfast pause, when the signal for work sounded, Ulm jumped up, packed his tools noisily, shoved his table locker up to his file bench, and shouted to the entire department: "Knock off! We strike!" He judged that only thirty-seven workers remained—managers and aides—and the works directors sent them home later in the day.[23]

Official accounts corroborate Ulm's account in general, as of 47,750 workers striking at noon on the twenty-eighth, Rumpler and AEG were cited among the factories struck already by that time. After five days, on 1 February the High Command placed certain factories, among them AEG and LVG, under military direction and ordered the workers there to resume work by 7:00 A.M. Monday, 4 February, or be subject to harsh punishment under the laws of siege. Factories assented to the induction of as many as 5 percent of their workers, and the Bavarian plenipotentiary at the inspectorate, Capt. Stabl, reported that this militarization of the factories and the inductions of exempted workers removed the bulk of the unruly elements. The War Ministry informed the kaiser on 5 February that the strike had disturbed the completion of new aircraft "only insignificantly," an assessment which appeared to substantiate Stabl's conclusion that the strike would have only a limited effect on airframe construction because of a surplus. Yet the War Ministry failed to say that the air force expected to lose 25 percent of monthly motor production as a result of the strike, which meant in fact that the completion of new aircraft had been seriously disrupted. In late February Stabl reported with obvious relief that apprehension of renewed unrest in the middle of the month had not been borne out, although the situation remained uncertain and unstable. He expected more strikes in the future.[24]

Appropriate measures were taken against future general strikes. In late March, for example, the Bavarian Engineers Inspectorate informed deputy general commands in south Germany that exempted workers, with the exception of important officials and white collar employees, would be inducted, commandeered labor would receive full wages, and the factories would be militarized and officers assigned to them as directors. Yet a report from Stabl submitted to the Bavarian War Ministry on 24 April alleged that the induction of unruly elements after the January strike had ultimately *hurt* production and taxed the aircraft factories to the limit. The workers, he believed, would inevitably falter sooner or later, as wages were no longer the stimulus they had formerly been. Food strikes became more likely as the workers toiled long and hard on insufficient food.[25] Prospects in labor relations thus seemed dim, in part because the remedy for the strike, induction of trained workers, had proved worse than the strike itself.

Finally, accidents also resulted in critical delays in aircraft production. On the night of 24/25 November, the North German Aircraft Works in Teltow, sixty-four aircraft, and forty motors were totally destroyed by fire. The flooding of the Dillinger foundry later that month interrupted the supply of armor plate to the Junkers Aircraft Works and thus the production of Junkers all-metal aircraft.

In attempting to counter these problems, the Inspectorate of Flying Troops resorted to more interference in the affairs of the aircraft industry through the increased coordination and centralization of procurement. In early October the Central Acceptance Commission ordered adherence to production quotas even if factories obtained more engines, workers, and material than they needed, as any surfeits were to be viewed as reserves. In November wood shortages forced factories to submit their requirements to the inspectorate's raw materials department and the association two months in advance in order to ensure their supply of commandeered wood from occupied territories. The association now managed supplies of steel, tin, and cable, while a special plant was under construction to manufacture oxygen for the aircraft industry, and the depot was experimenting at drying wood artificially. In early December the Central Acceptance Commission reiterated its insistence on adherence to its production programs, which would be formulated two to three months in advance with the firms. Failure to meet a production quota necessitated written permission from the commission to keep the same quota. Firms that had to release workers had to inform the commission fourteen days before the workers became idle. The BAs were instructed to ensure that factories did not employ unnecessary subcontractors and built as much as possible in their own plants, so as to concentrate production. In January 1918 written permission of the Central Acceptance Commission was required before a firm could place an order with a new subcontractor except for basic raw materials or standard parts such as screws, tanks, steel tube, and propellers. In February the aircraft depot's scientific section assumed control of the norms committee of the aircraft industry, which had previously been directed by the war trade association, and continued monthly distribution of some forty sheets of standards covering all areas of production and technology.[26]

The Central Acceptance Commission was also planning to eliminate contracts to various marginal firms during the year: Sablatnig, Germania, Kondor, LVG Köslin, Märkische, and Linke-Hoffmann after June 1918; Euler and Merkur after September; Albert Rinne after October; and SSW Nürnberg after November.[27] These measures were expected to be part of the demobilization, and the inspectorate well understood that the elimination of contracts meant the demise of these firms, at least as aircraft producers.

The inspectorate destroyed firms, but it also created them. The climax of its interference in the affairs of the aircraft industry occurred on 20 October 1917, when it negotiated the formation of the Junkers-Fokker Works in Dessau with a capital of 2.6 million marks. The merger was intended to facilitate the production of Junkers's armored biplane, the J1, which had been completed in prototype form in early 1917. In mid-February the aircraft depot had informed the then Junkers Works that it would soon order one hundred armored planes, so the factory should proceed as quickly as possible to mass production.

The planes, however, thwarted these intentions, because they proved impossible to mass-produce. Junkers had given no thought to ease of construction, and the metal construction necessitated four times as many workers as usual techniques. The inspectorate coupled the two manufacturers because it felt that Junkers had good technical ideas but lacked flying and mass production experience, both of which Fokker possessed. The union, which the inspectorate used "economic pressure" to create, was stormy and only partially successful. The first JIs began to equip some units toward the end of 1917, and the *"Möbelwagen,"* or "furniture vans," as their crews called them because of their slow speed and ungainly characteristics, were well suited in their strength for low-altitude attack duties. In March 1918 the inspectorate set the monthly production goal of JIs at 24–30, and these numbers were not attained until the summer of 1918, after the America Program. By that time Hugo Junkers and Anthony Fokker were hardly on speaking terms. Junkers, independent and scientifically oriented, had not appreciated the idea in the beginning, though he had no choice if he desired military contracts. Disturbed by the presence of Fokker's men in his factory, he withdrew increasingly to his research institute, where he could work in peace. Fokker, on the other hand, considered Junkers unsuited to the times, which demanded a practical more than a theoretical approach, and he later rebuked Junkers for refusing "to give up his all-metal construction for the sake of wartime expediency." After constant and fruitless arguments, Fokker's interest also waned. The inspectorate mediated between the two, and the merger survived for the duration of the war to produce a total of 227 JIs.[28]

It is evident that by late fall the Inspectorate of Flying Troops was encountering severe problems and resistance from the industry in its efforts to mobilize aircraft production. As further evidence of the checkered results of the military's efforts to prepare the industry for the 1918 offensive, two key areas of concentration during the America Program merit close consideration: the mobilization of the Bavarian aircraft industry and fighter development.

The Bavarian aircraft industry was considered crucial to the America Program because its lower stage of development offered the prospect of more significant increases than did north German factories. On 13 July Kogenluft politely advised the Bavarian War Ministry that Bavaria would supply two flying units and five fighter units of the program's seventeen flight and forty fighter units and suggested that the program's success depended upon the cooperation of all agencies, particularly the Bavarian Engineers Inspectorate and the Prussian Inspectorate of Flying Troops. The Engineers Inspectorate perceived that the fulfillment of the program depended most on an adequate supply of skilled workers and asked other inspectorates to give all their dispensable manpower to the flying troops and to the aircraft and motor industries.[29]

On 21 July the Engineers Inspectorate, in conference with the Prussian aircraft depot, determined that Bavaria was to receive 300 skilled workers for the aircraft industry and 700 for the motor industry. Although Bavarian production amounted to only one-eighth of total German production, they were to receive more than one-eighth of the labor force allotted in the program because the Bavarian industry was considered capable of relatively greater expansion. The Inspectorate of Flying Troops would conduct all contractual dealings with the factories, but the engineers intended to expand the Bavarian aviation inspectorate to monitor the BA and the growing aircraft factories and to station a liaison officer permanently at the Inspectorate of Flying Troops in Berlin. The Bavarian aviation inspectorate was requested to submit the BAs' estimates of the number of skilled workers the firms would require for the program.[30] The Bavarian aircraft factories and their subcontractors were requesting 1,490 workers; the aviation inspectorate deducted 15 percent as excess with some additional for employment of women as woodworkers and arrived at a total of some 1,250, or an increase of 200 workers per month. Since they were to receive only 300 workers during the program, this discrepancy was an early indication that the program's goals might be impossible to attain.[31]

The vital developments in the Bavarian industry in the second half of 1917 are described in detail in the reports of the Bavarian labor commission, which visited the factories from month to month.[32] In the five-month period from the beginning of the America Program to October, the Bavarian aircraft industry grew rapidly. Pfalz's labor force rose from 835 in July to 1,370 in September and was expected to reach 2,000 in three more months. In five months Rumpler's work force almost doubled from 276 to 500. BFW did not need to expand its labor complement of 2,000; rather, it needed to use them more efficiently. But the BAs encountered immense difficulties in rectifying the shortcomings cited in the labor commission's monthly reports and in persuading the factories that, to use the High Command's description in reverse, the front was not an endless screw that could forever produce skilled workers from the ranks of soldiers. The factories were slow to employ more rational work methods and to use their skilled and unskilled labor effectively. Furthermore, occasional failures of the military bureaucracy occurred, such as the Prussian inspectorate's upsetting manner of abruptly phasing out old types for new or its inability to supply SSW Nürnberg with contracts. In any case, production rose steadily through the fall. But winter would

inevitably halt this progress, and the following table based on statistics
from the official Bavarian history indicates the magnitude of this seasonal
disruption:

Bavarian Aircraft Production, November 1917–April 1918[33]

Firm		11/17	4/18
BFW	Workers	2,471	2,246
	Production	—	76 (+28 repaired planes)
Pfalz	Workers	—	2,000
	Production	165	111
Rumpler	Workers	649	659
	Production	24 (+7 repaired planes)	17 (+8 repaired planes)
SSW	Workers	178	243
	Production	(16 repaired planes)	15 (+19 repaired planes)

Monthly production had thus stagnated from November to April, and
undoubtedly had dropped in the intervening months. The Bavarian aircraft industry's failure to attain its production goals was a crippling blow
to the overall success of the America Program.

For the first time, however, particularistic conflict between Prussian
and Bavarian aviation agencies did not figure in the failure to achieve
mobilization goals. The Prussian authorities stopped attempting to gain
control of the Bavarian hinterland administration and concentrated on
the more positive goal of developing the Bavarian aircraft industry to
meet the needs of the front. The Bavarian agencies naturally appreciated
both aspects of this new approach. When SSW Nürnberg, on the brink of
partial closing, accused the Prussian inspectorate of discriminating
against Bavarian firms, the Bavarian War Ministry dismissed the accusa-
tion in light of BFW's and Pfalz's plentiful contracts.[34] A more dramatic, if
belated, transformation is scarcely imaginable.

A critical aspect of the America Program was the development of
superior fighter aircraft. Kogenluft informed the inspectorate on 12 July
that the numerical fulfillment of the America Program was no assurance
of aerial equality, much less superiority. Only technically superior machines could compensate for German numerical inferiority, and the per-
fection of present types, it advised, was not likely to achieve this. Kogenluft continued to recommend the curtailment of the development of
certain types, the standardized construction of only a few proven aircraft,
the expansion of the aircraft motor industry, and the development of new

motors in an effort to catch up with the allies. But, on 24 July, Kogenluft returned to its key point, stating to the inspectorate that the first task was the development of a new fighter.[35]

Germany's ace of aces, Manfred von Richthofen, attested to the serious condition of the German fighter forces in the summer of 1918. Richthofen had been wounded in the head while in combat in an Albatros D5 on 6 July. He sent the following letter to a close friend, Lieutenant von Falkenhayn of the Kogenluft staff, on 18 July, as he completed his convalescence:

> I can assure you that it is no longer any fun being leader of a fighter unit at this army [Sixth Army]. . . . For the last three days the English have done as they please. . . .
>
> Our airplanes are inferior to the English in a downright ridiculous manner. The triplane [Sopwith] and the two-hundred-horsepower Spad, like the Sopwith single-seater [presumably the Camel, which was just appearing at the front in July], play with our D5s. Besides better quality aircraft they have quantity. Our fighter pilots, though quite good, are consequently lost! The D5 is so antiquated and laughably inferior that we can do nothing with it. Yet the people in the homeland haven't produced any better machine than this lousy Albatros in almost a year and have stuck with the Albatros D3, with which I was already fighting in the fall of last year.
>
> We must unconditionally support and use every firm that produces a type merely somewhat better than this damn Albatros, even if its earlier conduct has been shabby and unreliable [a presumed reference to Fokker]. As long as Albatros encounters no energetic competition, we will remain sitting in our D3s (D5s). The English single-seater is faster and climbs better than our planes, and the English even have C-planes [a reference to the Bristol fighter], thus two-seaters, that the Albatros is not capable of overtaking, that overtake it [the Albatros] in a curve with the greatest of ease, against which one is simply powerless.
>
> What's going on with Fokker? He has two machines that are superior to the Albatros, and neither has been produced. There is his unbraced biplane with the stationary engine. It is unquestionably faster and has better qualities in the curve than the Albatros D5, and yet is not built. I believe Schwarzenberger [official of the Inspectorate of Flying Troops] is behind this.
>
> Furthermore, he [Fokker] has a triplane that is certainly no longer in the formative stages and has already shown exceptional climb and speed, that must be unreservedly supported and sent to the front in large numbers as soon as we have rotary engines.
>
> You would not believe how low morale is among the fighter pilots presently at the front because of their sorry machines. No one wants to be a fighter pilot any more.[36]

Richthofen proceeded to lament that shooting down planes was becoming more difficult, that it was so enervating and thankless a task with the Sixth Army that he could not blame those who declined to become fighter pilots. Fifty percent of them, after all, were dead before they received recognition or medals. His head was better, he was due to return to the front the next day, but he assured his friend that the letter was not a product of depression. It merely described true conditions at the front.

Richthofen, who has sometimes been portrayed as an unemotional executioner, was certainly suffering from some depression and apprehension about his return to the front. Any personal qualms were compounded by news that his *Jasta* had suffered some losses since 13 July. Nevertheless, his assessment of the circumstances was essentially correct. His mount remained nothing more than an updated and less reliable Albatros D3, although some accounts minimize the D5's deficiencies by stating that new high-compression engines offset some of its flaws. Richthofen dismissed the D5 as totally inadequate and insisted on competition to replace it with anything better.

The letter lays to rest the oft-repeated adage of German quality against Allied quantity and raises the critical question of why the German air force relied upon the Albatros series long after its prime. It has been suggested rather cynically that the D5 and D5a were ordered in vast quantities "presumably on the theory that sufficient numbers would overwhelm any opposition, even if of superior calibre." But this is patently absurd. The Inspectorate of Flying Troops on 24 July described the D5 as merely a lightened D3, whose performance was not sufficiently improved to warrant its production.[37] Kogenluft had observed in early July that mere modification of present types would not suffice even to attain aerial equality. The military authorities thus had no illusions about the worth of the Albatros D series by the summer of 1917. The plane was available and easily mass-produced with an abundance of ready parts and subcontractors. The America Program prescribed increased numbers of fighters; Kogenluft would obtain them, but not of the new types it desired. D5 orders were substantial: 262 in August, 250 in September, and 550 in October from the Johannisthal plant and 600 more from the Schneidemühl factory. The D5a, which appeared early in 1918, was stronger but heavier, and the modifications did not remove the structural flaws entirely. The most striking evidence of the D5's inadequacy is that the last production batch of D3s was ordered one month *after* the last D5s. Nevertheless, at the time of the great German offensive in the spring of 1918, Albatros D-planes comprised the majority of German fighter craft at the front, as the following numbers of fighters in late April show: 928 D5as (47.6 percent), 174 D3s (8.9 percent), 131 D5s (6.7 percent), 433 Pfalz D3as (22.2 percent), 171 Fokker Drls (8.8 percent), and 112 D-planes of miscellaneous type (5.8 percent).[38]

Richthofen's letter and the above statistics raise the possibility that there were better types available by the summer of 1917 and certainly by the fall and winter. The Pfalz D3-D3a series was the major supplement to the Albatros by April 1918. The first Pfalz D3s arrived at the front in the fall of 1917, went mainly to Bavarian units, and often served alongside the Albatros. According to British tests of a captured D3 in February 1918, its maximum speed was comparable to the D3–5 series, and it climbed slightly faster and answered the controls better than did the Albatros D5, although the Pfalz's roll rate was inferior. German pilots, however, regarded the Pfalz's maneuverability and general performance as inferior and preferred the Albatros. The Pfalz was not produced in higher quantities for two reasons: it did not offer sufficient improvement over the Albatros to warrant a changeover; and Pfalz's wood construction, though high quality, took longer than welded steel frames, produced heavier fuselages, and demanded more woodworking skills than were available to other manufacturers.[39]

As far as Richthofen was concerned, Anthony Fokker held the solution to German fighter inferiority in his triplane. His reference to an unbraced biplane with a stationary engine is enigmatic, as it could only pertain to an early version of a fighter that appeared in 1918, the Fokker D7. Yet this would have been quite early in its development, unless its evolution was delayed, as Richthofen intimated it was, by inspectorate officials working in the interests of Albatros. Fokker had always suggested that such a conspiracy was afoot to prevent him from displacing Albatros in fighter production.

The triplane's success was assured because it had Richthofen's support from its inception. Richthofen had shown Fokker a captured Sopwith triplane at the front in April 1917 before it was sent to Adlershof. Fokker relayed the information about the triplane to his chief designer Reinhold Platz, whom he instructed to design a triplane using a rotary engine, as Adlershof had a supply of 110-horsepower Rhones, while Fokker himself had a controlling interest in the German rotary engine firm Oberursel. Platz never saw the original Sopwith, so the design he produced was an original, of which the inspectorate ordered 320 after its test flight in July without the final results of its structural tests.[40]

Later in July, the aircraft depot distributed a circular inviting German manufacturers to inspect the Sopwith triplane with the incentive that it was prepared to grant contracts for test prototypes. Yet the English were already replacing the Sopwith triplane with superior biplane fighters like the Sopwith Camel and Se5, so the German manufacturers who undertook triplane construction—AEG, DFW, Euler, LFG, SSW, Pfalz, and Hansa-Brandenburg—were copying an obsolescent type. This situation explains why the Fokker was the only German triplane to see frontline service, none of the others advancing beyond the prototype stage. The depot's circular had done German fighter development a disservice, encouraging the manufacturers to waste time trying to copy an enemy design instead of proceeding independently to develop superior planes. Evidently the lesson of the Albatros D3—a mixed blessing in that it was superior to any current German craft, but the wing adapted from the French Nieuport had constituted its major flaw—had not been well learned. The Fokker triplane was successful because Fokker had seen the triplane early and his designer Platz never saw it and proceeded independently along lines of construction suited to his own genius.

The structural tests on the triplane were completed in August, and the plane was officially accepted by the army on 16 August. Its supreme asset, maneuverability, compensated for the numerous minor construction flaws that appeared. It became the favorite machine of Richthofen, its sponsor, and Werner Voss, another of Germany's great aces who was responsible for the triplane's fame. Then disaster struck at the end of October. Within two days two aces, Gontermann and Pastor, crashed in their triplanes, and a crash commission investigation found evidence of faulty workmanship in the wings and consequently restricted the use of the plane. Although the restrictions were lifted at the end of November and the DrI returned to operational use, production had been severely interrupted. Instead of the 173 craft in service envisaged by December 1917, only some 30 had arrived. All told, only some 320 DrIs were delivered before production ceased in May 1918. The craft lacked altitude performance, and the rotary engines lacked suitable lubricants. The triplane did not serve widely outside the Richthofen circus, and by May 1918 its two greatest proponents were gone. Werner Voss, an ace with forty-eight kills, fell to his death in an epic lone combat against a patrol of some of Britain's best pilots. Richthofen himself fell on 21 April 1918, and with his demise the triplane was eclipsed. On 27 February and 2 April, however, Richthofen had insisted on receiving some of "the new Fokker biplanes with high-compression engines."[41]

Fokker's new biplane, like the triplane, owed its existence in part to Richthofen's efforts. According to Hans Herlin, biographer of the German ace Ernst Udet, Lt. Konrad Krefft, the Richthofen squadron's technical officer, called Udet in later 1917 and informed him that Fokker had a new plane even better than the triplane. The High Command, however, wanted to "boot out" the Dutchman because his competition had spread rumors that he was shipping his money out of Germany and dealing secretly with the English. The High Command offered to let Fokker stay if he became a German citizen, but he declined. Krefft, at Richthofen's insistence, was assembling the fighter leaders to petition for an open competition for fighter prototypes from all German aircraft factories. "Did Udet want in?" "Naturally," came the reply. Fourteen days later Kogenluft agreed to the pilots' request and stipulated that the Mercedes 160-horsepower engine would be available to all entrants.[42]

At the Type D competition held at Adlershof in January 1918, Fokker entered five biplanes and two triplanes, Albatros four D5as, Pfalz four biplanes, Roland three, Rumpler two, Schütte-Lanz one, and SSW one biplane. After flying one of the biplanes—the V11 prototype—two days before the competition, Fokker determined that it was too sensitive a craft for the ordinary pilot. Working forty-eight hours without rest, he, designer Reinhold Platz, and a small crew lengthened the fuselage and added a vertical fin. The result was a superb aircraft, fairly easy to fly yet responsive and extremely controllable at altitude. After four days of comparison tests, during which manufacturers were forbidden to enter the field although the fliers stayed at their hotels in Berlin, the pilots unanimously judged the Fokker V11 prototype outright winner of the competition. General von Höppner asked Fokker how many aircraft he could build at once, then interrupted Fokker's reply, informing the Dutchman that he wanted four hundred as soon as possible.[43] Although the first Fokker D7s would not appear at the front until late April, three months later and mere days after the death of their most avid supporter, Richthofen, they proved to be the salvation of the German air force's fighter arm. The Fokker D7 possessed, as one authority noted, "an apparent ability to make a good pilot out of mediocre material," a tremendous asset with trained fighter pilots in increasingly short supply.[44] It was, and still is, widely regarded as the best fighter aircraft of the First World War.

The progress of single-seat fighter development during the America Program was thus extremely uneven: on the one hand the reliance on obsolescent Albatros planes during the entire period from June 1917 through April 1918; on the other, the introduction at the very end of the program of the superlative Fokker D7. Kogenluft had sought such a fighter in June 1917, but other craft had not met the requirement. The Fokker triplane, despite exceptional maneuverability which enabled it to serve well in the hands of superior pilots, lacked speed and climb and suffered from poor construction and difficult engine maintenance. Consequently, it was not mass-produced and did not see wide service. It was a deadly weapon in the hands of a Richthofen or Voss or Gontermann, provided it did not break up in mid-air.

A most noteworthy aspect of single-seat fighter development during the America Program was the increasing role of the pilots in the selection of the craft, culminating in the fighter competition in January. Manfred von Richthofen was instrumental in the evolution of the Fokker triplane and D7 and deserves credit for the accretion of the pilots' power in type selection, hitherto the purview of the Inspectorate of Flying Troops. The formalization of the pilots' power meant the erosion of the inspectorate's authority.

Although the evidence is inconclusive, there are grounds for the interpretation of fighter development during the America Program as the outcome of a struggle between two informal alliances—the inspectorate and Albatros on the one hand and Richthofen and Fokker on the other. The inspectorate may well have supported Albatros too strongly because of Fokker's previous shoddy construction and a reluctance to undertake a major change-over of type with the concomitant temporary disruption of mass production. Furthermore, the inspectorate's one initiative, the triplane circular, was abortive. Richthofen, who had long been desperate for a fighter to succeed the Albatros, believed that there was a conspiracy in the inspectorate, for whatever reason, to prolong the Albatros monopoly at the pilots' expense. The rumor campaign against Fokker, which threatened to ruin the Dutchman just when he was on the verge of creating his greatest craft, provoked Richthofen to retaliate quickly and effectively. He mobilized the other fighter pilots and challenged both Albatros and the inspectorate by approaching Kogenluft directly. Yet his plea was couched wisely in terms of an open competition, to which no one could reasonably object, although he was undoubtedly counting on Fokker to win the tests.

Yet any implication that favoritism was the determinant in Fokker's selection is erroneous. In 1958 Alfred Everbusch, one of the Everbusch brothers, owners of the Pfalz works, stated that "Richthofen and Krefft

Lt. Max Immelmann, the Eagle of Lille, with his Fokker monoplane. *Courtesy of United States Air Force Museum*

The Fokker DrI, the famed triplane. *Courtesy of Peter Grosz*

The Fokker E3, the best of the Fokker monoplane fighters of 1915–16. *Courtesy of United States Air Force Museum*

The Aviatik CI, a typical all-purpose craft of 1915. *Courtesy of Peter Grosz*

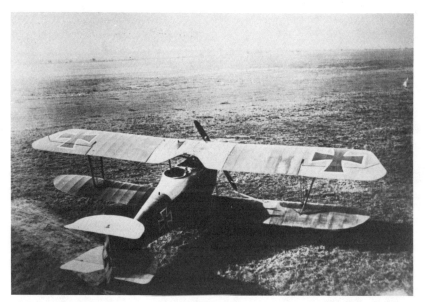

The Hannover CIII. The two-seat fighter from the rear, showing the observer-gunner's office. *Courtesy of Peter Grosz*

The Albatros C3, the most produced Albatros two-seater, saw service in 1916 and 1917. *Courtesy of United States Air Force Museum*

The Aviatik factory. Note the female workers. *Courtesy of Peter Grosz*

Seaplane repair workshop at an imperial dockyard. *Courtesy of Peter Grosz*

The Albatros DIII. Master of the air in the spring of 1917, it was the primary cause of Bloody April. *Courtesy of Peter Grosz*

The Halberstadt C12, a close-support and escort fighter, which began service in summer 1917. *Courtesy of United States Air Force Museum*

The Siemens-Schuckert RVIII, a giant plane that never flew. *Courtesy of Peter Grosz*

The Zeppelin-Lindau (Dornier) RsI, a gigantic three-engined seaplane that was wrecked in December 1915 before flight trials. *Courtesy of Peter Grosz*

The Pfalz D3, the Bavarian firm's contribution to the German fighter forces in later 1917 and early 1918. *Courtesy of United States Air Force Museum*

The Zeppelin-Lindau (Dornier) DI, Claudius Dornier's all-metal fighter, which competed unsuccessfully in fighter competitions in 1918. *Courtesy of Peter Grosz*

The AEG GIV, a day-and-night bomber of 1917–18. *Courtesy of Aviation and Space Division, National Museum of Science and Technology, Ottawa*

The AEG GIV, side view. *Courtesy of Aviation and Space Division, National Museum of Science and Technology, Ottawa*

were very strongly tied to Fokker, and personal sympathies and antipathies played a large role in aviation in the first world war."[45] Everbusch apparently forgot that Richthofen visited the Pfalz works for ten days in mid-December 1917 and was probably instrumental in obtaining more contracts for Pfalz's D3. The aces had been very close to Fokker in 1915, when he had produced the monoplane, but that did not save him from falling out of favor when the E-plane became obsolete. Richthofen had favored the Albatros when it had been the best fighter available; now he sought a new plane capable of equalizing the balance qualitatively over the western front, and he knew that Fokker had it. The open competition exposed Albatros as having done no further fighter development, as it could only produce modified D5as for the tests. The Fokker D7 won easily, and with its victory Richthofen had achieved a twofold conquest: he had obtained for his pilots the best plane and the right to select their own planes. The Type D competition was thus the culmination of a process that had begun with the great combat pilots' informal advice to the manufacturers in Berlin hotels, at their factories, or at the front.

Richthofen emerges here as more than Germany's greatest ace, a formidable combat leader. For him the responsibilities of command were not confined to frontline service, of doing the best with the materiel he was given, but encompassed doing all that was necessary to ensure that he and his men received the best materiel possible. His and Krefft's maneuvering in late 1917 also shows a touch of the politician. His character often appears to be unidimensional in most works—the ruthless leader of massed flights, a hero, admired by most, unappreciated by others who find him unchivalrous and cold, especially compared to his predecessor Bölcke. Yet 1917 and 1918 were not times for chivalry, and his heroism went deeper than previous authors have appreciated. They tend to ignore that he spent the bulk of his career fighting in outclassed planes, and they ignore his instrumental role behind the scenes in securing for German fighter pilots a plane that would enable them to hold their own on the western front for the rest of the war. The Red Baron cast a long shadow, and not merely because of his aerial exploits. To Richthofen's sponsorship of the Fokker D7, which appeared too late to save him, many a German combat pilot in 1918 owed his life.

The course of fighter development during the America Program illustrates that significant technological advances in aviation could not be created on command. The major types that came to fruition during the period from June 1917 to April 1918—the two-seat attack fighter and the long-range bomber—were the products of gestation that long antedated the America Program.

The C1 type—light, maneuverable, fast two-seat planes used in the attack and fighter roles—had been designed to meet an inspectorate specification of September 1916. The first type, the Halberstadt C12, entered service during the summer of 1917 and was supplemented during the fall by the Hannover C12. Later versions, the Halberstadt C14 and the Hannover C13 and C13a, appeared in time for the March offensive. These types formed the backbone of the protective or battle flights *(Schutzstaffeln* or *Schlachtstaffeln),* which were vital to the army's plans of close air support during the 1918 attacks. These planes served well and played an increasingly prominent role in the air and ground war from the fall of 1917 onward.[46]

The bombers—the Gotha G series and the Staaken R series—attained the culmination of their development and impact during the months of the America Program because of a concatenation of strategic and technological circumstances. Kogenluft revived the idea of attacking England in the fall of 1916—thus the Hindenburg Program's expansion of the bomber arm to 104 machines—as the Gotha G4, the first craft capable of the deed, entered production. Orders totaled 230—50 from Gotha, 100 from LVG, and 80 from SSW—with 30 to arrive by February 1917. The R-planes were expected to supplement the Gothas in the near future. The bomber campaign, named Turk's Cross, aimed, in grandiose fashion, to crush the morale and will to fight of the English by disrupting war industry, communications, and supply in southeastern England.

Material shortages, transportation crises, and unsatisfactory tests of the first production model delayed the arrival of the first Gotha G4 until March. The raids began on 25 May 1917. The next type, the G5, began to arrive in August, just as daylight raids over England became unfeasible, so from September through May 1918 the Gothas flew nineteen night missions over the island. A high-altitude version, the G8, was promised for the spring of 1918, but never materialized because the German aircraft industry lacked the resources to build the bomber in quantity.

The large Gothas (78-foot wing span, 39-foot length) and the huge R-planes (138-foot wing span, 73-foot length) represented a prodigious feat of technology and industry in those early years. The result of the efforts of the inspectorate and the Zeppelin Works at Staaken was the R6, the only giant bomber to enter serial production. Beginning in June 1917, eighteen were built: four by the parent firm, six by Aviatik, five by

Schütte-Lanz, and three by the east German Albatros Works. The R6s initially attacked in individual sorties in September and later in squadron strength of six or with the Gothas and flew eleven missions over England through May 1918. Altogether the Gothas of Bomber Squadron 3 dropped 84,745 kilograms of bombs in twenty-two raids with the loss of sixty Gothas; the R-planes, 27,190 kilograms with no losses due to enemy action. The raids failed to drive the English out of the war; they sufficed merely to goad the English into strengthening their home defense and creating a strategic bombing force of their own. The Germans, dismayed by the lack of results for their effort, especially in light of the drain from other production, ceased their raids after May 1918.[47]

At least the army's G and R-planes saw effective service. Despite the navy's urgent interest in multi-engine seaplanes, its efforts met with much less success. The relative absence of English patrol planes in the North Sea during the winter and spring had enabled the German armed seaplane force to concentrate on Flanders and unarmed reconnaissance craft to patrol the sea. Then, in the summer of 1917 the "Curtiss boats"—craft originally designed by the American Glenn Curtiss, improved by the English at their Felixstowe station (hence their English name "Felixstowe boats"), and powered by Rolls-Royce engines of 345–50 horsepower— appeared in force over the North Sea. The depredations of these large, armed craft prompted an increase in the importance of naval aviation and multi-engined craft. On 6 August 1917 the chief of naval flight units, Captain Kranzbühler, became the naval flight chief (Marineflugchef), subordinate to the Imperial Naval Office in technical and procurement matters and to the chief of the Admiralty Staff in operational matters. The command of the German High Seas Fleet established its own aviation commander that summer.

The administrative changes could not hasten the progress of multi-engine aircraft development. Gotha torpedo planes were underpowered and extremely vulnerable to shipboard fire during their launch runs, but were produced until the end of the war for want of better aircraft.[48] The G-planes proved inadequate for their duties: they needed more frequent overhauls after long flights than single-engine planes; they were unsuitable for long-range reconnaissance because they could not fly on one engine; and their poor steering when fully loaded made night and fog flying extremely perilous.[49] The R-plane remained primarily a subject of debate among the naval aviation agencies. In light of the extraordinary technical and production difficulties, the Naval Office doubted that the navy required an R-plane, since the best prospect, the Dornier Rs3, was still experimental. Naval flight chief Kranzbühler preferred a fighter seaplane to the R-plane, but the flight commander of the High Seas Fleet, Capt. Hagedorn, insisted on the R-plane, because the fleet required a long-range reconnaissance plane as a substitute for the Zeppelin before the English developed any of their own giant planes. R-planes were too important to let cost impede their development: large-scale production was impossible without substantial experience, yet they could amass sufficient experience only if they experimented with several craft. The Naval Office replied that technical difficulties, not cost, were its primary considerations. In an attempt to appease the High Seas Fleet, the navy did decide to order more R-planes to increase its experimental foundation, but it was too late to prevent further recriminations and internal dissension.[50]

In April the High Seas Fleet Command wanted to remove Kranzbühler from the position of naval flight chief, blaming him for the unavailability of R-planes. The state secretary of the Imperial Naval Office, Adm. Eduard von Capelle, explained that Kranzbühler was not at fault. Capelle reminded them that the army's control of engine production prevented the evolution of suitable large motors and that the fleet's earlier hostility to flying boats had impeded their further development and forced concentration on the twin-float airplane. They had tested Austrian boats and found them wanting; they had even considered copying the Curtiss, but the attendant difficulty was exacerbated by the dependence on the army for materials and skilled workers. If the fleet command insisted on removing Kranzbühler, it could approach the Admiralty Staff, but Capelle warned that such a step would unduly disturb further progress.[51]

Wisdom in this dispute resided with the Naval Office on all counts. First, an operational sea R-plane would take too much time to evolve. The Curtiss boats, an obvious standard of comparison, had been under development since 1908 and were equipped with engines some one hundred horsepower more powerful than those available to German designers. Second, Kranzbühler was not at fault, so there was no reason to make him the scapegoat. Third, the army's prior claim on the aircraft factories was not open to debate, and correctly so, as the focus of the air war lay with the army on the western front.

The test of the America Program was the success of the German air force in the spring offensives in the west. In March 1918 the air force had 153 flight units, 38 battle flights, 81 fighter units, and 7 bombing squadrons. Instead of forming 17 new flight units to increase their number from 183 to 200, the air force had reorganized the units. After the fall of 1916 some of them had first become protective flights and then battle flights, of which there were 38 in March 1918. Then 36 of the existing flight units were increased from six to nine craft each. The result entailed more of an increase in the number of C-planes than the 17 units originally planned. More significantly, the air force had 81 fighter units by mid-February; the 40 new ones, however, often were equipped only at half or three-quarter strength, with eight instead of sixteen planes.[52]

Production had not sufficed to supply all the planned units. In the first seven months of 1918, 1,009, 890, 1,360, 1,202, 930, 1,189, and 1,478 planes, respectively, were delivered to the air force.[53] Deliveries thus fluctuated wildly and were only beginning to approach 1,600, the minimal figure given by the War Ministry in July 1917, in July 1918. The official figures for motor production from January through July were 1,445, 1,145, 1,290, 1,530, 1,390, 1,430, and 1,420.[54] Average motor production of 1,379 and average aircraft production of 1,151 were in line with the 1,800 and 1,600 figures for motors and aircraft projected in the original minimum program, only much lower. In April, one of the best production months in the first half of 1918, motor production was 1,530 and aircraft production, 1,360. Thus at the deadline for the completion of the America Program, aircraft production in a good month still failed to reach the minimum goal by 140 planes.

The gravity of the situation just before the offensive was amply indicated by a proposal of 13 March from the inspectorate to pay Fokker, Rumpler, LFG, Albatros, Pfalz, and SSW a one-thousand-mark bonus for each plane accepted in March. The War Ministry accepted the proposal because of "the extraordinarily large need for fighter planes expected in the coming offensive."[55] A desperate measure was in order for the desperate offensive to end the war.

On 21 March frontline aircraft in the west totaled 3,668, a substantial increase over the 2,271 planes the German air force had had in early 1917. Against the Allies' 4,500 frontline planes, the German Army intended to use 2,000 and hold the rest in reserve. Forty-nine flight units, twenty-seven battle squadrons, thirty-five fighter units, and four bombing squadrons were concentrated to support the attacking armies. For the first two days of the battle, from 21 to 23 March, the air umbrella provided by the air force was quite impervious to enemy opposition; by the third day enemy opposition was more effective, and the battle flights began to suffer more casualties. Despite high attrition, the units were kept up to strength until 28 March, by which time the great assault had ground to a halt. The air service performed its tasks to the best of its ability; it would have done better had it had more operational units to deploy over the period of the battle, had its fighter force been equipped with better craft to prevent enemy encroachment into the airspace above the battle, and had it possessed more day bombers with which to disrupt enemy ground operations. Attrition of aircraft and crews was high. In the area of the Eighteenth Army alone, the losses of C and D craft in the two months from mid-March to mid-May were 324 and 135 respectively, of which 60 percent were not caused by enemy action. In January 1918 alone the air service lost 779 planes and 241 pilots and observers (179 dead) of approximately 4,500 aircrew at the front. These losses increased during the spring offensives, and Alex Imrie calculated that, based on 2,551 pilots at the front in May 1918, one-seventh of this pilot strength would have to be replaced every month.[56] The rear, however, was not equipped for these training duties. If the front was not receiving its allotments of fuel and aircraft, the rear was receiving even less.

The German home front, taxed to the utmost, was summoning its last reserves. Inadequacy—of labor, raw materials, transportation, manpower, and production—was the keynote of the America Program. Strive as the aircraft industry and the Inspectorate of Flying Troops might, they could not even attain the minimum goal of the program. In light of this harsh reality, the original aim of doubling aircraft and motor production to two thousand and twenty-five hundred appears even more utopian. Euler had been correct. Ruthless memoranda, proclamations, and organizational measures could not overcome irremediable shortages and exhaustion. And after the prodigious effort, the American threat of an aviation industry and aerial armada never materialized.

CHAPTER 6

To the Bitter End,
April–November 1918

THE CONDITION of the German air force and the aircraft industry in the spring of 1918 generally gave little cause for optimism. While the air force faced growing Allied numerical superiority at the front, at home the aircraft industry confronted increasingly severe shortages and a disgruntled labor force. Although there is an air of the anticlimactic to German efforts after May, the aircraft industry continued to evolve and mass-produce superior types, which the frontline pilots employed effectively during the closing months of the conflict.

Kogenluft and the Inspectorate of Flying Troops, discussing the future development of aviation on 8 April 1918, determined to emphasize the improvement of aircraft, especially fighter planes, rather than an increase in their number. This session, conducted in the immediate shadow of the failure of the America Program, thus arrived at a rather conservative goal: the mere maintenance of strength, rather than the doubling of monthly production prescribed in both the Hindenburg and America Programs. But this conference was only a preliminary to more extensive planning for the continuation of the war effort; formalization of the plans, as in the past, would take some two months, until early June. The air force General Staff did learn on 11 April that they could expect the continued support of General Ludendorff, who informed the War Ministry that its reductions of the arms industry were not to affect aircraft manufacture.[1]

The industry sorely needed such preferential treatment, because it was operating under difficult circumstances. Although the factories managed to secure sufficient varnish, steel tubing, and machines through the priority schedules, fabric supplies were rapidly approaching exhaustion. The factories were experimenting with substitute covering materials, but their best immediate prospect, silk, was not as strong as linen, did not take aircraft dope (paint) as well, and tended to crack under severe stress. At best it might be used for smaller machines like fighters. The general shortage of metals was extremely disruptive: the industry would have to reduce its demands for magnesium and aluminum, essential to aircraft production; and metal aircraft, such as the promising Dornier D1 fighter, could not be mass-produced. The persistence of the coal and transportation crises, which abated in May but then worsened in June, prompted the Bavarian representative at the inspectorate to advise caution in the formulation of future production programs. In his opinion the Hindenburg and America Programs' overestimation of German industrial capacity stemmed from the failure to allow for the inadequate supply of coal and other raw materials and the collapse of the transportation network. He sought to avoid the same mistake a third time.[2]

Bureaucratic procedures also hampered production. The inspectorate's specification of new contracts on short notice continued to disrupt the war trade association's dispensation of raw materials, but the struggle for technical superiority at the front made this problem unavoidable. On the other hand, the association's participation in decisions on wood allocation complicated wood procurement unnecessarily, so the War Ministry's raw materials department (Kriegsrohstoffabteilung, or KRA) instructed the inspectorate to relegate the association to the position of a dispensing agency.[3]

Perhaps the industry's most salient problem was labor unrest and shortages. In April rumors of the pending emergency induction of eligible reserves caused disturbances among the aircraft workers. Although the inspectorate intended to call up only "less important" workers and to replace any skilled workers with trained substitutes, by June the induction had irreparably worsened the shortage of skilled labor in firms subcontracting for the aircraft industry. The workers, who were demanding higher wages, more food, and reduced hours, often took time off on weekends without permission. In May a large number of exempted workers at Pfalz arbitrarily took sick leave, yet their skills were so sorely needed that they could not be fired. The firm could only report them to the BA and the deputy general command, which threatened the workers with induction if they did not return to work within the week. The punishment, of course, would harm production more than the crime did, as it entailed a permanent, not a temporary, loss of skills. The skilled workers thus derived substantial leverage from the shortage, for which there was no immediate remedy.[4]

The industry, air force, and aviation associations were attempting to train more skilled aircraft workers and engineers, but such efforts would bear fruit only in the future. Through articles in *Flug* the German Fliers League continued to instill in youth an awareness of the importance and tasks of the air force and, more practically, of the needs of the service and the industry for trained manpower. The industry, whose advertisements supported *Flug,* also contributed more directly to the training of prospective employees. In May 1918 the Hannoversche Waggonfabrik donated one hundred thousand marks to the technical institute in Hannover for the establishment of an aviation research institute, whose board of directors would comprise educators and industrialists. By the late fall of 1918 the military, industry, and technical institutes were sponsoring the creation of flight and aircraft mechanic training schools, the first of which was to be built on a field in Augsburg donated by the Rumpler works there. The school's board of trustees consisted of a representative of the inspectorate, two representatives from the factory, and the director of the technical institute in Augsburg. The labor shortage thus did appear susceptible to improvement, but the war would have to last far into 1919 before these remedies could take effect.[5]

In light of the labor problems and the worsening quality of materials, it is not surprising to find that complaints about "the careless work of the aircraft factories" were rife. The welding on Albatros fighters, unreliable gluing on LVG reconnaissance craft, and leaky gas and oil tanks on all makes prompted many a grumble at the front, while units equipped with the Friedrichshafen G3 twin-engined bomber filed numerous complaints of poor motor installation. Spare parts were often in such short supply that R-plane units were unable to undertake their missions in strength.[6]

The quality of the aircraft in service in the spring varied widely. Among the general purpose C-planes in service, the Rumpler C7, which was used for long-distance reconnaissance, was superlative. Its photo-reconnaissance version, the Rubilt, was capable of speeds of one hundred miles per hour above twenty thousand feet and therefore was virtually immune to interception by Allied fighters. The Albatros C12 gave efficient service, while the LVG C5 and DFW C5, though somewhat slow, possessed sufficiently good flight qualities for medium-range tasks. Both light C-types—the Halberstadt C12 and Hannover C12—were quality aircraft: the Halberstadt, light, strong, and maneuverable, was exceptional; the Hannoverana, though endowed with good climbing ability, was hampered by the unreliability of its 180-horsepower Argus engine. Of the three infantry, or J, planes, the all-metal Junkers was highly praised, as its crews had learned that the "furniture vans" afforded them absolute protection from ground fire. The AEG and Albatros J-types (infantry airplane, armed armored two-seat biplane) were both considered "useful," which can be interpreted to mean adequate, but no better. Of the fighters in service in April, the Fokker triplane maneuvered and climbed well, but lacked speed and view from the cockpit. The Albatros D5a, despite "good" flight characteristics, was inferior to enemy fighters; and the Pfalz D3a, though judged inferior to the Albatros by many frontline pilots, was still "useful."[7] These were the main craft upon which the German air force relied in the tactical air war of April 1918, and it is noteworthy that the priority fighter units, the most important element of the air force as the war became increasingly defensive, were equipped with no superior craft.

The introduction of the Fokker D7 in May provided the German air force with just such a superior craft. The D7's welded steel tubing fuselage and wooden wing with box spars proved ideal for mass construction. The inspectorate correctly assessed that Fokker's plant, which delivered 69 D7s in April, 118 in May, and 83 in June, could not produce the plane in sufficient quantities. The Dutchman's triumph was complete when the inspectorate, pursuing its policy of standardization, had the D7 constructed under license by Fokker's long-time rival, the Albatros Works, at a fee of 5 percent of the price of each airframe. With its larger facilities, Albatros would ultimately produce more D7s than the Fokker factory. Despite the effort at standardization, the D7s produced by each firm were different because the absence of workshop drawings for the original necessitated each factory's creation of its own jigs. When the D7 appeared at the front, it was not entirely problem-free. In early June inadequate dryness of wood caused some wing rib breakage in dives, and the summer heat occasionally resulted in exploding fuel tanks until better coolant was introduced. None of these difficulties, however, was sufficiently serious to force grounding of the plane, which had become quite indispensable after the grounding in May of 200 rotary-engine fighters, including the Fokker triplane, because of unreliable engine performance attributed to inferior engine oils. The D7 remained the mainstay of the German fighter forces until the end of the war. It was never bested by its Allied opponents, because the BMW engine vastly improved its performance, virtually halving the time to climb to 5,000 meters (16,400 feet) from 31.5 minutes with the Mercedes to 16 minutes. According to the official British history of the air war, the BMW gave the Fokker D7 a better rate of climb than any contemporary Allied plane in service and exemplified the maxim that "technical superiority, not necessarily of great degree, is a dominant factor in air warfare."[8]

As of the early summer then, German aviation technology proved capable of matching that of the Entente, but material and manpower shortages and labor unrest made prospects of dramatic increases in production uncertain. Under these dubious circumstances Kogenluft issued a new expansion program, and the inspectorate staged a second fighter competition in June.

On 6 June 1918 Kogenluft submitted a continuation of the America Program for the period from 1 July 1918 to 1 April 1919, which Ludendorff authorized on 11 June.[9] Although a dire shortage of fighter pilots and commanders prevented an increase in the number of fighter units, it was planned to increase the complement of planes in the battle squadrons and flight units from six to nine craft, and to add two more bombing squadrons and as many R-plane units as production capacity would allow. In addition to prescribing forty thousand more personnel for the air force, the plan required nine thousand skilled workers for the industry in order to raise monthly production to 2,300 airplanes and 2,875 motors. Perhaps more significantly, Kogenluft proposed to reorganize the Prussian Inspectorate of Flying Troops into an inspectorate of flying troops under Lieutenant Colonel Siegert for the training and replacement of personnel; an inspectorate of aircraft under Major Wagenführ, the previous head of the aircraft depot, for aircraft and equipment; and an inspectorate for aerial photography.

The reason for this strengthening of the air force and the industry was summarized by the naval liaison officer at Kogenluft in the following manner:

> Although only small numbers of American fliers have been active on the western front, mostly as fighter pilots, and the long-announced new planes have not materialized at all, still America's constantly increasing support in personnel and raw material deliveries, and recently through the copying of English and French types, will doubtlessly bolster the numerical superiority of the Entente.[10]

One can only marvel at Kogenluft's persistence. Having failed to attain the goals of either the Hindenburg or America programs, confronted with severe and increasing shortages and labor unrest, it was seeking to double production while fragmenting the agency that had been responsible for the execution of the previous programs. April's circumspection had yielded to June's optimism, perhaps because production invariably improved during the warm months. Yet it remains a mystery where the air force hoped to obtain forty thousand men and nine thousand skilled workers, when German manpower reserves were approaching exhaustion and the army was inducting all eligible men, including exempted skilled labor. In light of past failures and future prospects, the program can only be deemed unrealistic in the extreme. Kogenluft had apparently failed to learn from its experience, despite the admonition of the Bavarian representative at the inspectorate. Ludendorff, in his authorization of the plan, showed that he persisted in his determination to undertake programs that exceeded the homeland's capabilities.

If the magnitude of the planned expansion seems remarkable, the drastic modification of the homeland bureaucracy at such a critical time apears even more so. Kogenluft explained that the change would simplify communications and enable it to intervene more directly in the various affairs of the homeland bureaucracy.[11] The revamping would also relieve Siegert of some of his immense burden as head of an agency that had mushroomed from a few hundred men in 1915 to some fifty thousand in 1918. Yet bureaucratic language often conceals true intent, and there may have been more to this change than is initially apparent.

According to Maj. (ret.) Hans Arndt, writing in 1926, the Inspectorate of Flying Troops considered the fragmentation unnecessary and advised against it.[12] Of course, one could easily interpret this as a natural reluctance on Siegert's part to relinquish authority. A number of postwar sources lend credence to the necessity of Siegert's relief in asserting that the enormity of Siegert's task exhausted him,[13] and there is some small evidence to indicate that Siegert acknowledged by the summer that the war was lost and that it was necessary to prepare for peace. In private correspondence with Hugo Junkers in June, he observed matter-of-factly that the aircraft industry was preparing for peace.[14] Such an attitude was certainly alien to the old fighter, who had always been prone to vitriolic reproachfulness vis-à-vis the industry.

Had Siegert suggested that the new program, like those programs of the past, was impossible to achieve? Was the Bavarian representative at the inspectorate, in advising his superiors to be conservative in the formulation of new production goals, voicing not only his opinion but also that of the inspector? The new program was anything but circumspect, and a critical attitude on the part of the inspector would certainly have impeded his attempts to galvanize the industry to another gigantic effort.

The Organization of the Inspectorate before July 1918

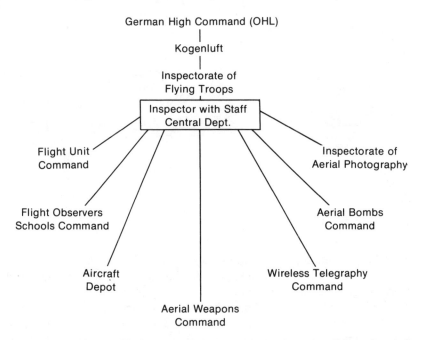

German High Command (OHL)

Kogenluft

Inspectorate of
Flying Troops

Inspector with Staff
Central Dept.

Flight Unit
Command

Inspectorate of
Aerial Photography

Flight Observers
Schools Command

Aerial Bombs
Command

Aircraft
Depot

Wireless Telegraphy
Command

Aerial Weapons
Command

SOURCE: W. Dieckman, *Die Behördenorganisation in der deutschen Kriegswirtschaft, 1914–1918,* p. 96

Kogenluft would undoubtedly have attributed criticism to exhaustion. Having failed to acknowledge that its past programs had been utopian, it undoubtedly blamed previous failures on the hinterland bureaucracy and the industry. The failure thus became one of will, and Siegert, as inspector, bore the responsibility in the eyes of the air force General Staff. Experts like Siegert, however, were too indispensable to be removed; consequently, the remedy was to brace his efforts through the direct intervention of Kogenluft. While the division of the inspectorate might cause more friction and duplication, as Arndt concluded after the war, Kogenluft was willing to risk all in its effort to spur the homeland to another enormous effort.

Kogenluft's reorganization of the inspectorate may have been prompted by the struggle over fighter development at the turn of the year. The tacit alliance between Richthofen, Krefft, and Fokker against Albatros and inspectorate officials like Captain Schwarzenberger had un-

The Reorganization of the Inspectorate, July 1918

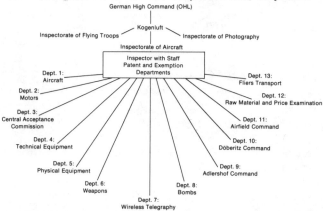

SOURCE: Kogenluft no. 3848 pers. F1 II, August 1918, stock no. 6470, AM, MA.

doubtedly included Richthofen's personal friend Lieutenant von Falken-hayn, who served in the technical department of the air force General Staff. Kogenluft had supported the fighter pilots' request for an open competition, which divested the inspectorate of some authority in aircraft selection. The fragmentation of the inspectorate may thus be interpreted as an attempt to decrease even more the inspectorate's power in favor of the frontline air force in the all-important area of fighter development.

A second single-seat fighter competition was held in June and July, the results of which have occasioned much debate among aviation historians. Prior interpretations have ignored the best summary of the selection process at the conclusion of the trials, which is found in the records of the naval liaison officer at Kogenluft.[15] Naval landplane aces also participated in the trials, as naval landplane units in Flanders had a fighter force of seventy to eighty-five airplanes during the summer months. At two conferences on 6 and 14 July, fighter pilots evaluated the planes according to the engines that powered them: the 160-horsepower Mercedes, the 185-horsepower BMW, the Oberursel (Rhone) rotary, the Siemens-Halske rotary, and the Benz 3b geared and ungeared engines. The first three categories were the most important, particularly the second, because the 185-horsepower high-compression BMW engine would prove to be superb.

The fighter aces recommended the following allocation: the Mercedes engine would go to the Fokker D7 and Pfalz D3a, although the naval aces still preferred the Albatros; the BMW to the Fokker D7 and Pfalz D12; the rotary Oberursel to the Fokker E5; the Siemens-Halske rotary to the SSW D4, although some considered the Pfalz D7/8 series quite good; and the geared Benz to the Fokker E5 and possibly the Aviatik D6. The ungeared Benz was not mentioned, probably because the poor performance of its craft prompted elimination of this category. The pilots, led by army aces Bruno Lörzer and Hermann Göring, the new commander of the Richthofen squadron, reached consensus on most selections. Both Lörzer and Göring were particularly impressed with the Fokker E5 parasol monoplane. Göring, cynical and cocky, dismissed the warning of inspectorate Captain Schwarzenberger that the wings might not retain their strength after three months' continual use with the jaunty reply that the front pilots could certainly win aerial superiority within that time. Ironically, everyone believed that the Zeppelin metal biplane, the Dornier D1, which had shed its top wing in flight on 3 July, killing Lt. Wilhelm Reinhard, then commander of the Richthofen squadron, was superior to most of the other craft, so Schwarzenberger agreed to promote construction of the Dornier fighter despite the accident. All the pilots also rejected the DFW, Schütte-Lanz, and Rumpler entries, especially the last, which Göring labeled a "criminal machine" worthy of distribution only to those pilots who insisted upon having it.

The naval liaison officer's report shows the subjectivity involved in the pilots' selection of fighters, as they often disagreed in their judgments of the same craft. Yet they were not being called upon to select a single new fighter; rather, they pointed out a number of possible types for production and development. Categorization of craft by engine was eminently logical, as engine production and shortages were the determining features of aircraft production, regardless of how good a particular type was. The inspectorate retained ultimate choice of what was to be produced, as only it could select among the types and engines. Furthermore, the inspectorate apparently did not confide entirely in the pilots, as Schwarzenberger promised to continue development of the Dornier metal fighter, although internal reports in April and May indicated that metal shortages would prevent production of that very fighter. In general, however, the procedures of the fighter competition in June and July judiciously juxtaposed the combat experience of the fighter pilots and the inspectorate's awareness of the production situation, while tempering the individual prejudices of the aces.

Despite a lack of concrete evidence, previous authors have attributed the selections of certain pilots to bribery. Bribery and graft never seem to be very far removed from aircraft procurement. Just before the war Albatros had been accused of bribing pilots with medals and small gifts, which, though mere pittances, were sufficient to cause an uproar from the competition. In 1915, the manufacturers' entertainment of the fighter pilots in Berlin became a common practice. By 1918 the favors occurred not only in Berlin but also at the front, as Anthony Fokker related that *Liebesgaben,* or "love gifts," were sent to the front with every consignment of aircraft. These gifts, which usually consisted of culinary delicacies, were, in Fokker's words, "an indirect form of graft." Fokker was also noted for his lavish gifts of silk to generals' wives for their dresses.[16] Yet how such expenditures affected aircraft procurement is impossible to determine, as difficult to ascertain as individual cases of bribery.

A. R. Weyl, for example, asserted that Ernst Udet, Germany's second leading ace, backed the Pfalz D12 in the June competition, resulting in rumors that Udet was "in league with" Pfalz because of the general dislike of the plane voiced by other pilots.[17] While the naval report did not mention Udet, it did show that all the pilots considered the Fokker D7 and Pfalz D12 equal, and the Pfalz gave a good account of itself when it arrived at the front in September 1918. In Weyl's account, the contrast between the attitude of Udet and the other pilots was the assumption necessary to lend credence to the rumor of Udet's attachment to Pfalz. In fact, there was no contrast, so if Udet was being bribed, his appreciation of the Pfalz did not set him apart from other pilots.

In an article on SSW airplanes, aviation historians Peter Grosz and Egon Krüger raise the possibility of bribery as a factor in the selection of th Fokker E5 *over* the SSW D4.[18] After relating that the D4 was a superlative craft, capable of outperforming the Mercedes-engined Fokker D7 on almost all counts, they attribute the SSW D4's failure to be a larger factor in the air war to the following reasons: delays in the production of serviceable Siemens-Halske Sh3 engines; the D4's more complicated and lengthier plywood construction process; and the bribes of rival manufacturers to aces, "perhaps the most significant factor" although "incapable of complete substantiation." This last reason, however, seems as superfluous as it is unsubstantiated.

Other authors have not resorted to bribery as an explanation. A. R. Weyl explained that although the SSW D4 vanquished the Fokker at the trials, the Fokker was produced because it was quite good, lighter, and smaller, used a less powerful engine, and was excellently suited to mass production—eighteen hundred workers could manufacture eight E5s daily at a rate of 2,250 man-hours per plane.[19] In a basic compendium of German aircraft of World War I, Peter Gray and Owen Thetford describe the SSW series as "without doubt . . . the best German fighters to reach operational status, yet . . . probably the least known." In their opinion engine availability determined the extent of D4 production, but they do note an initial antipathy toward the type's predecessor, the D3, on the part of the Richthofen squadron, particularly Hermann Göring. Gray and Thetford declared that only the efforts of another ace, Capt. Rudolph Berthold, who had obtained some victories on the D3, prevented the efforts of the D3's opponents to discredit the plane. Yet the authors show that opposition to the D3 in April and May was not capricious but quite justified, in light of piston seizures in the Sh rotary engine caused by low-grade castor oil. The engines had been improved and production of the D4 had begun by June, in time for the competition.[20]

Gray and Thetford do not discuss the June trials in any detail, stating only that the Fokker E5 was selected for its agility—take-off, climbing, and diving abilities. They do provide performance data on both planes, and based on their figures, one can conclude the following: the SSW climbed faster than the Fokker (four thousand meters in 9.1 minutes to the Fokker's 10.75 minutes), had a much higher service ceiling (eight thousand meters to six thousand meters), and had a longer flight time (2 hours to 1.5 hours), although the Fokker was some nine to ten miles per hour faster at ground level.[21] The SSW was certainly the better high-altitude fighter, but at altitudes around five thousand meters, where much air combat occurred, the Fokker was at least as good. The Fokker was thus cheaper, faster, and easier to manufacture and operate, and its engine was more reliable then the Siemens-Halske. If the Fokker's wings might not hold their shape long, a Saxon fighter unit observed in September that the SSW's best performance was short-lived and that its high landing speed limited its use to advanced pilots.[22]

The conclusion is inescapable: in light of Germany's stategic shortages of skilled fighter pilots, materials, and time, the Fokker E5 would have been the logical winner of the trial, *even if* it had been competing directly against the SSW D4. Yet the essential point here is that the two were not competing against one another. The SSW D4 was the unanimous selection for the Siemens-Halske Sh3 engine category; the E5, the unanimous selection for the Oberursel engine class. Both were deemed superior to the Fokker D7; beyond such generalizations, comparisons, though interesting, are misleading. There was no outright, definitive winner of the June–July fighter trials. The Fokker was to be the future mainstay of the German fighter forces; the SSW D4, provided the engine could be produced in quantity, would make an excellent top cover interceptor in addition to, not instead of, it.

Bribery could thus have had no effect on the choice of the Fokker as opposed to the SSW, as the choice never arose. This is not to deny the possibility of bribery; it is to say that its occurrence and effect on aircraft selection were impossible to determine. The outcomes attributed to graft in the cases of the Pfalz and Fokker can all be explained without resort to it.

In any case, Fokker had demonstrated his superiority again; the E5 was to succeed the D7. The E5 was rushed into production in July, and the first few arrived at the front in August for evaluation. By 5 August they equipped one fighter unit, but were then hastily withdrawn from operations on 21 August. Poor quality castor oil had resulted in engine seizures, and, more critically, wing failure had caused three crashes. Two explanations for these failures have been advanced, one from A. R. Weyl blaming the Fokker factory, the other from Fokker blaming the inspectorate.

In Fokker's effort at fast and cheap production, Weyl ventured, the box spars of the wings on production models were smaller than those of the prototype. Gray and Thetford suggest that the top and bottom surfaces of the spars were planed down after assembly, thus weakening the wing structure. An inspectorate commission discovered the smaller spar and ordered the wings strengthened on 30 August. Wagenführ, acting on the recommendation of Capt. Wilhelm Hoff of the inspectorate's scientific section, threatened Fokker with criminal proceedings on 3 September.[23]

Anthony Fokker's account differs substantially.[24] The inspectorate's regulations were designed for the standard externally braced wings and called for a strength of the rear spar proportionate to that of the front. Unlike most World War I aircraft, the E5's cantilever wooden wing required neither external bracing nor spars of proportional strength. Although the plane's wings had passed the sandbag strength tests, the inspectorate required Fokker to strengthen the rear spar. The result was an excessively rigid spar that did not flex, as it should have, but fractured under stress. After the planes were withdrawn from service and the wings tested again, they continued to meet the safety break tests, thereby baffling the "pure scientists" at the inspectorate. An annoyed Fokker complained that practical experience, not static deadweight tests, could discern the subtler stresses on a plane in flight. When Fokker subjected the wing to weight tests at Schwerin, he noted that the angle of incidence at the wing tips increased perceptibly under heavy loads, thus the load resulting from air pressure in a steep dive increased faster at the wing tips than in the middle of the wing. The resultant torsion, he surmised, would cause the collapse of the wing in combat maneuvers. The unwarranted strengthening of the rear spar, Fokker concluded, had resulted in an uneven deflection along the wing under stress. When Fokker brought this to the attention of the inspectorate, it initially consented only to allow the strengthening of the front spar to restore the original strength ratio between front and rear. Finally, it yielded completely and agreed to the original specifications.

Both of these accounts are plausible and consistent with the attitudes of Weyl and Fokker. Weyl regarded Fokker essentially as a profiteer and his factory as a travesty guilty of shoddy workmanship, while Fokker viewed himself as being in advance of the scientists, who did nothing but restrict the implementation of his practical designs. There is truth in both interpretations. The Dutchman did have a quick eye to profits and had established an industrial empire in aircraft and aircraft armaments manufacture that reached into Austria-Hungary, and the workmanship of his factory had often been of questionable quality. On the other hand, Fokker had often proved himself in advance of the authorities, first with his welded steel tubing construction techniques and later with his cantilever wings. The science of aeronautics was still in its infancy, so the essence of aircraft development remained experimentation, trial and error, at which Fokker and his staff excelled.

Although the documents do not enable a definitive resolution of the differences, Fokker's version would seem more nearly correct than Weyl's. If, as Gray and Thetford relate, it was simply a matter of excessive planing to clean up the spar assembly, then financial savings were not involved, as sawdust was not valuable. And since the flaw was easily rectified, the craft should have been back in production within a matter of days. Yet according to the most reliable accounts, the Fokker E5, redesignated D8, did not reappear at the front until the end of the conflict and in numbers too small to be effective. The extent of this delay would lend credence to Fokker's explanation.[25]

Perhaps the ultimate irony is that the poor quality of oil necessitated phasing out rotary-engined fighters, so that both the Fokker D8 and the SSW D4 were doomed to extinction by the end of 1918. If the rotary engine seemed the perfect power plant for a small, light, highly maneuverable fighter, all its advantages were negated by its unreliability if inadequately lubricated. Straitened circumstances, which had necessitated the use of all available material and prompted use of the rotary engine, now made its use impossible.

The demise of the rotary-engined fighter was confirmed by the last fighter trials held on 15–31 October 1918.[26] Because of the severe material shortages, the German air force intended to produce only one fighter type, equipped with the BMW 3a engine. The entry list of fifteen prototypes from eight firms was much reduced from the twenty-seven planes from nine firms in January and the forty-nine from fourteen factories in June. Of course, the large number in June had been excessive and wasteful. Firms which had never before built fighters entered the lists, although the domination of fighter development by Fokker, Pfalz, and Albatros amply indicated that tradition and experience were essential to the evolution of superior craft. The armistice intervened before a final selection was made, but the Fokker V29, a parasol version of the D7, was the front-runner. It was also planned to have the Rumpler D1, whose forerunner had performed so poorly in the June competition, produced with the Fokker for service in 1919, as it was the only plane to attain a height of 8,000 meters (26,300 feet). Although the selection of the Rumpler seems to contradict the premise of the necessity of experience, Rumpler's reconnaissance craft had long been noted for their performance at high altitude, and he had wisely concentrated on refining his earlier design.

The evolution of fighter design shows that despite material shortages and engine restriction, German aircraft technology progressed to the bitter end. Conditions were best suited to and placed a premium on an entrepreneur like Anthony Fokker, with his practical bents and willingness to have Reinhold Platz design craft that could easily be mass-produced within the limits of available materials. During the final months of the war, the Fokker factory demonstrated a remarkable ability to create planes that could be flown by average pilots yet were superior to their opponents. Designers who operated more scientifically, like Junkers and Dornier, proceeded with all-metal construction, even if raw material shortages prevented the mass production of their aircraft, and their efforts placed Germany far ahead of the Allies in metal aircraft construction at the end of the war.

Naval aviation technology also continued its strides. Dornier's Rs3 survived further trials, and he launched an R4 in October 1918, but the R-seaplane never saw active service. The disgruntled High Seas Fleet Command continued its agitation against flight chief Kranzbühler to the end of the war, and only the Imperial Naval Office thwarted its attempt to remove the chief from office.[27]

In the more critical area of single-engine floatplane fighters, Ernst Heinkel's efforts continued to be crowned with success. Friedrich Christiansen's exploits in the W12 earned him the Pour le Mérite on his thirty-eighth birthday in December 1917. He and Heinkel became friends, and the two proceeded to meet, in Zeebrugge, Warnemünde, or at the factory, to discuss the pilots' wishes.[28]

Heinkel's next craft, the W19, a longer-range and larger W12 with a 260-horsepower Maybach engine, appeared in January 1918. Forty of the fifty-three W19s delivered to the navy did not arrive until May and June of 1918 because the test plane broke a float in February and the test command feared that landings even on calm water might be hazardous. Yet such was the urgency that the High Seas Fleet Flight Command insisted on their delivery, presuming that strengthening the floats would prevent "further unfortunate accidents." In June the Borkum seaplane station vindicated this decision, reporting that not only was the big Brandenburg able to handle the English flying boats but also that it was faster and more seaworthy than previously believed, although landings at sea required good pilots. Although Brandenburg's installation hindered access to the temperamental Maybach engines, the W19 was clearly a success. During 1918 these fighters from Zeebrugge and Borkum, often accompanied by W12s, regularly engaged large British F2a flying boats from Felixstowe and Yarmouth.[29]

Yet perhaps the best of Heinkel's creations was the W29. Early in 1918 Christiansen met with him in Hamburg and advised that the maintenance of aerial superiority necessitated a successor to the W12. The Benz 150-horsepower engine was the only one available, and time was at a premium, so Heinkel created a monoplane version of the W12 by dropping the top wing and increasing the chord and span of the bottom one. The reduction in frontal area and drag gave an increase in speed of 10 miles per hour to 110 miles per hour and climb (two thousand meters in 13 minutes as opposed to 18.9 minutes for the W12). Christiansen was so pleased with the craft that he insisted on flying one of the first production series directly from Warnemünde to Zeebrugge for immediate operational use. The seventy-eight W29s produced enabled the Germans to preserve a competitive edge over the English. Later in 1918 Heinkel repeated his earlier enlargement of the W12 by designing the monoplane W33, a larger version of the W29 with a 245-horsepower Maybach engine, of which twenty-six were built.[30] All of the W series floatplanes were clean and functional designs, superior in performance. Heinkel's close relationship with Christiansen, reminiscent of Fokker's with Richthofen, was instrumental in his ability to fulfill the wishes of the naval pilots. His evolution of the W series exemplified two other circumstances: first, each naval aircraft design was closely based upon and evolved from a predecessor; and second, German designers had to compensate for the inability of the motor industry to produce high-powered engines with technical ingenuity.

The navy, though endowed with excellent single-engine planes, could never secure enough for its tasks of guarding minesweeping flotillas, guiding submarines through cleared minefields, and impeding English minelaying expeditions. In the southern part of the North Sea, where air warfare was continuous during 1918, inadequate production limited the increase in aircraft strength of Seaplane Unit I in Flanders (Christiansen's unit at Zeebrugge) from twenty-nine in 1917 to thirty in 1918. During the summer of 1918, factory deliveries of all seaplanes were two months in arrears, while inadequate repair facilities at the imperial dockyards, which also served as aviation supply depots, parts manufacturers, and training schools for naval engineers, resulted in the overuse and ultimately the loss of service aircraft. Even the later inclusion of private companies in repair contracts did not suffice to keep abreast of the work.[31]

As the navy's experience with small airplanes indicated, production, not technology, was the Achilles' heel of the German aviation effort. By September the industry was having difficulty securing precision machines for mass production from Wumba, its supplies of cable were inadequate, and canvas substitutes could not offset the textile shortage. The inspectorate of aircraft, in a desperate effort to obtain more ash and pine, attempted to procure wood independently. Metal supplies, which were seriously imbalanced with large amounts of lead and tin and small quantities of nickel, would suffice for only one more year, provided labor unrest and the coal supply did not worsen. At least quantities of metal tubing and synthetic rubber still sufficed to meet the needs of the aircraft industry.[32]

The labor situation in the factories was rapidly becoming more unstable. While factory managers sought to guard their precious skilled workers from the draft, management-labor disputes intensified. The workers sought shorter hours, especially on Sunday, but employers, fearing further disruption of production, refused their requests. The workers countered that they would produce better in their remaining hours at work, but to no avail; the two sides remained irreconcilable. Workers, irritated by food shortages, especially the inadequate deliveries of potatoes to the cities, made food forays into the countryside under the guise of "sick leave." In the opinion of the Bavarian liaison officer, only the leniency of the employers and the understanding of older workers enabled the avoidance of serious strikes, which would be inevitable in the coming winter without sufficient food.[33]

Notwithstanding such problems and a certain apprehension about a coming peace, some aircraft factories remained optimistic through September. In August 1918 the Rumpler Works, with 3.5 million marks share capital, announced a profit of 1.02 million marks in its first year as a joint-stock company (AG, or *Aktiengesellschaft*) and paid dividends of 12 percent. The firm was anticipating a second profitable year, although it realized that it would be overextended when peace came. In October the Bavarian Rumpler Works raised its capital from 1.0 to 1.5 million marks in order to complete its plant, but it postponed a major expansion because the new plant, which was so expensive at wartime prices, would go unused after the conflict.[34]

The disruptions also did not prevent the aircraft industry from increasing production through October 1918. The following table shows the production of Bavaria's two major aircraft factories in April and October 1918.

Bavarian Aircraft Production, April–October 1918[35]

Firm		4/18	10/18
BFW	Workers	2,246	3,000
	Production	76 (+28 repaired planes)	103
Pfalz	Workers	2,000	2,600
	Production	111	157

The table shows that not only were the firms able to increase their production but also that they obtained some thirteen hundred workers between April and October. Although it is impossible to determine how many of these were skilled workers, these figures indicate that neither the heights of production nor the depths of the manpower barrel had been reached. Figures are inadequate to determine whether the industry received nine thousand workers, and it is more likely that it did not. Nevertheless, the employment of women and youth had undoubtedly enabled the industry to make a serious attempt to reach the production quotas assigned in the America Program. Exactly this seems to have

occurred, as the production of the entire German aircraft industry increased dramatically during the warm months of 1918. The industry
produced 1,500 planes in July and 2,195 in October, while the German
motor industry delivered 1,420 and 1,915 motors in those months. Motor
production, if it lagged some 800 units behind the motor production
program in July, was nonetheless increasing.[36] Aircraft production in
October 1918 fell only some 100 units short of its projected goal for April
1919. Kogenluft's alteration of the inspectorate's bureaucracy had apparently not disrupted production, although it is impossible to ascertain
what influence it did have. The army may have pushed production beyond
judicious limits. After all, the industry had been on the verge of producing
1,000 planes in the early winter of 1916, and then its production was
halved by January 1917. To sustain such a pace of production during the
winter of 1918–19 would have been impossible, and the efforts of the fall
of 1918 would have been offset by a near total collapse of aircraft and
motor production during the winter, when coal, material, and food shortages would have crushed productivity.

The increasing supply of planes and motors and their steadily improving performance enabled the continued operation of the German air
force against vastly superior numbers. The German Army had been on
the defensive without respite since 8 August, the black day when the
British attack in the vicinity of Amiens put the Germans to flight. On a
twenty-five mile front the British and French had amassed their 1,904
aircraft, of which 988 were fighters, against 365 German planes, of which
only 140 were fighter planes. The available German fighter units, among
them the Richthofen squadron, fought without calculation and, though
they gave a good account of themselves, suffered terrible losses. The
British official history states that "the German air service was so roughly
handled that it was never able fully to recover," but it also acknowledged
that British aircraft production and engine deliveries in August 1918 did
not keep pace with the casualties on the western front.[37]

Aviation historian Alex Imrie takes issue with the interpretation that
the German air force never recovered, contending that the British official
history generalized in unwarranted fashion from the case of the Richthofen fighter wing, which was withdrawn after the debacle.[38] Imrie notes
that the formation was already far under strength on 8 August, with only
twenty-one serviceable machines as opposed to its usual complement of
fifty-two planes. If this large formation played little role during the rest of
the war, Imrie asserts that the effectiveness of the smaller fighter units,
the *Jagdstaffeln* of fourteen aircraft, increased in the last three months of

the war. *Jasta* Bölcke, for example, registered forty-six confirmed victories in September for the loss of only two of their own pilots, their highest total since their formation in August 1916; *Jasta* 50 recorded more than 50 percent of their victories at this time. Furthermore, *Jagdgeschwader* 2, another large unit, downed eighty-one enemy planes in seven days after 12 September for the loss of only two of their machines. The German fighter forces thus continued to exact a higher toll of Allied aircraft than they lost, and bombing and reconnaissance machines performed their missions, despite stringent fuel rationing and irreplaceable losses of men and materiel, right up to the end of the war.

Yet if the air service fought on, its spirit unbroken, the evidence that the war was drawing inexorably to a dismal end could not be ignored. Driven back from airdrome to airdrome, night bombers were pressed into service as tactical reconnaissance and ground-strafing machines, though the planes and crews were ill suited for ground cooperation flights. Fuel, as one bomber pilot related, often contained so much water that the engines coughed.[39] All the effort of the air force was futile, for the outcome of the conflict was a foregone conclusion.

Ludendorff, literally and figuratively at his wit's end, left his post of chief quartermaster general on 26 October. The front, though restored after the debacle of 8 August, was steadily being pushed toward Germany, while the home situation behind the army rapidly deteriorated. Collapse and revolution signaled the end for Germany, and the air force and aircraft industry plunged into the abyss. As the revolution gathered momentum, the War Ministry on 4 November decided to restrict the use of aircraft against the revolutionary forces to reconnaissance missions.[40] While the reason for this decision is unknown, it represents an appreciation either of the might of the airplane as a weapon, which was consequently not to be employed against other Germans, or of the unreliability of the rear echelons of the air service. The latter reason is more likely, for if the combat fliers were steadfast, the same could not be said either of the fliers replacement units or the industrial workers in Germany.

On the morning of 6 November several companies of armed men from Infantry-Replacement-Battalion 89 in Schwerin marched to the Fokker factory and ordered the workers to strike. Together they formed a workers' and soldiers' council that formulated a series of political demands for the Schwerin region, including recognition of the council by the old civil and military authorities, the removal of high administrators, the subordination of the officer corps to the council, the release of political prisoners, and the council's assumption of police powers.[41] Similar events occurred all over Germany. The troops of various fliers replacement units, such as those in Brunswick, Böblingen, and Gotha, initiated the formation of workers' and soldiers' councils in early November, while in Stuttgart / Unterturkheim the workers and soldiers stationed at the Daimler works formed a revolutionary council.[42] On 9 November a general strike affected practically all the factories in Berlin, and on 11 November World War I came to an end.

The German air force and naval air arm, though outnumbered, had continued to exact a toll of Allied aircraft to the conclusion of the war, because the aircraft industry continued to evolve superior single-engine aircraft. Four factors enabled the expansion of production until the end of the war: the increasing concentration on small airplanes; the more widespread use of new and speedy construction techniques such as Fokker's welded steel tubing fuselage; the rationalization of the industry and the introduction of more machinery, which probably offset the influx of unskilled workers; and finally centralized controls on the industry, which enabled the transfer of materials from firms that failed to meet their quotas to those that could increase their production. The industry could have continued to increase its production, given sufficient food for the workers, material for the factories, and transportation to move the materials to the plants and the finished planes from the plants to the front. Yet these favorable conditions were determined in large part by the seasons, the summer and fall months being the period of heightened productivity, the winter and early spring the doldrums. The German air arm would consequently have ceased to be effective in the winter and spring of 1919.

In November 1918 the aircraft industry comprised some thirty-six factories and departments with a labor force of forty to fifty thousand workers, with subcontracting companies employing some one-hundred thousand additional workers.[43] On 11 November 1918 the German army air force comprised 284 units of more than 2,700 combat aircraft—some 1,200 D types (single-seat fighters), 228 C1 (two-seat fighters), 1,017 C types (two-seat reconnaissance and all-purpose craft), 162 G (twin-engine bombers), and 6 R (giant) planes. While these totals differed from those in August 1918 (1,050 D, 1,016 C, 228 C1, 162 G, and 8 R-planes) primarily in a slight shift to D types, they showed a drastic decline from the 3,668 frontline aircraft listed on the western front in March of 1918.[44] Losses in the March and May offensives had apparently been too severe for the industry to recoup, although it was able to stabilize the situation once the army went on the defensive in August. Nevertheless, the air force at the end of the war had ten times more combat-ready aircraft, of far more sophistication and capability, than it had possessed in August 1914. German naval aviation had grown from nearly nothing to a force of 864 landplanes and seaplanes, the latter located at thirty-two seaplane stations in the North, Baltic, Black, and Mediterranean seas.[45] Now the air arm and the aircraft industry, grown large in war, faced a disastrous peace.

CHAPTER 7

Postwar Disaster, 1918–21

Wartime Calculations

ON 5 OCTOBER 1918, Wilhelm Siegert made a portentous entry in his diary: a satirical postwar scenario. He predicted that aviation would emerge as the most important branch of the armed services: The cavalry had been associated with the conservative Junkers; the navy, with "democracy"; so the air force, the most "revolutionary" weapon, would be associated with socialism. A parliamentary majority would be prepared to grant funds to the "independent socialist" arm, but, Siegert warned, the plethora of civilian government ministries requesting funds for aviation would prevent the army air force from obtaining a sufficient budget. Military aviation would be mired in absurdity: "Comrade Max's" naval staff, as Siegert scathingly referred to the navy's rebellious tendencies in the last days of the war, lacked an air expert; Oschmann, chief of the War Ministry's aviation department, would be on permanent vacation; and the inspector of aviation would be extemporizing before parliament on a subject about which he was completely ignorant. At the end of the scenario the Bavarian, Saxon, and Swabian (Württemberg) military plenipotentiaries discussed the inspector:

SAXON: What did that man really want?

BAVARIAN: Where possible, for a Prussian to be able to fly with a BMW motor.

SWABIAN: Or that Berlin be allowed to conduct correspondence with Daimler directly, without the Swabian War Ministry.

ALL TOGETHER: May the "Holy Particularism" protect us from him![1]

Wartime preparations for postwar military procurement and civil aviation confirmed Siegert's pessimistic conviction that particularistic and governmental conflicts might hinder the development of aviation.

Proposals for postwar military procurement revealed the continued strength of Bavarian particularism. As early as October 1917 the Bavarian aviation agencies contemplated the formation of a Bavarian aircraft depot (*Flugzeugmeisterei*) to preserve their independence from Prussia, although they acknowledged privately that they lacked adequate manpower to staff it. The depot would serve as intermediary between the Bavarian aircraft industry and the Prussian inspectorate.[2] Late in May 1918 at a conference with Major Wagenführ of the Prussian aircraft depot, Major Stempel of the Bavarian fliers replacement unit proposed the following procedures for procurement during the demobilization. The Prussian and Bavarian inspectorates would order aircraft jointly from the best types tested by a Prussian central acceptance institute. The factory with the best entry, regardless of its state, would receive the contracts, and promising small companies would produce the plane under license. Any firm that failed to produce its own successful craft within three years would no longer be eligible for licensed contracts. This procedure would aid less developed firms like those in the Bavarian industry while preventing the hoarding of raw materials. The Prussian market would provide sufficient contracts for factories like Pfalz, while the use of Prussian test facilities would save Bavaria the expense of creating its own.[3] The Bavarian authorities seemed to be most concerned with using the unfavorable circumstances in 1918 to wring particularistic concessions from the Prussians, who were powerless to refuse. Wagenführ agreed to the proposals in principle, but it is little wonder that Siegert grew more cynical about particularism as the war drew to a close.

In light of the expected postwar contraction of military aviation, commercial air transportation was just as significant for the future as the organization of military procurement. The airplane's demonstrated ability to transport substantial bomb loads reliably over distance made it possible to envision the modification of military craft for commercial purposes. Early in 1917 a study committee of an Austrian international air transport company (International Luftverkehrs AG) approached the Bavarian Transport Ministry requesting flight permits for a line from Constantinople to Hamburg via Munich. The committee reported that the Austrian and Hungarian transport ministries were prepared to issue the firm postwar airmail contracts.[4] When the Bavarian ministry relayed this request to the Prussian War Ministry, the latter responded on 28 April 1917 in the following manner:

The extent to which the airplane can be permitted to serve as a means of transportation depends upon the results of the discussion of a proposed air transport law.

It does not seem proper to make any concessions to a private company at a time when it is impossible to determine the extent of the restrictions on nonmilitary air transportation, because the private company could derive rights and demands from such concessions that would harm state interests.[5]

The War Ministry's real concern was not with the legality of the proposal, but rather with its potential for private infringement upon military prerogatives, which were equated with interests of state. The Austrian firm consequently received no license.

Serious discussion of air transport within the highest level of the German military establishment began in the fall of 1917, when Ludendorff agreed that Kogenluft would represent the German High Command in further discussions of air transport. Ever the ardent militarist, Ludendorff advocated the military direction and control of civil aviation, to the extent of using military subsidies to preserve competition within the aircraft industry. He proposed a central agency, evolved from Kogenluft and subordinate to the chief of the General Staff, which would administer and coordinate all aspects of aviation, military and civil.[6]

Concurrently with Ludendorff's deliberations, substantial financial interests in Germany became interested in commercial aviation. Through the imperial postal ministry the Deutsche Bank sponsored preparations for commercial aviation in conferences that included such notable personnages as Albert Ballin and Wilhelm Cuno of the Hamburg America shipping line and Arthur von Gwinner and Emil Georg von Staub of the bank's board of directors. In December 1917 AEG, which had shown an early interest in giant aircraft, founded the air transport company Deutsche Luftreederei with 2.5 million marks capital. The firm's directors moved rapidly to enter the commercial market because they believed that air links using multi-engined craft would be particularly useful over long stretches of water and in areas where other modes of transportation were unavailable or unfeasible.[7]

Kogenluft, determined to assure Germany a leading position in postwar commercial aviation, placed four planes at the ready on 8 February 1918 for experimental air mail flights, which began one week later. Then early in the spring of 1918 it permitted AEG to contact the Inspectorate of Flying Troops and any companies in "northern states," that is, Scandinavia, regarding the formation of an air transport line. In April AEG informed the Imperial Naval Office that it was ready to begin air transport tests at its own expense, using two-hundred-horsepower planes over short stretches. Both the Naval Office and the Imperial Office of the Interior encouraged the firm's efforts. Later, in October 1918, the Naval Office envisioned air routes not only to Scandinavia but also to Asia Minor and Persia, although it was not certain whether national interests would be sufficiently involved to warrant state-run aviation enterprises.[8] The highest agencies of the German government, both civilian and military, thus favored promoting commercial aviation. Their plans, however, were of a very general nature, the one firm point being the OHL's insistence on military control over civil aviation. Already, as Siegert had anticipated, a multitude of agencies was involved, in no coordinated fashion, in the preparation of postwar aviation.

The interest in commercial aviation on the part of the military and AEG stemmed from the necessity of creating a civilian aircraft market to compensate for a drastic reduction of military contracts. At a meeting of 7 November 1918, the inspectorate assured the industry that contracts would be honored and that a few firms would continue to produce warplanes through January 1919.[9] It was obvious that military contracts could support only a handful of small firms. Before the war the army had crushed any diversion of resources to civil aviation in its drive to develop an air arm and aircraft industry. Now a postwar civilian market was indispensable to sustain an industry bloated on wartime contracts. Yet these plans for the postwar era would be upset by the cataclysmic end of hostilities and the severity of the ensuing peace.

Contraction and Conversion in the Midst of Confusion, November 1918–June 1919

On 9 November 1918 the imperial government of Germany collapsed, and Kaiser Wilhelm abdicated. The heads of the socialist and independent socialist parties united in Berlin on 10 November to form a provisional government, the Council of People's Representatives, yet their consensus was tenuous, their power limited. They could not agree on the future form of government or on the merits of the socialization of industry. Furthermore, the spontaneous sprouting of workers' and soldiers' councils around Germany imperiled the central government's coherent exercise of power. These councils, which seized power locally in the November turmoil, did not necessarily adhere to the wishes of their own central council in Berlin, much less the new government, which many regarded as a mere advisory body. In December the First Congress of Workers' and Soldiers' Councils took the moderate path of supporting the government and future elections to a National Assembly. Incensed by this move away from revolution, the independent socialists attacked the congress's decision and resigned from the government. On 30 December the Spartacists, the most radical of the German socialists, took an open stand for revolution, socialization, and the prevention of elections to the National Assembly.[10] In this tense and uncertain atmosphere, the air force and aircraft industry, haunted by the specter of imminent revolution, groped for survival.

The armistice treaty of 11 November 1918 prescribed the immediate demobilization of the German air force and the surrender of 2,000 fighters and bombers, particularly Fokker D7s and night bombers. Hindenburg, maintaining that there were only some 1,700 D, C1, G, and R types at the front, asked that the number be lowered to 1,700, a figure which the Allies later accepted.[11] Yet even that number of planes was not surrendered. On 12 December, at the first meeting of the Allied Armistice Commission in Trier, the Allies acknowledged receipt of only 730 airplanes. The other 1,000 they had obtained were in such unfit condition—600 of them were completely unusable—that the commission refused to count them.[12] The German Army attributed its perfunctory compliance with Allied demands to disorganization during demobilization, mutinous conditions at the army flight parks and fliers replacement units, and continued fighting in the east, which necessitated the formation of additional units in December 1918. Yet the inspectorate would later confide to civilian agencies that the army had some nine thousand craft after the surrender of planes stipulated by the armistice.[13] Such statistics invalidate all the above excuses; the army simply refused to cooperate with the Allies.

The revolution had an immediate effect on the agencies in Berlin. On 10 November the Social Democratic Party's Berlin city representative began surveillance of the inspectorate in the name of the workers' and soldiers' councils. The next day an eight-man Soldiers' Council of the Flying Troops, ignoring Kogenluft completely and acting under orders from the Social Democrat Paul Göhre, the new undersecretary of state in the War Ministry, authorized the transformation of the inspectorate into the German Air Office (Deutsches Luftamt). They were instructed to use aviation in the interests of the people for commerce, transportation, and the delivery of food and mail. Göhre asked Siegert to head the new office, but Siegert declined because it would appear that he was trying to profit from the revolution. In any case, on 14 November the War Ministry's aviation department forbade him, as military personnel, to head the new office. The following day Siegert did suggest that the Air Office attempt to coordinate all aspects of aviation, including demobilization and material allocation. Siegert's gratuitous advice to the new government indicated that he was more concerned with the survival of aviation than with the principle of military control.[14]

Despite the council's orders to transform the inspectorate into the Air Office, the military agency continued to function under its old title. On the afternoon of 19 November it convened a conference on demobilization to advise the Association of German Aircraft Industrialists that they would have to confront squarely the conversion to peacetime production. Substantial stocks of materiel and the cessation of flight training made further purchases of new and repaired planes superfluous. The inspectorate did promise to honor current contracts, including those that the War Ministry had not yet reviewed. Yet, according to instructions from the demobilization office, these contracts would allow no profit, as they were intended mainly to enable the companies to retain their workers. If the aircraft factories obtained contracts from other governmental agencies, they would have to decrease their military aircraft contracts commensurately. By limiting contracts to the minimum necessary for relief, the state was sternly prodding companies to seek business from the private sector.

As alternative production pursuits the inspectorate suggested that diversified companies which built airplanes in departments or subsidiary plants could easily convert by transferring plant and workers to other areas of production. To aircraft factories it recommended furniture, woodwork, upholstery, and saddlery as suitable alternatives to aircraft production, with the cannibalization of half-finished craft and the production of commercial planes as possible supplements. When asked where the companies would secure the contracts, the inspectorate vaguely suggested "primarily from their communities" and offered the assistance of the war raw materials department in the War Ministry.[15] Furthermore, the military agencies were no help to the industry in its dealings with the workers' and soldiers' councils, which often issued instructions at odds with those of the military bureaucracy. The Leipzig and Hamburg councils, for example, forbade further aircraft production. The inspectorate, powerless to affect these circumstances, made no effort to intervene.

While a representative of the newly formed Bavarian Ministry of

Military Affairs (Ministerium für Militärische Angelegenheiten) at the conference considered the inspectorate's answers and efforts inadequate, one fact was clear—the industry had to convert to peacetime production without delay. The Bavarian criticized the inspectorate, but the Bavarian ministry also warned its factories that it was issuing no new orders and was under no obligations to fulfill its standing contracts. Firms with no prospects for peacetime production would be allowed to produce for the army in order to retain their workers, but Bavarian procurement agencies would monitor them carefully and use price reductions to force their conversion as soon as possible.[16]

After ten years of depending entirely upon military contracts for their livelihood, the firms were left largely to their own devices. These difficult conditions caused Hermann Dorner, technical director of the Hannover Railroad Factory's aircraft department, to advise air force Capt. Kurt Student, who inquired about employment in the aircraft industry in mid-November, to wait half a year, because the industry was then in the grips of a "fearful depression."[17]

While the inspectorate was divesting itself of old responsibilities, the new civilian government pursued its goal of forming an aviation office. On 26 November the Council of People's Representatives and State Secretary of the Interior Hugh Preuss jointly announced that a new Reich Air Office (Reichsluftamt) within the Office of the Interior would regulate civil aviation provisionally and assist the military agencies with the liquidation of military aviation.[18] Their description of the prerogatives of the Air Office was vague, and the man they chose to head the agency— August Euler—was just the type to arrogate more power to the position than was probably intended. He conceived of his tasks as wide-ranging: assistance in the liquidation of military aviation; the conversion and reduction of German aeronautical enterprises to small-scale civil aviation and an industry of small research workshops; and the regulation of aviation law and licenses.[19] Euler was the most logical choice among the industrialists to fill the position of undersecretary of state for air. As chairman of the Convention of German Aircraft Industrialists before the war, he had ardently, if unsuccessfully, promoted the development of civilian sport aviation in the face of staunch opposition from the Prussian Army. He was a long-time acquaintance of his superior in the Interior Office, Heinrich Albert, as both had played key roles in the prewar National Aviation Fund. Finally, Euler's wartime resistance to military measures was a definite asset in the person who would preside over the contraction of military aviation and the conversion to civil aeronautics.

Euler, however, thought only in terms of small-scale enterprises like his own marginal factory, which would be inadequate for the postwar development of German aviation. The small workshop was a relic of a bygone era, the age of Euler's successes before 1912. In his zeal to rescue aviation from the army, he might kill it with smallness.

Euler immediately contacted his old adversary Siegert to advise the inspector of the new circumstances, and the very tone of his letter manifested not a small touch of triumph at the reversal of position. After announcing that the Imperial Office of the Interior was now the authoritative agency for aviation, Euler advised that Siegert, Wagenführ, a representative of the Interior Office, and he would direct the liquidation of military aviation. He arrogantly and erroneously chided the inspectorate for doing nothing to ease the transition to peace and warned Siegert, "I will gladly serve you and Major Wagenführ, but I have not the slightest interest in wasting my strength against wanton opposition. . . . I request that you and Major Wagenführ make liquidation as easy a task as possible so that I need only to agree with you."[20]

Yet the new undersecretary of state for air would soon learn that the mandate of the government did not ensure the cooperation of the military authorities or of the federal states. As Siegert observed to Kogenluft on 27 November, the interest of imperial states like Württemberg in establishing their own air offices implied that the claims of Euler's central air office to authority were not universally recognized and consequently better ignored.[21]

In the midst of all the confusion, Lieutenant Col. Wilhelm Siegert took leave of the Prussian Inspectorate of Flying Troops on 13 December 1918. In resigning, the old warrior confided his feelings to his former adversary Euler:

> After almost ten years of practical and theoretical activity in aviation, I have decided, with heavy heart, to say good-bye.
> As I take this step, I think . . . of all who sacrificed their lives on the flying and battle fields for the steep ascent of the young creation.
>
> From the beginning "to fly" meant "to fight";
> First against prejudiced opinions;
> Then against wind, weather, and unpredictable material;
> Later for the palms of height, duration, and speed records;
> Finally against a world of enemies.
> The work of a decade is ruined.
>
> However, as the legend according to which the phoenix was able to rise from his ashes, so will the airplane rise from the dead, out of the world

conflagration, out of the rubble of the instrument of destruction to bind people together as the symbol of a new future.

To build it anew, I lack the necessary strength.

Furthermore, no old soldier belongs at the head of an organization to be created on a purely civilian and international foundation. He would remain—if not perhaps inwardly—at least outwardly tainted by his service to the old regime . . . and consequently could harm more than serve the good cause.

. . . After four and one-half years of duty uninterrupted by vacations or Sundays, I intend to devote some time to recuperation and the search for a new profession—away from the rustlings of the wings of the birds of the past war and the future peace.

My heartfelt thanks to all who enabled me to affect matters through their true willingness to sacrifice.

In "deliberation" we may have been of opposing views a thousand times; but when it came to the "deed," we were one.

I shall hold dear the memories of the flying man until my own last take-off for the realm of shadows.[22]

Late in 1920 Siegert served on a governmental commission assisting the Office of Aviation and Motor Vehicles, but he would never again serve the cause of German military aviation in an official capacity. He was replaced as inspector by Major Wilhelm Hähnelt, who had led an illustrious career, first as staff officer for aviation at the German Fifth Army at Verdun and then for the First Army at the Somme, and later as aviation commander of the Second Army in 1918. Hähnelt's appointment exemplified the postwar tendency to replace rear echelon bureaucrats with officers who had served in the air force staff's chain of command at the front.

One week later, on 19 December, Euler met with Hähnelt, Thomsen of Kogenluft, Major Sachs of the War Ministry, and representatives of the other central government agencies to discuss the prerogatives of the Air Office. The meeting essentially revealed that the Air Office had no authority in the liquidation of military aviation. The military representatives, particularly Thomsen, brooked no interference from the civilian agency, either in assessing and liquidating their equipment or in determining the legitimacy of other military aeronautical activities. The civilian officials could only urge the military's cooperation.[23]

The next day, 20 December, Euler conferred with representatives of all the major aircraft factories and aircraft industry trade associations. While Euler described the Air Office as a mediary between the industry and government, the agency's impotence in the crucial issuance of contracts reduced his assistance to the manufacturers to recommendations: that they see the inspectorate about outstanding army contracts and the Foreign Office about export licenses; that they cooperate with the workers and the new government; and that they enlist the aid of the industry's prewar trade association and its parent body, the Association of German Motor Vehicle Industrialists. The industrialists, who were unable to understand or control their new environment, were left in fear and disarray to muddle through their predicament. Complaints were rife about the instability of the inspectorate, whose rapid changes of personnel constantly invalidated contractual agreements, and about the capriciousness of certain workers' and soldiers' councils, whose insistence on the continued employment of workers in the absence of contracts threatened to ruin some factories. Haunted by the specter of bolshevism, they feared the imminent collapse of the German aircraft industry. All Euler could suggest was that they accept the inevitability of drastic contraction.[24] Yet his callous attitude left the impression that he welcomed the shrinkage. And perhaps he did. His small firm had recently suffered a most ignominious demise—French occupation troops in Frankfort used it as quarters for French troops and horses. With his factory ruined, he probably cared little that soon others would be too.

Such conferences, like the general events of the winter of 1918, unsettled the manufacturers, yet they fared variously. The Pfalz and Euler factories, which were located in the occupied zone, were lost. BFW also paid a severe penalty for the political disintegration, because the revolutionary government in Bavaria severed diplomatic ties with the German Foreign Office. At the end of November director Peter Eberwein requested repeatedly that the Prussian inspectorate pay for 1.5 million marks worth of planes and parts at the factory that it had ordered before the end of the war. The inspectorate advised him that it had no intention of paying a firm in a foreign country, because there was no guarantee of its ability to secure the materiel. BFW's complaints to the Bavarian Foreign Ministry availed nothing, and the firm found itself in severe financial difficulty: it owed 560,000 marks in state taxes and 2.75 million marks in war profit taxes, not to mention wages to its employees, but had no funds to pay the debts.[25]

Some factories continued aircraft production, while others began to produce goods like furniture and machine equipment. The Hannover Railroad Factory completed some two-hundred light two-seaters after the fighting stopped and even purchased some of its own planes from the air force in order to modify them for commercial use. The Fokker factory first manufactured boats—yachts, motorboats, canoes, anything that would float—but quickly found the competition fierce and the market flooded. A subsequent attempt to produce commercial scales failed dismally for lack of previous experience. Fokker's situation was commonplace. All ventures lost money, and only the diversity of his industrial empire—the aircraft factory at Schwerin, armaments factory at Reinickendorff, the Oberursel Motor Works near Frankfort, and a small seaplane factory in Travemünde—forestalled collapse. Fokker's losses, combined with his fear for his life during the revolution, convinced the Dutchman to leave Germany, an escape that was beyond his German colleagues.[26]

The uncertainties accompanying the armistice and political upheaval slowed progress on aircraft construction at SSW in November. The aircraft inspectorate canceled large contracts for one-hundred D4s, fifty trainers, and three R-planes, although the company painstakingly negotiated a small number of orders for D4s, prototype D6 fighters, and two R-planes. Its labor force shrank steadily: the design office declined from 40 to 10 men as the company finished current designs and began no new ones; a work force of 722 men and 175 women in September declined to 320 men and 30 women in December.[27] Although SSW, a large conglomerate, may have transferred aircraft workers to other branches, they were probably released, as competition in all areas of production was stiff.

Even in these dismal circumstances, there was hope. On 11 November, Hugo Junkers, undaunted by defeat, assembled his design and engineering staff to notify them that the firm would concentrate on civil air transportation. According to Junkers's biographer, Richard Blunck, Junkers's survival was due not only to this immediate decision but also to the very nature of the Junkers concern, a research enterprise that regarded mass production as a necessary but subordinate accessory. To East German historian Hans Radandt, however, Junkers was merely another monopoly capitalist whose war production enabled him to accumulate the capital for a virtual monopoly in aviation during the 1920s.[28] The truth lies between the two interpretations. If Junkers, an able inventor, was primarily interested in research, he was also an astute industrialist, who parlayed his inventions, from bath heater to aircraft engine, into substantial and successful enterprises. He emerged from the war with the capital, plant, and experience in the design and production of all-metal airplanes to make him the world's foremost authority on the subject. Unlike many other aircraft manufacturers, he was well prepared to look to the future.

The threatening disintegration of the German Empire and the haphazard restructuring of government from November through December 1918 impaired the efficient functioning of the old military agencies. Yet from the outset the army command, despite its apparently precarious position, brooked no challenge to its authority from the civilian agencies and replaced rear echelon bureaucrats who might exhibit conciliatory attitudes toward the civilians with staff officers with uncompromising positions toward the rear. Ironically, in Siegert's case, the conciliatory bureaucrat had once been a frontline commander, an uncompromising militarist, whose flexibility stemmed from his desire to preserve aviation at all costs, regardless of whether it were civilian or military. With the new government's creation of a civilian air office and its appointment of August Euler, erstwhile opponent of militarism, the stage was set for a civil-military struggle over aviation.

The disruption that ruptured the contractual lifeline between the German military establishment and the aircraft industry also prevented the new civilian authorities from stepping into the breach with contracts of their own. The aircraft industry was consequently left without state aid, other than relief contracts, and private markets in all areas were glutted. The aircraft manufacturers, frightened and disoriented, generally found that they lacked the liquid assets to pay their debts. The only potential untapped source of funds seemed to be commercial aviation. Yet here the industry would find itself caught in a civil-military conflict, given Euler's plans for civil commercial aviation enterprises and the army High Command's conception of commercial aviation as a vehicle to promote military interests. 1919 promised to be a troubled year for German aviation.

The Spartacist rebellion, which began on 5 January and was brutally crushed by government paramilitary troops ten days later, ushered in the new year in ominous fashion. Communist risings in March and April were also quelled violently. Underlying this sporadic violence was the disastrous economic situation in Germany—industrial life had collapsed, and the Allied blockade threatened to starve the nation. In the midst of this chaos, elections to the National Assembly confirmed the strength of the moderates, and when the assembly convened in Weimar on 6 February, socialists Friedrich Ebert and Gustav Scheidemann became president and minister president of the Weimar Republic. This new government reigned in an international limbo for three months until 8 May, when its representatives received the terms of the peace treaty at Versailles.

Through May civilian and military agencies were preoccupied with

establishing and controlling commercial aviation, while the aircraft factories struggled to survive. Despite the intermittent violence, the industrialists showed far less concern about bolshevism than they had at the
end of 1918. Apparently the government's ability to survive the chaos
and violence had allayed such fears. Matters pertaining to aviation once
again commanded their attention.

Kogenluft was dissolved on 21 January 1919, but the heart of the
agency, Col. Hermann von der Lieth-Thomsen, became head of the
aviation department in the War Ministry, thus continuing the practice of
replacing War Ministry bureaucrats like Col. Paul Oschmann with staff
types. The aviation department had at its disposal some six thousand
airplanes, of which it considered five hundred suitable for air transport.
Thomsen and Hähnelt of the inspectorate quickly decided to establish
four permanent airlines from Weimar, the center of the new government,
to Berlin, Dresden, Munich, and Stuttgart. Prussian troops would staff
the Weimar and Berlin-Döberitz stations with twenty-four planes; Saxon
contingents would staff Dresden; Bavarian, Munich-Schleissheim; and
Swabian soldiers, Stuttgart-Döblingen. The Bavarian Ministry of Military Affairs agreed to cooperate with these plans on 1 February. Then on
6 February the undersecretary of state in the imperial chancery, Curt
Baake, instructed the War Ministry to prepare a military air courier
service between Weimar and Berlin and the capitals of the independent
German states. The ex post facto nature of Baake's instructions suggests
that the army had decided to direct postwar transport aviation on its own
initiative.[29]

In a parallel effort, the aircraft industry and civil aviation agencies
were establishing their commercial aviation enterprises. On 30 January
German motor vehicle and aviation industrialists formed a commission to
examine the future organization and profitability of commercial aviation
and to discuss the liquidation of military aviation, from which they expected to acquire materiel and air bases.[30]

August Euler also presumed the imminent demise of military aviation. He was consequently shocked on 20 February to discover the army's
plans to establish the courier service. The accidental manner in which he
learned of the military enterprise—the Bavarian Ministry of Military
Affairs requested permission from the Air Office to participate in the
planned network—especially rankled, because the War Ministry had
previously promised to work closely with the Air Office. Of course, these
promises antedated Thomsen's arrival in the war department. Livid with
rage, Euler bombarded civilian agencies at the end of February with news

of the perfidy of the War Ministry and inspectorate. Air transport, he exclaimed, was supposed to be a civilian affair. The Air Office had licensed a number of civil air transport companies, the largest among them the AEG Deutsche Luftreederei with sixty-four planes and ten pilots. Yet these companies could scarcely survive competition with a state-funded army line. Euler questioned the wisdom of a military enterprise for other reasons:

> So substantial a military transport service as the army proposes could not remain secret, and the Entente could easily conclude that we still possess an excessive number of first-class military airplanes. Such a conception could ultimately cripple our embryonic civil aviation.[31]

He challenged the ability of a disintegrating air force, accustomed to the war's profligate waste of manpower and materiel, to conduct safe, reliable air transport. Yet here was the army, preparing military air stations for a permanent "imperial air courier service," approaching the armies of states—Bavaria, Württemberg, Baden, and Saxony—whose civilian agencies desired to establish air transport enterprises, and applying to the Ukrainian embassy for contracts for currency shipment to the East which the Foreign Office had reserved for private companies. Euler concluded that the army "was obstructing the development of civil aviation."[32]

The army seemed immune to Euler's pressure, and on 28 February the War Ministry notified the civilian agencies of the German government that it had prepared a daily military courier service for "state purposes" between Berlin and Weimar. Despite high costs, it also offered special flights over the two-hour route. Soon after the army's announcement the finance, economics, and postal ministries joined Euler in opposition to the military air courier service. Their opposition also had no effect on the army's plans, as Euler learned in a conference on 15 March with Maj. von Gilsa of the Defense Ministry, Capt. Helmut Wilberg of the War Ministry, and Captains Busch and Berthold of the inspectorate. Gilsa assumed a conciliatory attitude, granting the Air Office direction of civil aviation and even of the military courier service if necessary. Wilberg, however, was determined to preserve the military's control over its flight facilities and courier services, while Berthold was adamantly militaristic, insisting that only the army could guide civil aviation. Euler and the Office of the Interior challenged the right of the army to conduct the service and insisted on the civilian conduct of aviation transport. This encounter in the "internal air war," as Gilsa labeled the confrontation, resolved nothing.[33]

Late in April Captain Wilberg complained to chancery undersecretary Curt Baake that the civilian agencies did not understand the requirements of military aviation. The Entente had fully recognized the importance of aviation and was striving to maintain strong peacetime air forces, while Germany was allowing its air weapon to decline. Yet one could not afford to underestimate the importance of a strong air fleet for future mobilization. In earlier wars the first strong combat units had taken two or three weeks to reach the frontier; in the future, industrial centers would be attacked from the air within twenty-four hours of the declaration of war. Small countries would be held in check with no more than powerful air squadrons. Finally, a country's air defense could not be improvised from postal planes, but would have to consist of standing units of fighter aircraft. Wilberg was thus absolutely determined to retain control of the army's aviation facilities and to use the courier service to maintain military readiness.[34]

Colonel Thomsen also defended the air courier service, insisting that the government had requested it and that it would be cheaper than private or civil government enterprises and more reliable in times of upheaval. By avoiding a civilian state venture, Thomsen asserted, the army's line would enable the later establishment of a private monopoly. He consequently placed the units under Gen. Walther von Lüttwitz's command in Berlin.[35] Of course, Thomsen had made no attempt to explain how the service would lead to a private monopoly later, nor did he elaborate on the choice of monopoly, which departed from Ludendorff's wartime projection of competitive enterprises. But Thomsen's predilection shows how far apart the army stood from Euler, who was determined to create a competitive framework for civil aviation.

In a letter of 14 May to Minister President Gustav Scheidemann, Euler refuted all of Thomsen's claims. He continued to emphasize that the army's negotiations antedated Baake's instructions. He condemned the War Ministry's failure to collaborate with the Air Office, then repudiated Thomsen's claims that the military service would be cheaper and more reliable than civil enterprise. The cost of civil enterprise might appear greater, but it included everything, such as administration and insurance. Thomsen, Euler warned, was not taking into account the army's hidden costs, the expense of keeping troops at the ready, the high accident rate that one could expect with the military. The army was not so reliable in political turmoil: had not the Luttwitz corps had to wrest Döberitz airfield from other troops? Ultimately, the army's airline was wasteful and unnecessary.[36]

After five months of discussion, civilians and military men were no closer to resolving control of German commercial aviation than they had been in January 1919. While the army's attitude was not monolithic, the officers were prepared to assume control of civil aviation if it was necessary for the survival of military aviation. The army had been obstructionist from the start, toward the Entente in its refusal to comply with the armistice terms, toward German civilian agencies in its arbitrary actions. Its most conciliatory offer had been to allow civilians control of commercial aviation, provided they absorbed military personnel into their airlines. The army's preoccupation with civilian ignorance about military preparedness might explain its attitude, yet the sentiments were misplaced. From the beginning Euler had stated that he did not object to the army's performing purely military tasks; what disturbed him was its incursion into the civilian sphere. The misunderstanding lay in their definitions of what constituted "military tasks." The army regarded any undertaking that suited its purposes as a military one, ignoring any distinctions between civilian and military spheres, while the civilians considered it self-evident that postal and transport aviation were civilian matters, to be conducted by the Air Office and the aircraft industry.

The industry sorely needed any potential funds that air transport contracts might provide as it struggled through the difficult period from January to May 1919. The firms located on Johannisthal airfield had been unable to convert to other products, because their twenty-year contract with the airfield company stipulated that they could build only airplanes until its expiration in 1929, when the plants would become the property of the company. At the request of several major firms, the demobilization office interceded, and after two meetings the airfield company agreed to allow the factories to produce anything that did not damage the field.[37]

Conversion, however, proved no panacea. Furniture, automobile, and railroad production failed to compensate for the loss of aircraft contracts, because demand was lacking in all industrial spheres. Generally, where possible, the factories continued to produce airplanes, either for the army or for future civil aviation. The Bavarian aviation agencies were receiving equipment from BFW, BMW, Bavarian Rumpler, SSW, and the Zeppelin works at Lindau in June and July. BFW alone delivered two hundred finished airplanes to the Bavarian government at cost. In north Germany AEG transformed its G5 bomber into a passenger plane by adding a side door, more comfortable seats, and larger windows. Such modifications were not always sufficient, as the firm observed that engine noise still drowned out conversation. Five companies—Linke-Hoffmann,

DFW, Aviatik, Schütte-Lanz, and SSW—were building a total of eleven
R-planes at the end of January as part of the Prussian inspectorate's
wartime construction program. The inspectorate asked the demobilization office to allow the completion and modification of the craft for
peacetime uses at the prearranged prices, which ranged from 450,000
marks apiece for the Linke-Hoffmann to 750,000 marks for the SSW
craft. The office allowed the completion of nine of the planes as necessary
work on 20 January.[38] The suitability of such conversions remained to be
tested.

The Junkers factory showed no ill effects. When the Junkers-Fokker
Works dissolved in December 1918, Junkers assumed all the shares and
on 24 April 1919 actually increased the capital of the joint-stock company 900,000 marks to 3.5 million marks. During the intervening period,
the firm's production of its all-metal warplanes peaked, as it turned out
twelve of forty-seven monoplane D1 fighters in February, and eleven of
forty-four C11 attack fighters in March 1919. More important for the
near future, the prototype Junkers F13, an all-metal six-seater cabin
monoplane that was destined to become the most widely used transport
plane in the world in the 1920s, flew on 25 June. The plane was so good
that the Russians and Japanese employed it for military operations.[39]

Though struggling, firms did not collapse during this time. The most
significant loss that the aircraft industry suffered was Anthony Fokker,
who exploited the confusion of the revolution to smuggle six trains
carrying over 400 engines, 120 D7s, 20 D8s, 60 observation planes, and
tons of equipment and parts to Holland. He promptly established a new
factory there, although he left some of his assistants in Germany to
supervise his factories.[40] Despite the absence of outright bankruptcies,
the aircraft companies were in continued distress. One major company,
the Halberstadt Works, was sold to the Berlin-Halberstadt Industrial
Works in April so that it might continue airplane production. According
to the trade association, the industry could not give away excess machines, nor could they sell their materials, which were primarily partially
finished goods useful only for aircraft construction. Worse, no one, including powerful German raw material producers, seemed interested in
investing in the industry.[41] Historian Gerald Feldman noted that in 1918
certain German industrialists were convinced that heavy industry had to
enter finishing and manufacturing industries like aircraft production in
order to maintain its competitive position in the postwar international
economy.[42] This interest dissipated with the disappearance of markets for
airplanes. The industry was caught in an inescapable dilemma: neither

aircraft manufacture nor conversion provided profits. In May Euler estimated that the industry was losing 120–130,000 marks monthly.[43] The
Entente was barring German craft from foreign air exhibitions, thereby
effectively severing Germany from external markets. The industry lay
"fatally wounded," lamented the general secretary of the aircraft industrialists' trade association, and everything possible had to be done to save
it.[44] Yet no solutions presented themselves.

The disclosure of the Versailles treaty terms on 8 May ended the
discouraging limbo disastrously. The peace conditions allowed Germany
civil aviation, but on an unequal basis—Allied air transport, for example,
could fly over German territory, but the Germans received no reciprocal
rights. More critically, the Allies sought to crush military aviation permanently and aircraft production temporarily. Five articles—numbers
198–202 in Part Three of the treaty—were devastating. Article 198
forbade military and naval aviation, although the navy could retain a
maximum of one hundred unarmed seaplanes with one reserve motor per
plane until 1 October 1919 for locating undersea mines. Article 199,
while permitting the retention of one thousand aviation personnel until 1
October, ordered the demobilization of the air force within two months of
the ratification of the treaty. Article 200 gave Allied aircraft free passage
through and landing rights in Germany. Article 201 forbade the production and importation of aircraft and parts for six months after the treaty
entered effect, while article 202 instructed Germany to surrender all
military and naval aviation materiel to Allied and associated governments
within three months. The Inter-Allied Surveillance Commission stipulated by article 210 would ensure adherence to the treaty.[45]

Between 8 May and 23 June, when the German government accepted the treaty, aviation circles discussed the potential effects of the
severe peace terms on the future of German aviation and the most
appropriate forms of commercial aviation enterprises.[46]

One of the most salient features of Euler's stance in these meetings
was the assumption that the terms were not hard and fast, that the Allies
might adjust some of them in response to adroit diplomatic maneuvering.
Euler hoped to circumvent the Allies' proposed inequality for German
civil aeronautics and the prohibition of aircraft production by entering an
international aviation convention. He was convinced that the Allies
would allow Germany equality in international commercial aviation if
only to avoid obstacles to their own flights over Germany, and he presumed that articles 198–202, including the ban on manufacture, per-
tained to military and naval aviation, not civil aeronautics. While the

treasury representative agreed with Euler's optimistic position, most of Euler's colleagues did not. Maj. (ret.) Georg von Tschudi, director of Johannisthal field, warned that the ban on manufacture applied to all aircraft in order to prevent the military from using civilian planes, while Johann Schütte of the Schütte-Lanz company also doubted that the aircraft industry would be allowed to continue production. The head of the German Research Institute for Aviation and the representative of the Postal Ministry doubted that the Allies would permit Germany to "internationalize" its aviation, while the representative of the Interior Office suggested that the future held in store " 'inter-Alliedism' at Germany's expense," not "internationalism," because articles 201–2 were intended to paralyze all of German aviation.

If most of the civilian representatives did not trust to Allied leniency, German military officers trusted neither them nor the Allies. In fact, all the civilians agreed with Euler's refusal to allow the Air Office to compromise itself by espousing military interests in aviation at the peace conference. Euler further planned to use the Allies against the army by having the Foreign Office persuade them to allow civil aviation enterprises to take over military equipment and airfields. Capt. Helmuth Felmy of the War Ministry warned that the army would refuse to surrender aviation materiel to the assessment office, because the Allies would simply commandeer any equipment the civilians obtained. Felmy's statement showed that although the army no longer openly proposed to control German aviation, it still had no intention of assisting the civilians, whom it regarded as little better than a funnel to the Allies.

The Versailles terms had convinced the army that civil aviation was useless for its purposes. Wilberg had suggested as much in his conversation with Baake late in April when he referred to the impossibility of using postal planes as fighters. He consequently determined to flaunt Versailles openly. In a position paper on the future air force written for Gen. Hans von Seeckt, military expert at the German armistice negotiations and later head of the Troop Office (Truppenamt) of the one-hundred-thousand-man German Army (that is, chief of the General Staff), Wilberg proposed an air force of eighteen hundred airplanes and eight thousand men stationed at sixteen airbases. Impelled by the military-technical necessity of keeping pace with the Allies in military aviation, Wilberg was prepared to embark upon an extremely perilous course politically. It would have been impossible to hide so large an organization from surveillance, and Wilberg's proposal made no provisions for concealing the air force in any case.

The major focus of the discussion of commercial aviation enterprises was the concept of the mixed public-private venture. At the beginning of the year the governments of some smaller German states like Saxony and Bavaria had begun discussing this form of enterprise, and the representatives of the Bavarian Transport Ministry now proposed a Bavarian air transport company directed by the state and financed by private companies. They suggested this system as a model for other states to follow in forming a network across Germany.

Director Rieben of the AEG Deutsche Luftreederei found this approach inadequate and suggested a collective one. AEG was interested in a *"gemeinsamen Wirtschaft,"* or collective economy, in which the company enlisted the united efforts of governments, communities, and private interests. Rieben's concept originated with Wichard von Möllendorff, undersecretary of state in the Economics Office (later Economics Ministry), close acquaintance of AEG's director Walther Rathenau, and an engineer at AEG before the war. During the fall and winter of 1918–19 Möllendorff had expounded his corporatist ideas of autonomous economic associations for every branch of German industry, organized in a spirit of social cooperation by the Economics Ministry.[47] The Deutsche Luftreederei cooperated with a transport committee of the chamber of commerce and regional transportation associations in Weimar, while in Rhineland-Westphalia the mayors and chambers of commerce had coalesced to assist the company.

After the meetings Euler drafted a proposal for a combined enterprise that approximated Rieben's scheme but clearly diverged from the Bavarian by including the states in the financial responsibility for the project. Resolution of such divergences would have necessitated further conferences, but all these plans were futile.

Ideas of a *"Gemeinwirtschaft"* receded after 17 June, when the Entente presented Germany with the final peace terms. At the moment of truth, when it was finally clear that the terms were not open to adjustment, Euler was prepared to accept articles 198–202 on military aviation, although he feared that their fulfillment, which entailed the surrender of all airfields, would severely impair German civil air operations. He sensibly conceded that considerations of civil aviation were not such life and death matters as to prevent the signing of the peace treaty and counseled moderation to the German Foreign Office. Wilberg, however, recommended an open rejection of the Allies' conditions, which he found completely detrimental to German national security. In Euler's opinion, any such declaration would not save military aviation; it would merely arouse the mistrust of the Allies and make matters more difficult for civil aviation.[48] Euler was correct. The treaty had to be accepted, whatever the consequences. Although debate over the terms caused the fall of the Scheidemann cabinet on 21 June, a new cabinet accepted the Versailles treaty on 23 June and signed on 28 June.

In the first six months of 1919, commercial aviation had been the focus of attention of the aircraft manufacturers and of civilian and military agencies. It was consequently the arena that showed most dramatically the alteration of the military-industrial relationship. Despite friction and conflicts of interest, the prewar and wartime ties between the army and the aircraft industry had been symbiotic, with the army as consumer and the industry as producer. Now the two were competing in commercial aviation, as the army used warplanes to usurp transport contracts from the aircraft factories' airlines. The army seized any excuse to run an air service because it regarded such ventures as being in the national interest. In reality nothing could have been further from the truth early in 1919. Any evidence of military participation risked arousing swift and immediate Allied retribution. The army's direction of air transport was not even in its own interest, much less the national interest, as Wilberg acknowledged under the pressure of the treaty. The aircraft industry and the civil aviation agencies, both newly independent of the military, sought to act on the coincidence of their interests in the mixed enterprise, which avoided socialization while utilizing the wartime experience of state guidance of industry. The Versailles treaty initially appeared to foster the separation of German military and civil aviation and thus to offer the opportunity for a civil aviation and aircraft industry independent of the military. In reality it would administer a crushing blow to a languishing aircraft industry and shackle civil aviation just as it prepared to escape from the German Army.

Collapse, July 1919–Spring 1922

The signing of the Versailles treaty signaled the death knell of the German air force and aircraft industry of World War I. By the time the treaty entered effect on 10 January 1920, the remaining old guard of Germany's first air force had followed Siegert's precedent and retired from the army. Col. Hermann von der Lieth-Thomsen departed on 11 August 1919; Lt. Gen. Ernst Wilhelm von Höppner, on 30 September; and Maj. Wilhelm Hähnelt, the last inspector of flying troops, on 31 October 1919. Only

Maj. Felix Wagenführ, the head of the aircraft inspectorate, remained as head of the aviation peace commission, the liaison between the German Troop Office (Truppenamt) and the Inter-Allied Aviation Inspection Committee that arrived in Germany in September 1919. On 8 May 1920, Gen. Hans von Seeckt, chief of the Troop Office, proclaimed the official dissolution of the German air force with the epitaph, "The arm is not dead; its spirit lives."[49] Seeckt knew well how alive military aviation was. In every end there is a beginning, and the future German Luftwaffe was already alive in the minds of the Troop Office's military aviation experts—Capts. Kurt Student, Helmut Wilberg, and Wilhelm Vogt.

Nevertheless, the dismantling of German military aviation was the central occurrence of this period. The Inter-Allied Aviation Inspection Committee began its duties on 22 February 1920, and under its direction the Germans ultimately surrendered approximately fifteen thousand aircraft and twenty-seven thousand engines. Yet the pace of aviation disarmament was too slow to satisfy the commission, which possessed evidence of continued aircraft manufacture in Germany. The six-month prohibition of construction stipulated at Versailles was due to end on 10 July 1920, but in June 1920 the control commission persuaded the Ambassadors Conference in London to continue the restrictions. The ban on production would not be lifted until three months after the commission deemed that Germany had fulfilled the disarmament provisions and had destroyed or yielded all materiel.[50]

The Germans persisted in their efforts to circumvent the treaty's provisions. An aerial police employed former air force personnel and military airplanes, among them Fokker D7 fighters. As these police were obviously a nucleus for a future air force, the Ambassadors Conference ordered the force disbanded on 8 November 1920 and forbade the police to use airplanes. The prohibitions of aerial police and aircraft manufacture were repeated in a disarmament note of the Paris Agreements of 29 January 1921 and in the London Ultimatum of 5 May 1921.[51]

Once again, the Allies could justify continuation of these penalties with evidence that German aircraft manufacture had not ceased. German manufacturers established branches abroad—Junkers and Heinkel in Sweden, Dornier in Holland and Italy—which provided them with a limited outlet, while they maintained their design offices in Germany. During 1920 Claudius Dornier, who continued to design small seaplanes with some fifty men at Seemoos, began work on his large flying boat, the famous Dornier Wal ("Whale"), at an Italian subsidiary of his firm after the Allied control commission's protests had forced him to scuttle a new six-passenger flying boat off Kiel in April 1920. At the Karl Caspar firm in Travemünde, Ernst Heinkel designed seaplanes for foreign powers and had the parts assembled in Sweden, where the navy had been buying his floatplanes since the end of 1918. Finally, the debut of the all-metal transport plane Junkers F13 in the spring of 1921 provided ample proof of Germany's continued progress in aircraft production.[52]

The French in particular were sorely disturbed by what they witnessed. Indeed, a comprehensive report on German aviation issued by the French undersecretary of state for aviation on 18 January 1921 had probably prompted the disarmament note of 29 January. He was not disturbed by the government's appropriation of 12.5 million marks to commercial aeronautics in 1920, essentially because German commercial aviation remained marginal.

More crucial and threatening was the continued progress of German aviation technology. While the inspectorate's aircraft depot was no longer there to dispense scientific and technological information, the Scientific Society for Aviation and local aviation societies now provided liaisons among aviation specialists and engineers, while the factories' technical laboratories were in close contact with one another. As the report observed, "The constant effort and goal of the German aeronautical industry is to get away from anything of an empirical nature. . . . It is only necessary to visit the factories of the Junker[s] or Zeppelin corporations in order to see just how little empirical formulas are admitted in their industries." These procedures were producing the most significant strides in postwar aviation technology: a new AEG twin-motored aircraft, which had broken the world altitude record with eight passengers aboard; Zeppelin's continued development of R-planes; and Junkers's five-seat "advanced experimental all-metal limousine" (the F13), which the French report called "the craft of the future."

Although the aircraft factories had undertaken other forms of production in order to survive the postwar financial crisis, the report cautioned that larger factories like Junkers and Zeppelin had retained most of their original personnel. These circumstances led the French undersecretary to conclude:

> From the time the Junkers and Zeppelin corporations can put their aircraft on the market, commercial aviation will progress with an incredible swiftness. . . .
> To place the enormous number of factories capable of producing aviation equipment on a footing to produce new material will require no more

than three months; to enable them to produce again at full capacity, no more than nine months to one year. Consequently, the terms of the treaty of Versailles which forbid all aeronautical construction in Germany for six months will have no appreciable effect on the subsequent volume of Germany's aeronautical production. The only present restriction to Germany's assuming aviation supremacy is her financial and economic situation.[53]

The French had two choices: they could recommend lifting all the Versailles prohibitions, or they could attempt to postpone the inevitable resurgence of German aviation for as long as possible. The first choice was out of the question, so they pursued the second course.

Yet French fears were exaggerated. The undersecretary was more sanguine about the prospects for revival of the German aircraft industry than most German manufacturers. In fact, the large majority of German aircraft companies, including many prominent firms, collapsed or left aircraft production.[54] The Rumpler Works was dissolved on 25 June 1919, Edmund Rumpler turned to automobile construction, and perhaps the most gifted German manufacturer of high-altitude craft was lost to aviation. Although the French report credited Aviatik with developing transport planes in 1920, in fact Aviatik had already converted primarily to tractor production. The company was dissolved in December 1921. The Halberstadt plant also failed in its production of agricultural machinery and was sold to the Saxon security police in 1920. LVG was liquidated early in 1920, the Zeppelin works at Staaken was closed, and the Gotha Railroad Works, which failed in its attempt to reenter railroad construction, was bought by an automobile factory in 1921. AEG, SSW, and the Hannover Railroad Factory all disbanded their aircraft departments. What was left of the Fokker aircraft works closed in 1921.

The Inter-Allied Control Commission's technical report confirmed these developments by indicating that practically all the old firms turned to the production of other implements, primarily agricultural machinery, furniture, rolling stock, automobiles, and canoes.[55] For those firms which converted successfully, the extension of the production prohibition ensured a long hiatus before the issue of serial contracts, and with every passing day their prospects of reentry into aircraft production declined. Consequently, although the association of German aircraft industrialists listed all the old firms on its roster in April 1921, most of them were in fact lost to aircraft manufacture forever. Although the German government awarded the aircraft manufacturers association 150 million marks in July 1922 as compensation for losses of profits and wages suffered from the

London Ultimatum's continued restrictions,[56] there was never the possibility of compensation for the general collapse of the industry from 1919 through 1921.

Ironically, the continued aviation restrictions ultimately redounded to the benefit of the German Army. Möllendorff and his program of the collective economy fell victim to the change in cabinet after the struggle over acceptance of the Versailles treaty, while Euler was first routinely ignored by the Foreign Office in the discussion of peace terms and then forgotten. Late in the summer of 1919 the Air Office became the Air and Motor Vehicle Office, which was further submerged in the Transport Ministry's railroad department in October 1920. Euler resigned in December 1920, to the relief of many aircraft manufacturers who erroneously blamed him for the failure of German aviation policies and the continued ban on aircraft production.[57] Euler's departure meant that the staunchest defender of an independent civil aviation was gone, as the old eagle, Germany's first licensed pilot, retired to a life of obscurity until his death at the age of eighty-eight in 1958. His successor in the Transport Ministry's aviation department, Capt. (ret.) Ernst Brandenburg, winner of the Pour le Mérite as a bomber commander during the war, was perfectly willing to use German civil aviation as a vehicle for the reconstruction of the German air force.[58]

The Allies' attempt to destroy German military aviation aided its survival at the expense of German civil aeronautics. The German Defense Ministry's secret rearmament project in Russia enabled it to evade the total ban on military aviation, while the restrictions on commercial aviation forced the few remaining German aircraft firms back into the clutches of the army if they desired contracts. Junkers, for example, after constant French harassment forced him to suspend the operations of his airmail line late in October 1921, agreed to construct an aircraft and aero engine plant in Russia for the army. In 1922–23 the army approached Albatros, Heinkel, and the new Arado Company for the Russian venture, and though their deficiencies forced it to rely temporarily on Anthony Fokker in Holland, the future connection was established. The Allied bans restored the symbiotic relationship between the military and industry, which had disintegrated in the crisis of early 1919, at a much more rapid rate than might have occurred had they left German civil aeronautics alone to prosper in peace. The restrictions had severely crippled the German aircraft industry and the air arm, but the few firms that survived and the new ones that arose in the 1920s were invariably and indissolubly linked to the German Army in the clandestine rearmament of the Reich.

CHAPTER 8

The Inept Ally:
Austro-Hungarian Aviation, 1914–19

THE STORY of wartime Austro-Hungarian aviation is one of inadequacy and dependence upon Germany. At the declaration of war the army could muster thirteen flying companies with forty-eight frontline and twenty-seven training planes; the navy, five frontline and seventeen training craft. From the very beginning of the conflict, limited production facilities severely restricted the size of the Austro-Hungarian air service. At mobilization the entire aircraft industry employed only 218 workers, of which 150 worked at the Lohner factory. The new Lloyd factory in Budapest and the recently founded branches of German factories, the Aviatik and Albatros works, were little better than workshops. The industry's inability to replace aircraft losses in the first days of the war necessitated the continued procurement of aircraft from Germany despite German complaints that Austro-Hungarian orders disrupted supplies to their units.[1]

When German supplies of forty-eight craft from August to December did not suffice to meet frontline demands, Col. Emil Uzelac, the army's aviation commander, raised his estimate of the requisite minimum domestic production from forty-six to sixty. Such production levels were not remotely possible. Although the labor force of the Austro-Hungarian industry quadrupled to 824 by the end of the year, it produced only sixty-four aircraft from August through December. Monthly deliveries actually declined from twenty-four to seven planes because of the transition to new types. In light of these figures, the assessment of Austrian aviation historian Col. Erich Kahlen that "it was extremely difficult to raise monthly production to forty-six planes by the end of 1914" displays

167

a mastery of the art of understatement.[2] Uzelac presumed continued reliance on Germany and forecast that the industry would attain full capacity at the earliest in June 1915.

The army aviation authorities took measures to bolster the air arm, yet their very actions often impeded increases in production and deliveries. Uzelac wisely ordered the expansion of the airship unit's small installation at Fischamend into an aviation arsenal. On the other hand, the airship unit had placed contracts for the development of twin-engine G-planes with domestic firms in August 1914 and insisted upon pursuing the matter despite the industry's total inability to develop such a sophisticated aircraft. By ignoring the necessity of coordinating frontline demands with industrial capability, the unit wasted valuable industrial effort on a doomed venture. The War Ministry's refusal to authorize the training of sufficient test pilots for fear of creating a postwar surfeit of pilots delayed acceptance of the few aircraft produced. Finally, the lack of a system of prepayment until the middle of 1915 undoubtedly hindered the firms' procurement of raw materials. It is little wonder that the official history of the Austro-Hungarian army in World War I mentions the

The Organization of
Austro-Hungarian Military Aviation, August 1914

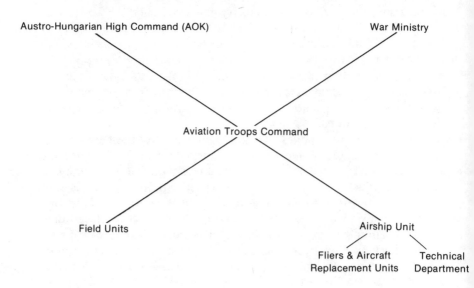

SOURCE: *Das Luftfahrwesen*, p. 31, fol. no. 19a, LA, OK.

aviation troops in 1914 only once, and then to observe their embryonic state. The army air arm and the aircraft industry had failed to meet even minimal expectations.[3]

During the first five months of 1915, the limitations of the Austro-Hungarian aircraft industry, despite growth, encouraged more reliance on Germany. Although arms magnate Baron Karl von Skoda founded the Austrian Aircraft Company (Österreichische Flugzeugfabrik, or Öffag) in Wiener-Neustadt early in 1915, the industry, laboring under delays in material procurement and rising material prices and wages, never managed to deliver more than 29 airplanes monthly. In June a substantial increase in aircraft prices of 7,500 crowns, to 19,500 crowns per plane helped the firms to cover their costs but did little to affect the rate of production. Unfortunately for the air service, the indispensable shipments of craft from Germany arrived erratically, and German units in the field on the southeastern front seldom allowed direct acquisition of their planes. From August 1914 to April 1915, only half of the 139 aircraft and 185 motors ordered from Germany arrived. German factories refused to sell their blueprints to Austrian firms, although they did train small numbers of Austro-Hungarian aircraft workers after January 1915. In May Colonel Uzelac went to Germany himself in order to procure aircraft from Camillo Castiglioni's Hansa-Brandenburg factory, which the German Army had released for German naval and Austro-Hungarian production. After severe prewar difficulties with monopoly in the aircraft industry, the Austrian authorities might have been concerned that Castiglioni had substantial investment in the Austrian Albatros works in Vienna and in the Hungarian Aircraft Factory (Ufag), a new firm in Budapest. If they were disturbed, they said nothing, silenced by their desperation to procure any capable warplanes.[4]

From July through November 1915 the army ordered 156 craft at a total cost of over 4 million marks from Brandenburg, which delivered punctually, sending 148 planes by the end of the year. In December the Austrian aviation command acknowledged its dependence upon Brandenburg for modern, fast planes.[5] Brandenburg used this leverage to dictate comparatively high prices to the Austro-Hungarian Army, which had no choice but to pay them, because insufficient domestic production jeopardized not only the outfitting of new companies but also the continued supply of units already in the field. Only once, in September, did domestic firms deliver more than 46 airplanes, and they never approached the goal of 60 set late in 1914. There were months in which Hansa-Brandenburg delivered more planes than the entire Austro-

Hungarian industry, a circumstance that the monarchy's air service could ill afford in the face of a rapidly expanding air war.

Italy's declaration of war against the empire on 23 May 1915 forced the aviation troops to redirect their major effort to the southwestern front. The air service consequently faced opposition on three fronts with a production base inadequate for one. The service did enjoy the continued support of the High Command (Armeeoberkommando, or AOK), which proclaimed on 2 June the "extraordinary importance" of military aviation for the course of the war.[6] It then gave Uzelac staff officers of aviation in the field. Yet the crucial issue was whether this favorable disposition would affect priorities in the allocation of labor and material. The air service and aviation industry, relegated to secondary status behind artillery and motor vehicles, had not been able to attract sufficient skilled workers, engineers, or officers with technical training. Tired of "surreptitious dealings" and "daily begging" to obtain the factors of production, the aviation command requested the formation of a central industrial agency in the War Ministry to assist its acquisition of skilled manpower and materials.[7] The request was ignored.

The Italian war further compounded the army's difficulties in aviation by bringing the naval air arm into the conflict, thereby putting more pressure on Austria-Hungary's limited resources. During the summer of 1915 the army and navy sought unsuccessfully to set procurement norms for aircraft and motors. Both services considered the other's claims disruptive and unjustified, particularly the army, which lay claim to all motor production through August 1916 in order to form fifteen new flight companies totaling 180 planes. The navy desired to expand to a force of 300 craft by procuring 163 aircraft as rapidly as possible.[8]

To resolve the dispute the High Command appointed a committee of representatives from the General Staff, War Ministry, the naval section in the War Ministry, and the aviation troops command to establish guidelines for aircraft procurement. On 22 January the committee established the following rules for the distribution of planes: the navy could procure from Lohner, Albatros, Öffag, and Ufag, although it could obtain no more than one-third of its monthly quota from any single factory (at Albatros this was reduced to one-sixth); the army could rely upon Aviatik, Lloyd, the Wiener Karrosserie Fabrik (WKF), the Fokker factory in Germany, and three other insignificant firms. Most critically, the army obtained the rights to the entire production of Hansa-Brandenburg, from which the navy could buy only 6 airplanes. The navy would be allowed to procure a total of 264 airplanes from February 1916 through January 1917 at a monthly rate increasing from 16 to 31 planes.[9]

These norms presumed a tremendous increase in production during 1916 over the 467 airplanes delivered in 1915, of which 186 had come from Germany. These numbers had sufficed to replace losses and to equip a total of eighteen flight companies, a flight officers training school, and eight replacement companies by the end of 1915. The army had fallen twenty-two companies short of a prewar timetable set in January 1914 by chief of the General Staff Franz Conrad von Hötzendorff, who had planned to have forty flight companies by early 1916.[10]

There was little likelihood, however, that the industry would perform much better in 1916. Even the best factories labored under severe difficulties. Early in 1916 Lohner's production was disrupted by delays in expanding its plant and securing raw materials and workers. Ufag's plant was described as "limited, poorly utilized, and lacking in any systematic process." Workmanship was quite good, but the plant was overcrowded and difficult to monitor, the assembly was unsystematic, and a procurement office was lacking.[11]

A shortage of skilled labor was one of the most severe impediments to production. In January 1916, just when the factories were submitting lists of sorely needed skills, the War Ministry's personnel department was preparing to induct exempted personnel born in the years 1878–97. After remonstrations from the industry and the aviation department that this "catastrophic" measure would cause the industry "to collapse like a house of cards" from the loss of its most important technicians and foremen, the War Ministry allowed the industry to retain its exempted personnel. In Budapest the navy secured workers for Ufag from the Hungarian Ministry of Defense just in case the induction became a reality. The army secured the assignment of 200 eighteen-year-old inductees in April and 613 skilled workers in June to the industry, and it inaugurated long-range training courses for youth fourteen to seventeen years of age. Yet the shortage of skilled labor persisted, and in answer to requests for 5,125 skilled workers in 1916, the aviation department received only 2,857. Furthermore, availability, not appropriateness, determined the distribution of skilled labor to the industry, as the personnel department sent primarily woodworkers, not the metalworkers that the industry sorely needed.[12]

These problems notwithstanding, the Austro-Hungarian aircraft industry produced 807 aircraft in 1916. While not the 1,000 planes credited to it by the official history, this represented a substantial improvement over the 281 aircraft produced in 1915. The individual firms had also grown substantially, as the following table shows:

The Austro-Hungarian Aircraft Industry[13]

Firm	Labor Force	
	August 1914	January 1917
Albatros	16	1,177
Aviatik	36	903
Lloyd	16	544
Lohner	150	342
Mag	——	74
Öffag	——	804
Thöne & Fiala	——	93
Ufag	——	1,036
WKF	——	372
Hansa-Brandenburg (Germany)	——	638
Total	218	5,983

This growth did not suffice to keep pace with the escalation of the air war in 1916, so the expansion of the army air arm was limited to nineteen flight companies (numbers 19–37) ar d seven fighter companies. The empire's pilots, such as aces Capt. Godwin Brumowski and Sgt. Julius Arigi of the army and Lt. Gottfried Banfield of the navy, acquitted themselves well against increasing odds, but Austria-Hungary could maintain only a limited aerial presence.

In order to compensate for these deficiencies, Lt. Franz Reichelt went to Berlin in April 1916 to establish and command aircraft acceptance organs in the office of the AOK's plenipotentiary. Yet as the army formalized its aircraft procurement bureaucracy in Germany, the German armed forces' increasing demand for airplanes reduced its exports to Austria-Hungary to ninety-five craft in 1916. Camillo Castiglioni's connection to Germany consequently became more important than official military channels, as his three companies—the German parent firm Hansa-Brandenburg and its license producers Austrian Albatros and Ufag—became the primary channel for the flow of German technology to Austria-Hungary.

After the spring of 1916, the Austro-Hungarian air arm relied primarily on the Castiglioni conglomerate. The Brandenburg C1 was the army's standard reconnaissance plane from the spring of 1916 until the end of the war. The D1 was the mainstay of the fighter force from the fall of 1916 until the middle of 1917, despite the plane's early reputation as a *Sarg*, or coffin. The navy relied on the Brandenburg CC flying boat fighter and the large bomber-reconnaissance K-boat in 1916 and 1917. As alternatives to the Brandenburg craft, the navy had only a few Lohner L-boats; the army, Lloyd and Aviatik reconnaissance and fighter planes.

The conglomerate attempted to capitalize upon this dependence with requests for higher prices. In order to recover losses of almost 250,000 crowns suffered in the first half of 1916, Ufag requested and received a substantial price increase from 38,000 to 60,000 crowns per flying boat from the navy in July 1916. When Ufag sacrificed aircraft safety in its haste to produce the more expensive boats, the navy, hard-pressed to maintain its frontline strength, had no choice but to accept the craft. When approached by Albatros, the army reacted differently. Albatros cited dramatic increases in material prices, the rapid introduction of new types, and excessive tax rates as justification for its request. The army replied with a minuscule raise to a standard price of 28,740 crowns per plane, which allowed a profit of 900 crowns per plane based on an annual fabrication of three hundred planes.[14] In fact, profits would be nonexistent, since no Austrian factory produced three hundred planes a year.

The services' disparate responses to these requests for higher prices exacerbated the interservice rivalry, as Brandenburg attempted to cancel its army contracts to tend to the more lucrative naval offers. After lengthy disputes, the AOK merely confirmed its adherence to the 1916 norms, according to which the army claimed all of Brandenburg's production and allowed the navy only a few prototypes from the company. Ironically, the army's victory was purely academic, because in 1917 and 1918 the German Navy monopolized Brandenburg's capacity, forcing the Austro-Hungarian armed forces to rely entirely on Ufag and Albatros. Furthermore, the Hindenburg Program prohibited the previous system of exporting aircraft frames, and the Prussian military authorities were more reluctant to grant export permits for aircraft materials and plant machinery.[15] Reduced to their own limited resources, the Austro-Hungarian aviation forces were doomed to impotence; their interservice conflicts over materiel, to futility.

In 1917 pressure for price increases continued to agitate the industry's relationship with the armed forces. Although the army raised its prices in February to thirty-two thousand crowns for single-seaters and thirty-three thousand crowns for two-seaters, some firms requested further raises one month later. By June 1917 the factories were insistent, as they labored under sizable pay raises to placate an increasingly strident

labor force and regulations providing for more costly health insurance
and for wage payments to workers in case of legitimate absences or
unavoidable work stoppages. The aviation arsenal admitted that the costs
of aircraft production exceeded the army's prices, and a special military
price commission confirmed the necessity of a price increase. Yet the War
Ministry courted disaster by adhering to current prices, while the naval
section, in a reversal of its previous price policies, refused the Brandenburg conglomerate price increases in October and December 1917. Apparently the War Ministry was not yet assured of sufficient funds to cover
further raises.[16]

Such severe stringency was detrimental to aircraft production. As the
cost-of-production factors climbed, the allowance of little or no profit
seriously squeezed the aircraft factories, not only impeding wartime
production but also robbing the industry of the accumulation of reserves
necessary for postwar survival. Profit per plane in Austria-Hungary,
where serial deliveries were small and production problems great, needed
to exceed that in Germany, but it did not. Judicious price increments
might have served the armed forces as levers to encourage more efficient
production, but, as the navy's earlier experience with Ufag had indicated,
the existence of Castiglioni's near monopoly of aircraft production in
Austria-Hungary effectively deprived the armed forces of the price
weapon.

The army's policies generally did little to solve production problems.
During the summer of 1917 the deficient organization of exemptions
compounded the aircraft factories' difficulties. There was no central
agency to distribute workers to industry, and the labor collection offices
were directed by businessmen who ignored the special needs of the
aircraft industry. Consequently, precision lathe hands often performed
large-scale work in metal munitions factories, while the aviation industry
had to use large-scale lathe hands to perform the precision work of
turning motor cylinders. Skilled furniture makers and carpenters passed
their time in frontline companies "making ingenious war mementos to
amuse themselves," while the aircraft industry had to utilize ordinary
carpenters for extremely intricate work. Yet the aviation command's
repeated pleas for the creation of a central labor exchange to facilitate the
more judicious allocation of skilled labor were still ignored.[17]

On 10 August an exasperated and desperate aviation command
requested the War Ministry's permission to suspend the directors of
negligent firms and replace them with military officers and plant crews of

nineteen to thirty soldiers to frighten the industry to better efforts. The
War Ministry demurred on legal grounds: it could completely militarize
the factories, but it could not take such halfway measures.[18] The aviation
command could threaten the firms with total militarization, but the
ministry wisely shied away from such drastic measures, which would
certainly have harmed production.

In September 1917 the High Command adopted a measure that was
intended to unify the organization of the air force under its control and
improve the coordination between aircraft procurement and the demands
of the front. It established a General Inspectorate to assume control of
aviation affairs in the rear from the War Ministry. In Germany the High
Command had attempted to circumvent the War Ministry in aviation by
granting the air force a procurement bureaucracy independent of the War
Ministry. Yet the Austro-Hungarian method of superimposing the new
agency on top of the existing hierarchy was more comparable to the
German High Command's superimposition of the War Office on the War
Ministry in the Hindenburg Program. The results were also similar, as the
General Inspectorate merely complicated command in aviation.[19]

In light of such rampant military and industrial inefficiency, it comes
as no surprise that monthly aircraft deliveries were erratic. After a low
point of 37 aircraft in January, deliveries rose to 135 in May, only to
plummet to 67 in June because of strikes and shortages. They attained a
maximum for the year of 211 in August, then gradually declined to 142 in
November—and stopped altogether in December because of severe
winter shortages![20]

The armed services' plans for expansion in 1918 reflected the shift-
ing fortunes of production. In July the army and navy were optimistic.
The navy still sought to raise its force to three hundred planes, but now
requested fifty planes monthly to compensate for higher attrition. The
army's aviation arsenal was determined to strive for the consistent production of four hundred aircraft monthly.[21]

Franz Reichelt, the aviation representative in Berlin, used the conditions in Germany as a basis to estimate the industry's labor requirements. Skilled workers in Austria-Hungary were less numerous, specialized, and qualified than in Germany, so that the same task required
25–30 percent more workers. Calculating that the industry required 34
workers to produce one plane per month, Reichelt concluded that the
aircraft industry needed a total of 13,600 workers to produce 400
airplanes a month and the motor industry an additional 14,800 workers to

raise its production from 254 to 600 monthly.[22] Yet the aviation department had obtained only 2,900 workers in 1916 and 4,529 more in 1917 as of October.[23]

The technological prerequisites for such an expansion were also lacking. Although the small number of academically trained engineers in the Austro-Hungarian industry probably made the German practice of technical reports unnecessary, the arsenal might have shared the proceedings of its research institute with the firms. Of course, one of its best scientists, Theodor von Karman, was preoccupied with the development of helicopters rather than warplanes. In any case, Austrian factories were reluctant to exchange information and did not entrust their research to the aeromechanical laboratory at the state technical school in Vienna, because its director, Professor Richard Knoller, had designed a mediocre reconnaissance plane and was consequently regarded as a competitor. The most beneficial arrangement would have been the dissemination of the German technical reports in Austria, but German firms adamantly refused.[24]

Undaunted, the aviation agencies, presuming the monthly production of 400 planes, continued their plans in the fall to double their units to a total of ninety-five companies of 410 reconnaissance and 566 fighter aircraft. Yet the AOK was not satisfied. Not only did it desire the monthly production of 750 planes and 1,000 motors in 1918, it also insisted on having twin-engined G-planes and armored infantry (J) planes. It did not propose where to obtain the craft. The Austro-Hungarian industry could not produce them, and the hard-pressed German industry would not. The aviation arsenal, aware of the insurmountable difficulties yet reluctant to contradict the High Command, concluded through some unknown process of reasoning that the numbers could be achieved.[25]

The chimerical nature of these plans defies belief. The arsenal postulated a total of 14,375 skilled workers to produce 750 airplanes monthly, only 1,000 more than Reichelt had judged necessary to manufacture 400. Where it would secure the workers remained a mystery. Furthermore, plans to manufacture so many craft while absorbing the potentially disastrous effects of a looming coal shortage were patently absurd. Production did not suffice to attain the goal of sixty-eight flight companies and three G-plane squadrons by the end of 1917. There were sixty-six flight companies and one G-plane squadron, but no company had more than 60 percent of its designated aircraft or pilot complement. The intensifying air war on the southwestern front during the tenth through twelfth battles of the Isonzo (May–November 1917) occasioned the fame of Austrian aces like Frank Linke-Crawford and Benno Fiala von Fernbrugg, but consumed more materiel and thus made it even more difficult for the industry to keep abreast of frontline demands.

Ultimately, the disastrous effects of the winter coal shortage in December brought the arsenal to its senses. Pressured from above, buoyed by the production increases during the summer, it had lost perspective. By 11 December, however, the arsenal calculated that under the most favorable circumstances deliveries from December 1917 through April 1918 would total only 1,040 planes with none in December. It expected only 500–800 aircraft because of problems in motor production and in the installation of machine guns on the planes.[26] Conceding that its reach had far exceeded its grasp, the arsenal grimly prepared to face the final year of the war.

From January through March 1918 the Austro-Hungarian aircraft industry, crippled by coal and transport shortages, inadequate aircraft prices, and the induction of skilled workers, delivered 506 aircraft.

On 6 January the arsenal complained to the General Inspectorate that no measures had been taken to assure coal deliveries to the factories. During the previous winter the Ministry of Public Works had ignored the factories' repeated requests for coal, and the government had done nothing about the shortage of rolling stock, which had been evident as early as the fall of 1915. After receiving no coal for months, the Lohner plant closed at the beginning of January. Phönix, the successor to the Albatros company, was rotating workers around ovens to keep them warm, but they would not stand for that much longer. Öffag and Ufag would also have to close down soon. Even the arsenal's workshop at Fischamend had had no electric current since the middle of December 1917. The arsenal attributed the crisis to "lazy" civilian officials, whom it cursed as "worse than middle-level aircraft factory workers." On 23 January the General Inspectorate termed the coal and transportation situations "insupportable," as the shipment of merely two hundred cars ot coal daily to the factories—the minimum necessary to maintain the current inadequate levels of production—was impossible. More than a month later, on 2 March, the AOK assured the inspectorate that it recognized the importance of aviation and would place the aircraft industry on the priority lists for coal.[27] Considering the inefficacy of the AOK's recognition of the importance of aviation and promises of full support to the industry the previous year, the measure was tardy and paltry, to say the least. Only the arrival of warmer spring weather would alleviate the effects of the coal shortage.

To compound the air arm's difficulties, the full effect of the War Ministry's refusal to increase prices was felt simultaneously. On 18 February the arsenal warned that a complete cessation of aircraft production was imminent unless prices were raised immediately to forty thousand crowns for single-seaters and forty-two thousand crowns for two-seaters. The failure to obtain higher prices had seriously impaired the manufacturers' ability to satisfy their increasingly strident workers. When Ufag's workers struck in February, the firm had few options at hand. The severe shortage of trained workers prevented firing them, and a lockout would only further disrupt production and possibly spread the wage movement to other factories in Budapest. The factory was forced to grant a 50–75 percent wage increase for special work, although it did manage to introduce the piecework wage system for all serial production.[28]

Shortly afterward, however, Ufag's trade association, the Budapest machine factories, requested release from the conditions of the war service law, the removal of military directors and commandeered soldiers from the factories, and the elimination of government labor complaint commissions. In the manufacturers' opinion, the military and the commissions had given labor a disproportionate advantage over them, resulting in the "extraordinary growth" of the labor unions. This "first sign of a new kind of strike . . . a strike of capital," convinced the arsenal that the industry's complaints were justified, that the factory directors were caught between escalating material prices and labor demands on the one hand, and the War Ministry's intransigence about aircraft prices on the other. If the army was going to capitulate to the workers' wage demands, the arsenal reasoned, then it should acknowledge justified requests for higher prices.[29] In March the War Ministry was able to raise the prices of aircraft to forty-four and forty-five thousand crowns, and there is no further record of so-called capital strikes in the aircraft industry.

Finally, the industry lost valuable labor in a general induction of men born in the years 1894–99 that was announced in January. Late in April the AOK promised not to weaken the industry by repeated inductions of skilled labor, an assurance which was itself proof of the factories' repeated losses of skilled manpower. The AOK, robbing Peter to pay Paul, was using workers taken from the industry to staff its air units.[30]

In light of such precarious circumstances, the Austro-Hungarian aviation agencies found their excessive dependence upon Camillo Castiglioni increasingly onerous and dangerous. The navy paid dearly for its complete reliance on his firms. Despite warnings from the head of the naval section in the War Ministry, the navy had based its entire construction program for the year on untested and in part undetermined aircraft types from Castiglioni. His companies consequently received contracts "of an unnaturally significant quantity and correspondingly high value": Brandenburg obtained 7.9 million marks of contracts; Ufag, 7.8 million crowns; Phönix, 3.5 million crowns; and BMW in Germany, which Castiglioni acquired in 1918, 10.3 million crowns in advance. After the failure of such ventures as a new 350-horsepower flying boat, the construction program was a shambles, and the navy was left with aircraft that "in no way met the stated demands." On a visit in May 1918 a German naval inspection team attributed the Austrian navy's inferior equipment to the absence of competition, and in June the navy blamed Castiglioni for its "critical shortage of suitable and capable airplanes."[31]

The army was fortunate to have alternative airplanes such as Öffag's version of the German Albatros D3 fighter and the Aviatik Berg aircraft. On 2 March, however, rumors reached it of a plan to unite all Austro-Hungarian aircraft companies in a monopoly. The prince of Bourbon and Parma was allegedly to be the president of the concern, but the AOK wanted to know who was behind the venture. Without hesitation, the agitated aviation agencies labeled Castiglioni the culprit. He already controlled more than three-fourths of Austro-Hungarian aircraft production, the Öffag and Lloyd companies excluded, and some businessmen believed that he had "authoritative influence" over the arsenal. The aviation command suggested three measures to prevent his complete monopolization of aircraft production: the use of "all legally and morally permissible means" to hinder his further subordination of aircraft factories and, if possible, to draw his own firms from his grasp; second, the promotion of Skoda's Öffag works; and finally, increases in the productivity of the military aircraft works at Fischamend. The command concluded shrilly:

> Castiglioni must be immediately inducted and sent to a service post, for example, with the eastern corps in Palestine, that hinders any commercial transactions with the rear. Though presently exempted from the navy, he is liable to service. Exemptions are supposed to be for people whose service in plants promotes the army's acquisition of war materiel. . . . Castiglioni's exemption is actually injurious.[32]

Despite the considerable ire of the aviation command, there was not the remotest possibility that Castiglioni, twice decorated for his services to the empire, would be inducted. A dramatic expansion of the arsenal's workshops at Fischamend was also unlikely, as industrialists believed that

Fischamend's well-equipped and supplied operations already interfered with the expansion of the private factories. The command resolved to promote Öffag as a counterweight to Castiglioni's firms when the opportunity arose.

Yet the mere creation of such an opportunity depended entirely upon the army's ability to obtain prototypes of competitive aircraft from Germany. It consequently turned to Germany to procure models and materials through the aviation (L, or Luftfahrt) contingent, an exchange of materials, materiel, and designs which had been established on a semiannual basis early in 1917. The German Army used the contingent to prevent Austro-Hungarian orders from disrupting its mobilization, while the Austro-Hungarian Army, by ordering through German procurement agencies, obtained the same prices and faster acceptance of export permits. The great bulk of the exchanges occurred from Germany to Austria-Hungary, as the latter sought to obtain all types of aircraft from Germany.[33]

The AOK's highest priority in 1918 was the procurement of G-planes. The arsenal suggested Ufag's licensed production of Friedrichshafen twin-engined craft, but the aviation command selected Öffag in order to thwart Castiglioni's attempts to "limit . . . the Austro-Hungarian Army's freedom of disposition of its contracts." After May 1918 the aviation command planned to procure ten to fifteen planes monthly from Friedrichshafen through the L contingent until Öffag began production. The arsenal presumed from the outset that it would take at least eight months, until January 1919, to produce the plane domestically. All G-plane contracts were canceled on 8 November 1918.[34]

If G-plane manufacture would have proved difficult in Austria-Hungary, the production of metal airplanes was impossible because of shortages of metals and metalworkers. Nevertheless, the AOK showed a fervent interest in armored infantry planes and all-metal aircraft during 1918. At the end of 1917 the War Ministry had undertaken to procure a few Albatros or AEG armored J-planes as models, but had dismissed the all-metal Junkers craft as entirely too difficult. Consequently, when the AOK insisted on the Junkers in June 1918, the War Ministry waited until September to order aluminum Junkers J-planes and C-planes from Berlin. These orders were canceled on 31 December 1918. The AOK's consideration of the Junkers planes was part of a wider interest in producing all-metal airplanes in Austria in 1918. In April the Zeppelin company inquired whether the Austrian military would support its construction of a metal airplane factory at Lochau, near Bregenz, Austria. Although the aviation command condemned the enterprise as impossible, negotiations continued with Zeppelin in Berlin during the summer, goaded by the navy's warnings that Castiglioni had obtained a license to produce Junkers metal planes through his connections with Anthony Fokker, Junkers's business partner. In the end, neither enterprise materialized.[35]

Other attempts to secure German aircraft failed. Despite the inability to manufacture or import steel tubing, the AOK was determined to have the Fokker D7 license produced in order to standardize production on one superior fighter plane. It rejected the Pfalz D12, though the excellent Pfalz was built primarily of wood and was thus far more suitable than the Fokker for production in Austria-Hungary. Early in the fall of 1918, the AOK, still adamant about the D7, recommended an attempt to produce the Fokker entirely out of wood.[36] Of course, the entire matter was academic by then.

The confusion within the Austro-Hungarian military over these license procurement ventures was evident. The AOK, judging solely from the perspective of the front, pressed for planes that were beyond the capacity of the domestic aircraft industry to produce even under license. The aviation command, aware of the realities and limitations of production through its direct contact with the arsenal, realized from the beginning that some of these ventures were impossible. The General Inspectorate usually agreed with the aviation command's prognoses, while the War Ministry acted to delay unpromising ventures until they were no longer feasible. While these agencies could not dissuade the AOK from its projects, their half-hearted execution of its unrealistic plans ensured that they wasted little effort on them.

Confusion reigned even in purely domestic procurement projects. Aircraft consistently failed to meet expectations. Orders of new aircraft were often insufficient for tests. Contracts on standard craft were occasionally canceled in anticipation of the production of untested craft, the subsequent failure of which condemned the service to reliance on obsolescent planes. If the new plane was successful, the service invariably had difficulty choosing which older types to phase out in order to avoid interrupting production at too many plants. After so many failures of projected airplanes, the arsenal had actually become reluctant to push firms to produce new types because of the financial losses inherent in the transition to new planes. In August 1918 it did resolve to encourage the companies, even at the expense of their profits, to proceed energetically

The Organization of
Austro-Hungarian Military Aviation, October 1918

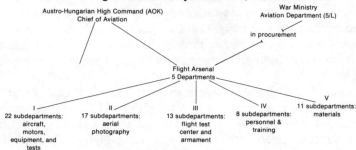

SOURCE: *Das Luftfahrwesen*, p. 30, fol. no. 19a, LA, OK.

with the testing and production of better aircraft.[37] But it was too late, for they could not escape their present circumstances quickly. For example, the long-serving Berg fighter had lost the confidence of its pilots by August, but it could only be phased out gradually in order to ensure the continuation of deliveries. Furthermore, its intended replacement, a new Berg fighter and the wood Fokker D7, were still on the drawing boards. Austro-Hungarian service pilots were condemned to fight in obsolete craft for the rest of the war.

The High Command's tendency to push reliance on Germany to unrealistic extremes not only increased confusion in procurement but also resentment toward Germany. The reports of the Austrian plenipotentiary in Berlin on German innovations had often been disparaged by Austrian agencies, who insisted that they had found "something better." The "something better" invariably turned out to be a dismal failure.[38] Now, in August 1918, aircraft designer Julius von Berg protested the acquisition of licenses for German planes which he considered inferior to Austrian types, because it would crush Austrian creativity and reduce domestic companies to mere branches of the German industry. Instead of "supporting" and "trusting" the Austrian industry, the army was sending the money it needed to Germany and depressing exchange rates and state finances in the process.[39] The memorandum struck a responsive chord at the arsenal, yet in fact Berg was railing against a long standing fait accompli. Since 1914 the domestic industry had been nothing more than an adjunct to German firms, and if the reliance on Germany did stifle and dishearten trained Austrian engineers, there were too few of them to matter.

During the spring and summer of 1918 the army's aviation agencies became so desperate for airplanes that they even attempted to procure aircraft from Russia. After the Treaty of Brest Litovsk a purchasing commission from the arsenal arranged for the procurement of nearly four hundred aircraft and motors from the Anatra Works of Odessa in the Ukraine. Yet after delivering some material and training aircraft, the Anatra Works became another mirage. It could neither control its workers nor obtain raw materials.[40]

In the midst of these mishaps, the AOK acknowledged in June the failure to achieve its expansion goals for the first half of the year. It had intended to have one hundred companies with 1,080 planes; it had only seventy-seven companies with 684 combat planes, having received only 627 planes from March through May 1918. Late in August the General Inspectorate attributed the failure to strikes, labor and transportation shortages, and particularly the failure of the civilian authorities to supply the factories with coal. They were incurring heavy losses from an increasingly superior enemy. Aircraft production and the air arm had to be expanded, even at the expense of other forces.[41]

Such exhortations were worthless, as the flight companies fought at only 50–60 percent of their strength during the summer. The collapse of the Piave offensive in June, in which the aviation forces participated effectively, dashed any lingering Austrian hopes for a successful prosecution of the war.

Nevertheless, the aviation agencies began as usual to prepare for further expansion. During July and August an arsenal commission visited all the factories to estimate their potential for expansion. To raise production to 460 aircraft per month, the commission hoped to increase the labor force of the industry by 3,000 to 10,300 workers and to double coal supplies to two thousand tons monthly. Yet it was dismayed by the actual conditions in the factories. It saw empty space and unused plant caused by shortages. Labor was increasingly unreliable, as outbreaks of unruliness and "hoarding expeditions" disrupted production. At Fischamend, absences, vacations, and desertions had depleted the work force by one-third, and those soldiers left were too undernourished to perform heavy work.[42]

After four years of war, Austria-Hungary was clearly coming to the end of her resources, both human and material. This reality was reflected in the final measures and plans undertaken during the fall of 1918. In the middle of September the AOK assumed direction of all front and rear aviation agencies in an attempt to concentrate the organization of aviation at the highest possible level and eliminate the previous divisions of competence among the AOK, War Ministry, General Inspectorate, and the aviation command. The war ministry's sphere would be limited to the direction of economic, administrative, and technical matters, and it would conduct independently the distribution of material and equipment to the industry. The War Ministry and the AOK, which had replaced the General Inspectorate with its own chief of aviation, would determine procurement programs together. The arsenal would continue to monitor procurement, production, and repairs. The General Inspectorate's disappearance resulted from its failure to unify aviation, so the AOK assumed the task. But it was too late to make any difference. On 25 September, at the last recorded conference to plan the future of aviation, all the Austro-Hungarian agencies acknowledged that the aviation industry would receive neither the coal nor the manpower it so desperately needed.[43]

The air service, hard-pressed, struggled on. The industry had acquired some fifteen hundred workers since the middle of 1917 and maintained its production from June through October, delivering 183, 220, 217, 202, and 398 aircraft. Its total deliveries for the ten months of 1918 were 1,989 planes, which constituted an increase of one-third over 1917. Yet this effort barely kept pace with attrition during the last year of the war. The air service failed to expand beyond some 600–700 combat planes.[44] Austro-Hungarian aviators, outnumbered, their aircraft outclassed, paid for the inadequacy and ineptitude with their lives. Fortunately for them, the war ended on 4 November 1918.

The postwar contraction in Austro-Hungarian aviation was disastrous. With the dissolution of the monarchy, the new national governments assumed military authority within their borders and consequently responsibility for all unpaid and undelivered contracts. They were generally unresponsive to the needs of the firms. The Austrian Aero-Club, whose members included Uzelac and Castiglioni, met with the demobilization commissar in January 1919 to establish guidelines for the transition to peace. The government asked the factories to continue work without profit in order to assure their workers of wages for a minimum of six months. Current aircraft contracts would have to be completed for civil aviation. As of March 1919 the industry's attempts to sponsor commercial aviation failed, and so it ceased to exist. Phönix became a lumber company, Aviatik an oven factory, and WKF returned to chassis production. In Hungary Bela Kun's communist government nationalized all the aircraft factories, which did not survive his regime.[45] The empire's most famous aviation industrialist, Camillo Castiglioni, became an Italian citizen but continued his business activities in Central Europe. During the postwar inflation he acquired and lost a financial empire. He died of bronchial pneumonia in Rome on 24 December 1957 at the age of seventy-six.

Industrial and military inefficiency and the consequent necessity of reliance on Germany were the three most critical factors determining the evolution of Austro-Hungarian military aviation. The industry, saddled with high taxes, inadequate administration, and shortages of materials, trained engineers, and workers, was hard-pressed to expand from its small base during wartime. Shortages of metal and metalworkers were particularly crippling. The workmanship of Austro-Hungarian wood-workers compared favorably with that of the Germans, but the former frequently labored with inadequate and worn equipment.

The confusion within the military establishment impeded its coherent assistance to the fledgling industry. The inept execution of labor exemptions, the stringent price restrictions, and the uncoordinated price policies of the army and navy—all were symptomatic of the general military disarray. The German air force had its own bureaucratic problems, but they were never as severe, primarily because of the superior organization of the German Army and because the army's control of aviation procurement effectively restricted interservice conflicts. Also, the German Army clearly accorded to the aviation industry a much higher priority than did its ally.

Finally, while German assistance was indispensable to the Austro-Hungarian air arm, the desire to emulate, even to outdo, German achievements compounded the latter's problems. In the Hindenburg and America programs, the German air force sought to double its production under difficult circumstances. The Austrian agencies, not content to contemplate merely doubling production, determined to quintuple it under worse conditions, as if to prove that they could excel their overbearing ally in one area. Such ambitions were pathetic, especially since they could not be realized without heavy reliance on the German nemesis. Consequently, intensifying wartime pressures merely served to underscore the inadequacies of the military establishment and the aircraft industry in Austria-Hungary.

Conclusion

DURING WORLD WAR I the airplane developed from a novelty to a major weapon of war. In the Armageddon of static trench warfare on the western front and Sisyphean struggles in the east, the airplane played an increasingly important role, particularly on the critical western front. By 1915 it was the primary implement of reconnaissance and artillery observation and an occasional vehicle for bombing attacks. Attempts to deny opposing aircraft access to the air space over and behind one's lines led to individual aerial combats in 1915, which erupted during the great battles of 1916 into encounters between opposing formations. Aerial supremacy became a major goal of the opposing armies, and its attainment and maintenance required a speedier technological evolution and industrial expansion than had ever before been necessary or possible in warfare.

In the last two years of the war the plane was a staple in the arsenals of the belligerents. Over the North Sea and the Channel German and English naval aircraft contested the air space; on the southwestern front Austro-Hungarian craft confronted the Italian air arm over land and the Adriatic Sea; on the eastern front and over far-flung battlefields of the war, the airplane served usefully. On the western front, decisions to increase production in 1916 ensured heightened struggles for aerial superiority in 1917 and 1918. The last of the fabled individualistic aces fell in 1917, relics of a transitional era before the mass production of warplanes.

Massed formations of airplanes now became commonplace, as indicated by the much publicized German fighter circuses and battle wings *(Schlachtgeschwadern)* of light attack fighters in 1917. The battle units, which often attacked in waves from altitudes as low as one-hundred feet, were used in critical infantry engagements at the decisive point of attack.

186

They exemplified the High Command's emphasis on highly coordinated tactical air support for ground operations, and tactical aviation became a significant weapon of mass warfare like the machine gun. The emergence of strategic bombing, particularly the German raids on England in 1917 and 1918, added a further important dimension to warfare.

From the beginning of the war the Entente's superiority in manpower and resources placed a premium upon the efficiency of the Central Powers' aviation mobilization. Bureaucratic fragmentation in Germany and Austria-Hungary, however, impeded the development of the air forces. The execution of exemptions, for example, reflected inadequate coordination, as war ministries proposed regulations and subordinate agencies like deputy general commands in Germany disposed of them, often emasculating the orders in the process.

The most salient administrative schisms were between the front and the rear, and between the services and the states. Tension between front staffs and rear echelon bureaucracies was inherent in their respective duties. Military staffs, close to the fliers and directly responsible for the conduct of battle, desired as many quality aircraft as possible and tended to underestimate technological and industrial limitations to the fulfillment of their wishes. Procurement agencies, confronted daily with shortages of manpower and materials and management-labor strife, could not keep pace with the front's ever increasing demands for superior aircraft. General Staff attempts to eliminate the division by taking control of the hinterland bureaucracy may have spurred the efforts of the rear, but at the price of subsuming these tensions within the staff's bureaucracy.

Interservice rivalry was also inherent in the military structure. In Germany the Prussian Army's dominance made military-naval tensions over aircraft procurement comparatively mild, although the navy, with the aid of Bavaria, thwarted Prussian designs to form a German air ministry. In Austria-Hungary, the army was also the dominant force, but the complete inadequacy of domestic aircraft production led to constant interservice friction over aircraft supplies. Yet strife between the front and rear and between the services was certainly no worse in Germany and Austria-Hungary than in France and England. French aviation historian Georges Huisman considered the former conflict the major flaw in wartime French aviation, while in England continuous army-navy conflict over aviation finally forced the formation of an air ministry.[1]

Where the empires suffered in comparison to England and France was in the inadequate centralization of their states. The federal nature of Germany, particularly the Prussian-Bavarian dichotomy, and the dualism of the Hapsburg monarchy complicated and confused aviation mobilization more than did the centralized structures of the English and French governments.

The success of the Central Powers' air effort depended primarily upon the German Army's mobilization of its aircraft industry. The Prussian Army's policies, though haphazard, enabled it to maintain control over the German aircraft manufacturers and to mobilize the German aircraft industry adequately, if not always efficiently. The war forced the Prussian aviation bureaucracy to intervene directly in industrial affairs, but it did so without any overall strategy and with only the general aim of increasing the capability of the aircraft industry. The War Ministry attempted to abridge patent protection and, perhaps most importantly, as historian Rolf Dumke has suggested, injected itself into hitherto sacrosanct management-labor negotiations by granting unions far greater rights and generally supporting the workers in crucial wage disputes.[2] In bringing collective bargaining to the aircraft industry, the army acted as an "agent of revolution from above," as Gerald Feldman observed,[3] however or portunistic its motives. By 1915 the recognition that the airplane and the aircraft industry were crucial to the German war effort was reflected in credits to the industry and its relatively high wage scale. Furthermore, the industry grew from fourteen to twenty-six companies in two years and increased production from some thirteen hundred planes in 1914 to seven to eight thousand in 1916.[4]

The German air service might have acquitted itself better had it not been the slowest of the great powers to standardize its aircraft. The Prussian Army coerced firms which proved incapable of creating their own designs into licensed production. Otherwise, any company's craft that met the requirements was accepted, regardless of the atrocious difficulties in supply and repair that such a policy created. The German air service consequently possessed similar aircraft of differing construction instead of having the best plane license-produced by other firms. During this period the army did not press the industry to improve plant organization and to use machinery to insure uniform mass production, while the aircraft manufacturers were not about to disrupt production by introducing these techniques unless the army forced them. Yet only rationalization would enable the efficient replacement of skilled craftsmen with unskilled labor.

The English and French, on the other hand, rapidly standardized their aircraft. The French Army swiftly conquered its aversion to standardization, ordered the licensed production of certain aircraft, and required that the parts for the same type be interchangeable, regardless of manufacturer.[5] The English, using a mixture of state and private enterprise with extensive licensed production and subcontracting, progressed rapidly. The massive Royal Aircraft Factory, a combination research institute and factory which was militarized in October 1915, disproved the German maxim that state factories could only reproduce designs en masse. English companies also "tackled the problem of large output by adopting the French *système globale* which consists in having a vast quantity of minor parts made by smaller firms, under rigid inspection by the staff of the head firm, and assembling these items at the head firm's own works."[6]

Yet the Achilles' heel of the German aviation effort was not standardization, but aircraft engine production. German aircraft production through 1916 kept pace with the French and exceeded the English, but Germany fell further behind the French in engine development and manufacture. In the three months from October through December 1914 the French industry delivered 429 airplanes; in the five months from August through December the German aircraft industry delivered 694 and the English 193. French aircraft production apparently exceeded German only slightly then and through 1916, when German aircraft production was approximately 7–8,000 and English 5,700.[7]

In engine production from August through December 1914 the Germans outproduced the French and British combined, delivering 1,035 motors to 870 for France and 100 for England. Yet in July 1916 French engine production totaled 1,550, German 720, and English 515. In the crucial year 1915 German errors combined with Entente good fortune to ensure German inferiority in engine production for the rest of the war. French production shot ahead rapidly to almost 1,400 monthly by the end of 1915, but German manufacture stagnated at below 500 monthly until the last quarter of 1915, when it rose to 650. Daimler's near monopoly of production limited expansion, but a series of erroneous decisions by the inspectorate, which suffered from a paucity of engine experts, produced near disaster. On 16 November 1914 it decided against the development of motors of more than 150 horsepower to avoid disturbing production. This decision, while prompted by limited production capacity, delayed the evolution of more powerful engines, a key factor in better aircraft performance. In 1915 the inspectorate declined the Benz 240-horsepower engine and later ordered 500–600-horsepower (!) engines for R-planes, thereby arresting motor evolution and production for another year.[8]

While the Germans floundered, the Entente drew on foreign resources in the form of Swiss engineer Marc Birkigt's work for a Spanish firm funded with French capital. His efforts produced the Hispano-Suiza 150-horsepower V-eight water-cooled engine, which would power successful fighters for the rest of the war, as its horsepower was augmented to keep pace with the demands of the front.

The Germans, unable to keep pace with the combined efforts of the English and French, resorted to a defensive aerial strategy except in rare cases. Their survival also required technological superiority, which was not always possible in a struggle against powers endowed with substantial technological resources. The British and the French possessed the materiel and manpower to be aggressive in the air, though such aggressiveness occasionally entailed a callous squandering of lives, especially by the English, whose craft were often inferior to the Germans during the first part of the war. Only in the late spring of 1917 did the English finally capitalize on the benefits of standardization to produce superlative fighter aircraft, which pressed the German air service ever more harshly during the last two years of the war.

German aviation mobilization in 1917 and 1918 was plagued by administrative confusion and inefficiency, the breakdown of transportation, and shortages of raw materials and labor. The German High Command's attempts to order industrial developments failed, admirably illustrating Karl Helfferich's maxim that an economy could not be ordered about like an army. In this context, the efforts of Kogenluft and the inspectorate to exorcise administrative barriers to a smoothly functioning mobilization did not meet with complete success. Although they generally succeeded in coordinating the industry and its raw material and labor supplies, their orders to the factories were sometimes ill-advised and were often ignored or even disobeyed by disgruntled manufacturers.

Though German aircraft production rose during the last two years of the war, it did not keep pace with that of the Entente. Entente superiority increased markedly in 1918, primarily because of English efforts. After producing 13,766 planes in the entire year of 1917, a few hundred fewer than the Germans, the English surpassed that number in the first six months of 1918, building 25,000 aircraft before the armistice, while Germany could manage only some 17–18,000. At the armistice England and France were each manufacturing some 2,800–3,000 aircraft monthly, compared to a German maximum of slightly below 2,200. Approximate totals of wartime production for the combatants were the following: Austria-Hungary, 4,200 aircraft; Germany, 43,000; England, 48,000;

France, 52,000; and Italy, 12,000. Furthermore, American manufacture of some 16,000 combat engines and 12,000 airplanes between August 1917 and November 1918 portended disaster for Germany had the war continued into 1919.[9]

The reasons for the English upsurge and German inability to keep pace in 1918 are numerous and instructive. First, the English aviation industry grew from 60,000 workers in August 1916 to 174,000 in November 1917, then to 347,000 at the armistice, nearly twice the size of the French aviation industry's total of some 180,000 employees. The statistics for labor dilution (that is, the replacement of male skilled workers with women and youth) were 31.7 percent in August 1916, 40.1 percent in November 1917, and 46.1 percent in October 1918. In the summer of 1917 the number of workers required to produce one plane per month in England was 120, and 1 of every 15 workers was estimated to be the absolute minimum proportion of skilled to unskilled workers required in the industry.[10]

The German aviation industry was much smaller, dilution was less, and productivity higher. The German industry employed at most 140,000 workers in the summer of 1917—40,000 in the aircraft factories, 30,000 in the motor plants, and 40–70,000 in subcontracting firms. It did not expand significantly in the last year of the war because it could not obtain sufficient skilled labor; consequently, by the war's end the English industry was approximately *two and one-half times* the size of the German. Available statistics indicate that at no time was there more than 25 percent dilution with female and youth labor. Yet, compensating for the small size and less dilution was the higher productivity of the German aircraft industry.[11] In the summer of 1917 22 workers, 14 in the aircraft industry and 8 in subcontracting firms, not 120 as in England, produced one plane a month. In 1918 the obvious barrier to keeping abreast of English production was the nearing exhaustion of the supply of skilled labor, food, and raw materials.

While it appears logical to state that Germany would have done better had the military instituted more licensed production of simpler aircraft types, this transition would have been difficult, ill advised, and probably impossible. The aircraft depot's pressures for rationalization of the aircraft industry in late 1917 and early 1918 are evidence that the introduction of jigs and other machines to facilitate the efficient replacement of skilled with unskilled labor had been rather limited. This in turn meant that licensed production remained a problem. Although the inspectorate forced it upon companies during the Hindenburg and America programs, inexperience and recalcitrance stood in the way of efficiency. Consequently, for want of either blueprints or appropriate skills, companies occasionally designed their own copies of the licensed aircraft, as was the case with Albatros's production of the Fokker D7.

The relatively complex structure of many German aircraft did not lend itself to machine production by a predominantly unskilled labor force. The English and French preferred simpler production techniques, designing single parts for quantity manufacture and better utilizing machine work in aircraft production. The Entente could rely on more powerful engines to provide increased performance, while the German motor industry's failure to meet its competition necessitated more sophisticated aircraft structures to achieve the same end. A shift to machine production would have required large numbers of skilled toolmakers, which Germany undoubtedly lacked. Finally, individual aircraft firms used production techniques unique to them out of necessity. Pfalz's production of wood fuselages, for example, was geared to the abundance of excellent woodworkers in the Rhineland Palatinate, and variations in German regional economic development would have hindered the reproduction of its aircraft by firms located elsewhere. In 1917 and 1918 drastic adjustments in the modes of operation of the industry would have meant severe dislocation and a corresponding decline in production. Germany was approaching the upper limits of her productive capability in aviation during wartime.

Both the English and German motor industries experienced severe difficulties in delivering approximately forty-one thousand aircraft engines. Production of French motors under license enabled the English to overtake German production. The French produced the astounding total of eighty-eight to ninety-two thousand motors, more than compensating for any English difficulties. Repeated English reliance on untried engines as the basis for production programs resulted in continual crises of engine production from 1917 onward. It mattered little, however, because by the armistice the French engines like the Hispano-Suiza three-hundred-horsepower V-eight and the American Liberty engine would have sufficed to bear Entente aviation to victory had the war continued into 1919.[12]

The most praiseworthy German accomplishment in engine development was the invention in July 1917 of the BMW 185-horsepower high-altitude engine that powered later versions of the Fokker D7 so effectively. Otherwise, because success with rotary engines eluded Germany, continued demands of safety, reliability, and repair confined German aviation to dependence on the six-cylinder in-line motor and so limited performance. Daimler's continued near monopoly also made it immune to pressures from the military to promote licensed production, and in 1918 the company could still refuse to open its ledgers to inspection by the army. In any case, the official history of German aircraft motor production concluded that the deleterious effect of food, material, and labor shortages on motor production would have made it impossible for the German air force to influence the course of the war in 1919.[13]

Despite all these problems, the German Army and the aircraft industry accomplished a remarkable feat in the maelstrom of total war; they had evolved an important combat arm and its industrial foundation from small beginnings. From August 1914 to November 1918 the German aircraft industry produced some 43,000 planes for the army: some 700 from August to December 1914; 3–4,000 in 1915; 7–8,000 in 1916; 14,000 in 1917; and 17,000 in 1918 through November.[14] The industry produced another 1,740 seaplanes for the navy during the war.[15] Kogenluft and the inspectorate promoted the expansion and the concentration of aircraft production. The number of companies and the amount of their share capital grew from seventeen with 3.2 million marks capital in 1914 to thirty-six with 36 million marks capital in 1918, while the largest companies, which had employed fewer than a thousand workers in 1914, employed three and four thousand aircraft workers in 1918. The profits and dividends of the best firms had risen substantially: Aviatik, for example, paid dividends of 8 percent in 1913, 20 percent in 1914, and 25–30 percent in 1917.[16] The army had exercised a decisive influence on the development of the aircraft industry to their mutual benefit—it had received its planes, and the industry its profits.

Certainly the two most significant soldiers in the military-industrial relationship were Col. Hermann von der Lieth-Thomsen and Lt. Col. Wilhelm Siegert. The commanding general of the air force, Lt. Gen. Ernst Wilhelm von Höppner, who won the coveted Pour le Mérite with Thomsen on 8 April 1918, seems to have provided the tact for his forceful subordinates. His history of the air force, published between his retirement on 30 September 1919 and his death on 25 September 1922, gave him prominence, yet Thomsen and Siegert were the soul of German military aviation.

Thomsen, first chief of field aviation and then chief of staff of the air force, had been the principal architect of German aviation since his prewar tour of duty on the General Staff. He deserves much of the credit for the mobilization of German aviation during the war. Col. Max Bauer,

Ludendorff's éminence grise, praised Thomsen as a tireless, energetic, and capable officer with an extraordinary understanding of technology. He lauded Thomsen's "great service in the development and production of airplanes and the training and use of the flying troops." Bauer observed:

> We argued constantly about questions of raw material and labor, and his aggressive manner made him feared in all quarters. But what he did and said was essentially clear and justified, and I would only have wished that there were such men everywhere. I have always openly admired him, particularly from a human standpoint. He stood up for his subordinates on principle and at all times; in short, he was an unafraid, courageous, and intelligent man with a warm heart for the army and particularly for his fine troops.[17]

Siegert, who had been instrumental in the formation of the first bomber units and of the office of chief of field aviation, who as inspector had been responsible for the mobilization of the aircraft industry and the air arm for most of the war, was rewarded for his prodigious efforts with obscurity. If Siegert occasionally wielded his power inappropriately, this abrasive, imaginative officer had borne the immense burden of military-industrial relations upon his shoulders for nearly four years and deserved more recognition than he received. His position was the most taxing and thankless of all: as the intermediary between the staff at the front and the industry in the rear, the inspector could satisfy neither. Siegert died in obscurity in Berlin on 26 January 1929 at the age of fifty-seven.

Under Siegert's guidance, the inspectorate essentially rationalized the German aircraft industry. It began this process in 1915 with the imposition of more efficient accounting and management methods on some factories and the promotion of aircraft production at large companies. The inspectorate's measures in 1917 and 1918—the introduction of industrial norms and of equipment and procedures for mass production and licensed production, the amalgamation of companies, and the closing of small, inefficient, and out-of-the-way plants—constituted a determined effort to rationalize the industry under wartime pressure.

The key to this effort was the inspectorate's formation of the war trade association of aircraft manufacturers. In an analysis of the German war economy, Ulrich Nocken observed that where private trade associations did not exist or were at an early stage of organization, the government created or expanded them, thereby increasing the power of the private organizations while simultaneously expanding the ability of the government bureaucracy to control and coordinate industries.[18] In the case of the aircraft industry, the private trade association, through which smaller firms could still oppose the army's promotion of large-scale enterprise, was simply pushed aside and replaced by one which the inspectorate controlled. The bureaucracy, not the private organization, benefited, as did certain powerful companies like the Albatros Works.

Previous studies have described rationalization as a movement of the 1920s and 1930s. Robert A. Brady's study conceived of it as a post-1923 phenomenon of retrenchment and reorganization, then systematic modernization of plant processes, albeit with some antecedents in war-time controls.[19] Edward Homze's study of the interwar aircraft industry concentrated on the Air Ministry's promotion of cooperation, not competition, within the industry, of the division of companies into categories for development and production, and of systems of complexes built around a parent plant during the 1930s.[20] It is now evident that although the planning and orderly procedure which Brady associated with the rationalization movement were not present during the war, when rationalization was undertaken hastily with an eye to expansion and not retrenchment, the measures taken by Kogenluft and the inspectorate should be viewed as the first rationalization of the industry. Though competition was still regarded as indispensable to aviation progress, the inspectorate's exceedingly close ties to Albatros, which produced some 40 percent of all German aircraft during the war, indicated that agency's tendency to favor the large producer at the expense of competitive procurement. Albatros and Hansa-Brandenburg represent the pro-totypical parent companies; Fokker, Pfalz, and Junkers, specialist companies; and BFW, a licensed producer. Thus there was specialization in the industry before the end of the war, and these antecedents certainly did not escape the attention of Air Ministry planners in the 1930s.

The army's exertions and the consequent evolution of the industry show clearly that the airplane, besides the submarine, was the most significant new technological weapon in the German arsenal. Tactical aviation was indispensable to the army and navy, while strategic aviation, if secondary during the war, held devastating promise for the future. Yet the importance of the airplane has been difficult for some historians to accept. G. W. F. Hallgarten, for example, allowed that "while the airplane belonged to the most progressive weapons of battle, in the First World War it had not yet attained the same significance as the tank and played only a minor role."[21] Hallgarten claimed that the tank decided the war solely on the grounds that Ludendorff attributed his request for an armistice to the tank. In fact no single weapon decided the war, and Ludendorff, whose nerves were extremely fragile by the end of the war, was less able to cope with the tank than were his soldiers. What Hallgarten ignored was that the German High Command accorded priority to the airplane, and not simply because of metal shortages but essentially because the airplane was more indispensable to the German war effort than the tank.

In contrast to the German experience, Austro-Hungarian aviation efforts never left the ground, figuratively speaking. Yet the administrative confusion and industrial poverty of Austro-Hungarian aviation should not obscure a most critical point—aircraft production increased to the end of the war, while the production of other weapons peaked in the first half of 1917 and declined thereafter.[22] Within its domestic context, therefore, the Austro-Hungarian aircraft industry acquitted itself well. Austria-Hungary lacked the industrial foundation to build a substantial aircraft industry during the war and was unable to utilize fully what German assistance was granted to it. Camillo Castiglioni's near monopoly of production did provide a lifeline to an efficient German firm, but left the armed forces at his mercy. The military bureaucracy, inexperienced in technological and industrial matters, was often an inadequate and unrealistic guide to the struggling industry. Schemes for licensed production of German aircraft in 1918 remained stillborn, and besides the Brandenburg airplanes, only the Albatros D3 was built in any numbers in the dual monarchy. The necessity of adapting German planes to Austrian engines raised a further barrier to interstate licensed production, in sharp contrast to the substantial English manufacture of French aircraft and engines throughout the war.

Yet the relationship between Germany and Austria-Hungary is not comparable to that between England and France, because Austria-Hungary lacked the industrial resources to employ German aid as the English used French assistance, while the Germans lacked the expertise of the French in aircraft engine technology. The palpable threat of enemy forces on French soil forced the French to share their knowledge, a goad the Germans lacked. Finally, the French and English were able to draw upon others—the Italians for Caproni bombers and the Americans for Glenn Curtiss flying boat designs—while the Germans and Austro-Hungarians were forced to be self-sufficient. In fact, the relationship between Germany and Austria-Hungary was more analogous to Franco-Russian ties, in which a dominant air power sought to assist a feeble one in its development of aviation. Both Russia and Austria-

Hungary possessed a small number of aircraft designers and a rudimentary industry incapable of the sustained development and mass production of quality aircraft. As a result, despite prodigious amounts of Allied assistance, Russian and Austro-Hungarian aviation developed little during the pressures and scarcities of wartime.

A final question concerns the war's effect on aviation science, technology, and production. A French Army expert on aviation during World War I, Albert Étévé, observed that the exceedingly rapid growth of aviation left insufficient time to verify developments and to comprehend technological and industrial difficulties.[23] British aviation historian Harald Penrose asserted that aerial progress was not as great as many claimed, that despite the evolution of more precise mathematical calculations on structure and improved controllability and stability of aircraft, basic aircraft structures did not change.[24] East German aviation historian Gerhard Wissmann contended unreservedly that the war hindered the progress of aviation science and technology because capitalist systems and imperialistic wars, of necessity, hinder scientific progress. The war forced aviation to "live from hand to mouth," resulting in piecemeal improvements "leaving the aerodynamically unfavorable conception of the externally braced wooden biplane" basically intact. What work was done lacked logical conclusions. Progressive concepts that would take years to mature did not interest the manufacturers or the military, and by 1918 material and labor shortages ensured the rejection of progressive projects like the all-metal airplane. If the war prompted increased funds for aviation, scientific agencies like the German Research Institute for Aviation received precious little of them. Finally, the emphasis on large serial production limited the possibilities for further progress.[25]

Some German aircraft manufacturers held more positive opinions. Ernst Heinkel suggested that the four and one-half years of war equaled six years of peacetime evolution.[26] Perhaps the most accomplished scientist among the German manufacturers, Hugo Junkers was convinced that the war would hasten technological and industrial development enormously.[27]

In fact, the war both hindered and promoted the evolution of aviation science and technology. From the very beginning it arrested the contact with France that had been essential to the German aircraft industry. While technological diffusion from France to Germany did not cease entirely, as German efforts to copy the Nieuport sesquiplane attested, copying captured aircraft and using captured engines were poor substitutes for obtaining blueprints and material specifications under license. So while the war exerted more pressure for speedy technological progress, it eliminated some of the prewar avenues to such advancement. The necessity for haste did not allow sufficient time to verify developments, ponder facts, and draw logical conclusions from them, circumstances to which flawed aircraft like the Albatros D5 amply attested. Wartime shortages did place a premium on ease of construction, not incorporation of the most advanced aviation knowledge, and hindered pursuit of concepts like all-metal aircraft.

Left to their own devices, German manufacturers pursued their own methods of construction quite successfully. They generally resisted wartime pressures more than did their Entente counterparts, who compromised greatly with wartime necessity by keeping their structures simple and wooden and relying primarily upon increased engine power for improved performance. German manufacturers like Junkers and Dornier did not relinquish their pursuit of advanced aviation knowledge, though they functioned in more deprived circumstances than did Entente designers. Fokker's reproach to Junkers, that the older man refused to compromise his all-metal construction with the wartime necessity of simplicity for mass production, is the best proof of the scientist's perseverance under adverse conditions. Consequently, German aviation technology at the end of the war was clearly superior to that of the Entente. Albatros's introduction of the plywood semimonocoque fuselage structure (a monocoque structure is one in which the outer shell carries all or much of the stress) on its fighters, Fokker's welded steel tube fuselages, Dornier's and Junkers's all-metal aircraft, the cantilever wings of Fokker, Dornier, and Junkers craft—all are major examples of German pioneering efforts. The war enabled the manufacturers to test their ideas at the public expense and the German Research Institute for Aviation to accumulate and disseminate knowledge that wartime coordination had made available to it. The army and navy encouraged and promoted the development of the giant R-planes. The haste and pressures of wartime may have favored the innovative trial-and-error designer like Anthony Fokker, but they did not halt the efforts of his more scientific colleagues. If the emphasis on mass serial production sometimes impeded innovation, the German industry, lacking powerful engines, had to rely more on technological progress than did the Allies in the quest for air superiority.

One point is not debatable: wartime markets fueled the tremendous expansion of the aircraft industry and its transition to large-scale serial production and rationalization. Yet what the war provided, the peace rescinded.

A postwar contraction of the aircraft industry was expected, but the conditions under which it occurred—economic collapse exacerbated by the Versailles treaty—made it more severe and abrupt than had been imagined. Governmental palliatives to ease the decline—a few military contracts, suggestions to build other products for market—failed. Military contracts were sparse; other markets, glutted. Under these circumstances, governmental insistence on retention of workers exacerbated the already intolerable strain on the young industry. The rise of commercial air transportation, the most likely means of survival for a few firms, was stunted first by economic dislocation, then by Versailles and subsequent restrictions on German aviation. Initially these circumstances resulted in competition for air routes between the military using surplus aircraft and the aircraft industry; ultimately they drove the army and the few companies that survived back together in secret military ventures in Russia. By then, however, barely a handful of German aircraft companies remained. The contraction in Austria-Hungary was more devastating, as the aircraft industry disappeared.

The essential difference between contraction in the losers and in the victor states was that the latter was more gradual and less severe. For example, the English government also sought to minimize unemployment by forbidding a general discharge of munitions workers, although it ordered the abolition of all overtime work and a reduction of the work week. The Ministry of Munitions allowed "war break clauses," in which the aircraft companies could extend three months' output over six months after the end of the war. Consequently, the government was still accepting delivery of almost three hundred aircraft weekly in May 1919. 1920 proved to be the year of crisis for the aircraft industry. With the economy in a slump and the worsened lack of demand, final payment of the wartime excess profits tax came due. This tax, which pegged the level of wartime profits to prewar earnings, had restricted the amount that the prewar aircraft companies could earn. Now major pioneering companies like Sopwith and Airco collapsed under the burden, though in collapse they often gave birth to heirs, as Sopwith did to the Hawker and Airco the De Havilland firm. The Air Ministry aided the aircraft industry by deciding to preserve a ring of sixteen competing aircraft companies.[28] This last statistic is the best indication that the contraction in England was less severe than in Germany, as the German industry shrank to fewer than one-third that number of firms. English government attempts to ease the contraction were more effective because the victors could establish break clauses untrammeled by domestic political and economic collapse and international constraints. Government contracts had nourished the growth of the German aircraft industry. As their absence meant economic starvation, by 1921 the World War I German aircraft industry was no .nore.

Yet if the World War I German air force had ceased to exist officially in 1920 and the aircraft industry in 1921, the two left a legacy that would endure through World War II. Allied shackles on German aviation endured in the civilian realm until 1926 and in military affairs until their repudiation by the Nazi regime, but they did not prevent the rebirth of the German aircraft industry and the air force. The new industry's guiding designers included Hugo Junkers, Ernst Heinkel, and Claudius Dornier, who had survived by concentrating on scientific and technological advances and civil aircraft, while not relinquishing the development of military airplanes. After a trailblazing career in commercial aviation during the 1920s, Hugo Junkers lost his aircraft factory to the Nazi state in 1933 and died two years later at the age of seventy-six. Heinkel and Dornier lived to play a major role in aviation during World War II. For Heinkel, success followed success, from transport aircraft like the Heinkel He70 Blitz ("Lightning") in the early 1930s to military airplanes like the He111 bomber, mainstay of the wartime Luftwaffe. Camillo Castiglioni's chief designer for Hansa-Brandenburg survived his former employer by one year, dying in 1958. Claudius Dornier's giant R-seaplane designs culminated in successful commercial seaplanes during the interwar period. He also manufactured warplanes for the Nazi regime. After passing his company on to his son and namesake, Dornier died in 1969, the last of the great pioneer designers.

The military connection arose with the aircraft industry in clandestine rearmament ventures in Russia and in close ties between Lufthansa and the German Army. From Holland Anthony Fokker supplied German units in Russia with his superlative fighters during the early 1920s. He continued his phenomenal success until his untimely death at the age of forty-nine in 1939 from a postoperative infection. The continuity in the German military establishment between World War I and II was both personal and theoretical. In retirement Hermann von der Lieth-Thomsen served as head of the Moscow branch of the German Army's agency in charge of coordinating secret contracts with Russia from 1923 until 1928. He spent the years from 1928 until his death in 1942 at the age of seventy-five almost completely blind. Younger officers of the first war played significant roles in the second: Hermann Göring was the commander, however inept, of the Luftwaffe; Ernst Udet, inspector of fighters and dive bombers in the Nazi regime until his suicide in 1941; and Kurt Student, the architect of the German paratroop forces in World War II. The legend of Manfred von Richthofen lived on in *Jagdgeschwader* Richthofen No. 2, formed by special order of Adolf Hitler on 14 March 1935. The Luftwaffe inherited its predilection for tactical over strategic aviation from the World War I German air force. The material and manpower shortages, the success of the close air support, and the disappointment with the results of the bombing of England in World War I certainly encouraged the decision that limited strategic resources made a force of many small tactical aircraft preferable to one of fewer and larger strategic ones. This legacy, manifest in the Luftwaffe's early blitzkrieg victories won with closely coordinated air and armor and ultimately in its inability to strike at the English and Russian heartlands, is the best evidence that the foundation of German aviation in World War II was laid in World War I.

As Wilhelm Siegert had predicted, German aviation had arisen, like the phoenix from its ashes. But his bird of peace had a Doppelgänger, which did not bare its talons openly until the 1930s. It was the bird of war, whose day would come again in 1939.

German Military
Aircraft Procurement, 1914–18

STATISTICS on wartime deliveries, particularly during the last two critical years of the conflict, differ greatly, depending upon the source. The most official and widely accepted figures are the following: 1,348 aircraft in 1914; 4,532 in 1915; 8,182 in 1916; 19,746 in 1917; and 14,123 in 1918 for a total of 47,931 airplanes.[1] However, the figure for 1917, which implies average monthly deliveries of 1,645 aircraft, is inflated, as the inspectorate indicated monthly procurement of more than 1,500 airplanes only in mid-1918.[2] On the other hand, the total for 1918 seems insufficient, because some twenty important firms produced approximately 3,300 more aircraft in 1918 than 1917.[3] Hence the following totals, which appeared in an East German aviation journal in 1953, might seem more reasonable: 694 aircraft delivered by eighteen companies from August to December 1914; 2,950 by twenty companies in 1915; 7,112 by twenty-six companies in 1916; 13,977 by thirty-four companies in 1917; and 20,971 by thirty-six companies through November 1918 for a total of 45,704 airplanes.[4] The author may have had access to the files of the German aircraft industry's war trade association, which the Deutsches Zentralarchiv has not opened generally to researchers. Nevertheless, now the figure for 1918 seems excessive. If one accepts the inspectorate's figures of monthly procurement from January through July 1918 (1,009, 890, 1,360, 1,202, 930, 1,478),[5] then deliveries in the four months through November would have had to exceed 3,000 aircraft. Yet two sources put construction in August and October at 2,195, and others estimate monthly production during the summer of 1918 at 2,000 aircraft.[6] Consequently, the procurement of some 14,000 airplanes in 1917 seems reasonable, but the figure for 1918 should be reduced to approximately 17,000 planes delivered through November 1918. A more definitive conclusion awaits the release or discovery of new documentation.

The Expansion of
German Aircraft Factories, 1914–18

Factory (location, date of formation)	Year	Employees	Deliveries	Workshop Area (m²)
A. Prewar Aircraft Factories				
Albatros GmbH (Berlin-Johannisthal, 1909)	1914	745	338	12,824
	1915	1,235	846	19,932
	1916	2,070	1,011	25,882
	1917	2,680	2,097	28,392
	1918	3,140	1,950	37,502
Luftverkehrsgesellschaft mbH (Berlin-Johannisthal, 1910)	1914	450	300	25,000
	1915	920	1,020	25,500
	1916	1,750	720	25,800
	1917	2,200	1,680	42,000
	1918	2,200	1,920	42,000
Rumpler Werke AG (Berlin-Johannisthal, 1908)	1914	400	109	6,000
	1915	700	210	14,000
	1916	1,200	486	28,000
	1917	2,000	901	37,000
	1918	2,300	1,400	38,200
Fokker Flugzeugwerke (Schwerin, 1912)	1914	110	32	3,300
	1915	480	260	——
	1916	950	675	——
	1917	1,400	798	——
	1918	1,850	1,500	18,000

B. *Prewar Aircraft Department of Another Enterprise*

Allgemeine Elek-	1914	200	20	1,000
trizitäts	1915	600	91	——
Gesellschaft	1916	1,400	220	——
(Berlin-	1917	2,300	615	——
Hennigsdorff,	1918	3,200	454	26,000
1913)				

C. *Wartime Aircraft Factory*

Mercur-Flug-	1915	70	——	2,000
zeugbau,	1916	490	370	——
GmbH (Ber-	1917	1,010	450	——
lin-Neukölln,	1918	1,465	600	14,000
1915)				

D. *Wartime Aircraft Department of Another Enterprise*

Hannoversche	1916	460	3–17 monthly	3,600
Waggon-	1917	1,515	18–60 monthly	7,000
fabrik AG				
(Hannover,	1918	1,940	100 monthly	14,000
1915)				

Siemens-	1915	120	——	1,000
Schuckert	1916	——	250	——
Werke	1917	——	350	——
(Siemensstadt,	1918	750	380	15,000
1915)				

SOURCES: Draft, "Geschichte der deutschen Flugzeugindustrie" (compiled by the inspectorate of aircraft, summer–fall 1918), IIa and IIb. *Entwicklungsgeschichte, Statistik der Flugzeugfabriken, 1914–1918*, pp. 80–148, IL 234/32, MA.

CRITERIA FOR SELECTION: Group A represents the type of company (seventeen) that built most of Germany's wartime aircraft, so the four firms listed are among Germany's best factories. AEG was the more important and productive of the two firms in category B, while Mercur was the most productive factory in group C for which relatively complete statistics were available. Finally, of the seven firms in category D, Hannover was chosen for its productivity and SSW for the importance of the parent company.

Wages in an Important Berlin Aircraft Factory, 1914–17

A. Hourly Wages (in Pfennige, Index: 8/14 = 100)

Position	Date	8/14	1/15	7/15	1/16	7/16	10/16	1/17
Fitter[a]	Wage	75	86	98	114	130	147	179
	Index	100	115	131	152	173	196	238
Carpenter[b]	Wage	66	69	87	101	115	128	149
	Index	100	120	132	153	174	194	226
Lathe hand	Wage	100	100	110	125	152	170	200
Unskilled	Wage	59	62	62	72	94	102	125
worker	Index	100	105	105	122	159	173	212
Seamstress	Wage	35	38	45	55	67	78	94
	Index	100	109	129	157	191	223	269

B. Average Hourly Wages and Average Hourly Real Wages

Date	Wage	Index	Cost of Living Index[c]	Real Wage
	(Pfennige)	(8/14=100)	(8/14=1.00)	
Carpenter				
8/14	66	100	1.00	100
8/15	90	136	1.40	97
8/16	161	244	1.87	130
1/17	196	297	2.20	135
Fitter				
8/14	87	100	1.00	100.0
8/15	96	110	1.40	78.5
8/16	164	189	1.87	101.1
1/17	202	232	2.20	105.0

Lathe Hand

8/14	92	100	1.00	100.0
8/15	120	130	1.40	92.9
8/16	175	190	1.87	101.6
1/17	212	230	2.20	104.5

C. Annual Income

Position	Date	1914	1915	1916
Carpenter	Wage (marks)	2,179	2,793	5,397
	Index (8/14=100)	100	126	247
Fitter	Wage	2,480	2,978	5,164
	Index	100	120	208
Lathe hand	Wage	2,304	3,318	5,620
	Index	100	144	244

SOURCE: Reichstagskommission zur Prüfung von Verträgen über Kriegslieferungen, 3d meeting, 11 January 1917, pp. 51–52, apps. 4, 5, K10–4/2540, AM, MA.
[a]Based on the average wage of five fitters.
[b]Based on the average wage of seven carpenters.
[c]Based on Gerhard Bry, *Wages in Germany, 1871–1945*, pp. 440–45.

Raw Material Prices for an Important Berlin Aircraft Factory, 1914–17

Material	Date	1/8/14	1/8/15	1/8/16	1/1/17
Steel tubing	Price (marks)	0.80	1.10	1.52	4.32
(1 m)	Index (8/14=100)	100	125	190	540
Aluminum	Price	2.20	4.75	5.28	5.50
(1 kg)	Index	100	216	240	250
Oak (m³)	Price	156.00	250.00	350.00	400.00
	Index	100	160	224	256
Steel	Price	16.25	22.75	29.50	36.00
(100 kg)	Index	100	140	182	222
Iron	Price	13.50	18.00	26.00	30.00
(100 kg)	Index	100	133	193	222

SOURCE: Reichstagskommission zur Prüfung von Verträgen über Kriegslieferungen, 3d meeting, 11 January 1917, pp. 52–53, app. 6, K10–42540, AM, MA.

German Aircraft Motor Production, 1914–19

SOURCES differ (though not greatly) on aircraft motor production. The two most likely totals are presented in the charts below, both of which are found in reliable sources. The first table is based on figures from the last inspector of flying troops, Colonel Hähnelt; the second is found in the official history of German aircraft motor production from 1910 to 1918.

German Aircraft Motor Production, 1914—19

Time	Stationary in-line Engines	Rotary Engines	Total
(8–12) 1914	748	100	848
1915	4,544	493	5,037
1916	6,930	892	7,822
1917	10,364	836	11,200
1918	13,757	1,758	15,542
Total	36,343	4,106	40,449

SOURCE: Walter Jost, Friedrich Felger, eds., *Was wir vom Weltkrieg nicht wissen*, p. 183.

German Aircraft Motor Production, 1914–19

Time	Production
8/1914–12/1915	6,007
1916	7,823
1917	12,029
1918	16,412
Total to 10/30/18	41,012
Total to 12/31/18	42,271
Total to 2/28/19	43,486

SOURCE: J. A. Gilles, *Flugmotoren, 1910 bis 1918,* p. 185.

The Construction Inspectorates (Bauaufsichten—BAs) and Their Factories, Summer 1918

BA 1. Albatros-Gesellschaft für Flugzeugunternehmungen mbH, Berlin-Johannisthal.
BA 2. Luftverkehrsgesellschaft mbH, Berlin-Johannisthal.
BA 3. Ago-Flugzeugwerke GmbH, Berlin-Johannisthal.
BA 4. Rumpler Werke AG, Berlin-Johannisthal.
BA 5. Luft-Fahrzeug-Gesellschaft mbH, Berlin-Charlottenburg.
BA 6. Mercur Flugzeugbau GmbH, Berlin-Neukölln.
BA 7. Automobil und Aviatik AG, Leipzig-Heiterblick.
BA 8. Deutsche Flugzeugwerke GmbH, Leipzig.
BA 9. Gothaer Waggonfabrik AG, Gotha.
Otto Schwade und Co., Erfurt (repairs, some license construction).
BA 10. Hannoversche Waggonfabrik AG, Hannover.
BA 11. Halberstädter Flugzeugwerke GmbH, Halberstadt.
BA 12. Ostdeutsche Albatroswerke GmbH, Schneidemühl.
BA 13. Fokker Flugzeugwerke, Schwerin.
BA 14. Allgemeine Elektrizitäts Gesellschaft, Flugzeugfabrik, Hennigsdorf.
BA 15. Daimler-Motoren-Gesellschaft AG, Abteilung Flugzeugbau, Stuttgart-Sindelfingen.
BA 16. Flugzeugbau Friedrichshafen, Manzell.
BA 17. Luftschiffbau Schütte-Lanz, Abteilung Flugzeugbau, Mannheim-Rheinau. Albatros-Militär-Werkstätten, Warsaw.
BA 18. Linke-Hoffmann Werke AG, Breslau.
BA 19. Albert Rinne Flugzeugwerke, Berlin-Rummelsberg.

BA 20. Bayerische Flugzeug Werke AG, Munich.

BA 21. Pfalz-Flugzeug-Werke, Speyer.

BA 22. Germania-Flugzeugwerke GmbH, Leipzig.

BA 23. Kondor-Flugzeugwerke, Essen.

BA 24. Ottowerke, Flugzeug und Maschinenfabrik GmbH, Munich (accessories).

BA 25. Luftfahrzeugbau Schütte-Lanz, Zeesen.

BA 26. Märkische Flugzeugwerke GmbH, Bork.

BA 27. Siemens-Schuckert-Werke, Transformatorenwerk, Nuremberg.

BA 28. Euler-Werke, Frankfort on The Main.

BA 29. Norddeutsche Flugzeugwerke, Berlin-Teltow.

BA 30. Hanseatische Flugzeugwerke Karl Caspar AG, Hamburg-Fuhlsbüttel.

BA 31. Automobil und Aviatik AG, branch in Bork.

BA 32. Siemens-Schuckert-Werke, Abteilung Flugzeugbau, Siemensstadt.

BA 33. Flugzeugwerke J. Gödecker, Mainz (repairs).

BA 34. Luft-Verkehrs-Gesellschaft mbH, Köslin.

BA 35. Ludwig Alter Werke, Abteilung Flugzeugbau, Darmstadt.

BA 36. Junkers-Fokker-Werke AG, Dessau.

BA 37. Bayerische Rumpler-Werke AG, Augsburg.

BA 38. Franz Schneider Flugmaschinen-Werke GmbH, Seegefeld (repairs).

BA 39a. Flugzeugwerke Richard Götze, Kommandit-Gesellschaft, Berlin-Teltow (accessories).

BA 39b. Sablatnig-Flugzeugbau, Berlin.

BA 40. Nürnberger Schraubenfabrik und Fassongrekerei, Nuremberg (accessories).

BA 41. Berliner Unterlieferanten (twenty subcontracting firms), Berlin.

BA 42. Flugmaschinen Rex Gesellschaft mbH, Cologne-Bickendorf (repairs).

BA 43. Zeppelin-Werke GmbH, Staaken.

BA 44. Bleichröder Flugzeug-Industrie, Bleichröder a. Harz.

BA 45. Walter Steiger und Co., Burgrieden bei Laupheim i. Württemberg (accessories).

Austro-Hungarian
Military Aviation, 1914–18

Aircraft Deliveries

Year	From Austro-Hungarian Factories	From German Factories	Total
1914 (8–12/14)	64	48	112
1915	281	186	467
1916	732	95	827
1917	1,272	32	1,304
1918 (1–10/18)	1,989	0	1,989
Total	4,338	361	4,699

SOURCE: *Das Luftfahrwesen*, p. 35, fol. 19a, LA, OK.

Aircraft Motor Production

Year	1914	1915	1916	1917	1918	Total
Production	72	440	854	1,230	1,750	4,346

SOURCE: J. A. Gilles, *Flugmotoren, 1910 bis 1918* p. 185.

Abbreviations Used in the Notes

Abt. Abteilung (department or unit)

a.D. ausser Dienst (retired)

AEG Allgemeine Elektrizitäts Gesellschaft (General Electric Company)

AM Archiv der Marine

AOK Armeeoberkommando (Austro-Hungarian High Command)

BA Bundesarchiv (Federal Archive, German Federal Republic)

BB Bayerischer Beauftragter (Bavarian delegate)

BdMFA Befehlshaber der Marine-Flieger-Abteilung (chief of naval flight units)

Bevoll Bevollmächtigter (plenipotenitiary)

BFW Bayerische Flugzeugwerke (Bavarian Aircraft Works)

BKA Bayerisches Kriegsarchiv (Bavarian War Archive)

CdAS Chef des Admiralitätstabs (chief of Admiralty Staff of the Imperial German Navy)

CdE Chef des Ersatzwesens (supply chief, Austro-Hungarian Army)

CdGS Chef des Generalstabs (chief of the General Staff of German Army)

DFW Deutsche Flugzeugwerke (German Aircraft Works)

DLZ Deutscher Luftfahrer Zeitschrift

DM Deutsches Museum (German Museum, Munich)

DMA Demobilmachungsamt (demobilization office, Germany)

DVL Deutsche Versuchsanstalt für Luftfahrt (German Research Institute for Aviation)

FEA Fliegerersatzabteilung (fliers replacement unit)
Feldflugchef chief of field aviation, Prussian Army
    Flars Fliegerarsenal (aviation arsenal, Austro-Hungarian Army)
  Flkmdo Flottenkommando (fleet command)
   Fluba Flugzeugbauaufsicht (aircraft construction inspectorate, Bavaria)
      FS *Flugsport*
     Fzm Flugzeugmeisterei (aircraft depot)
      GC Peter Grosz Collection
   GIdL Generalinspektor der Luftstreitkräfte (general inspector of the air force, Austro-Hungarian Army)
  GIdMV Generalinspektion des Militärverkehrswesens (General Inspectorate of Military Transportation, Prussian Army)
  Hptm. Hauptmann (captain)
  Idflieg Inspektion der Fliegertruppen (Inspectorate of Flying Troops, Prussian Army)
     IdV Inspektion der Verkehrstruppen (Inspectorate of Transport Troops, Prussian Army)
    IFW *Illustrierte Flug Woche*
      II Inspektion des Ingenieurkorps (Inspectorate of the Engineer Corps, Bavarian Army)
   Iluft Inspektion des Luftfahrwesens (Inspectorate of Aviation, Bavarian Army)
    Iluk Inspektion des Militär-Luft- und Kraftfahrwesens (Inspectorate of Military Aviation and Transportation, Prussian Army)
  IMLuK Inspektion des Militär-Luft- und Kraftfahrwesens (Inspectorate of Military Aviation and Transportation, Bavarian Army)
    JEH *Journal of Economic History*
    JFW *Jahrbuch für Wirtschaftsgeschichte*
     KA Kriegsamt (War Office)
   KAdL Kriegswissenschaftliche Abteilung der Luftwaffe (Military Science Department of the Air Force)
   KAdM Kriegswissenschaftliche Abteilung der Marine (Naval Science Department)
   KbKM Königlich bayerisches Kriegsministerium (Bavarian War Ministry)

KbMFMA Königlich bayerisches Ministerium für Militärische Angelegenheiten (Bavarian Ministry for Military Affairs)

Kdflieg Kommandeur der Flieger (flight commander, German Navy)

Kgl. Ung. Königlich Ungarisch (Hungarian)

KKdH Kaiserliches Kommando der Hochseestreitkräfte (Command of High Seas Fleet)

kl. Klasse (class)

KM Kriegsministerium (war ministry)

KMAD Kriegsministerium Allgemeines Kriegsdepartement (War Ministry, General War Department, Prussian Army)

Kmdo Kommando (command)

KM / 5M (later KM / 5L) War Ministry, Aviation Department, Austro-Hungarian Army

KM / MS Kriegsministerium / Marinesektion (War Ministry, Naval Section, Austria-Hungary)

KM/OK–MS Kriegsministerium / Operationskanzlei—Marinesektion (War Ministry Operations Chancery, Naval Section, Austria-Hungary)

KMZD Kriegsministerium Zentraldepartement (War Ministry Central Department, Prussian Army)

Kogenluft Kommandierender General der Luftstreitkräfte (commanding general of the German air force)

KpKM Königlich preussisches Kriegsministerium (Prussian War Ministry)

KRA Kriegsrohstoffabteilung (War Raw Materials Department, Prussian War Ministry)

KuK Kaiserlich und Könliglich (referring to Austro-Hungarian ruling dynasty, the Habsburgs)

LA Luftfahrtarchiv (Aviation Archive, Austrian War Archives)

LFG Luftfahrzeuggesellschaft

LFT Luftfahrtuppen (Aviation Troops Command, Austro-Hungarian Army)

LSA Luftschifferabteilung (airship unit, Austro-Hungarian Army)

Lt. Leutnant (lieutenant)

LVG Luftverkehrsgesellschaft (air transport company)

MA Militärarchiv (Military Archive, German Federal

Republic)

MAF Marinearchiv Flugwesen (Naval Archive, Aviation, Austrian War Archive)

MBA Marinebaufaufsicht (Naval Construction Inspectorate, Austro-Hungarian Navy)

MFAA Ministerium für Auswärtige Angelegenheiten (Bavarian Ministry for Foreign Affairs)

MFB Marineflugzeugbauleitung (Naval Aircraft Construction Directorate, Austria-Hungary)

MFC Marineflugchef (naval flight chief, German Navy)

MGFA Militärgeschichtliches Forschungsamt (Military History Research Office, German Federal Republic)

MLA Marine-Luftfahrt Abteilung (naval flight unit)

MLG Motorluftfahrzeuggesellschaft

MR *Marine Rundschau*

MVO Marine Verbindungsoffizier (naval liaison officer)

ND Nachlass Hermann Dorner (Personal Papers of Hermann Dorner)

NE Nachlass August Euler (personal papers of August Euler)

Oberlt. Oberleutnant (lieutenant)

Öffag Österreichische Flugzeugfabrik (Austrian Aircraft Company)

OHL Oberste Heeresleitung (German High Command)

OK Österreichisches Kriegsarchiv (Austrian War Archive)

OMZ *Österreichisches Militär Zeitschrift*

RdI Reichsamt des Innern (Imperial Office of the Interior, Germany)

REA Riesenflugzeugersatzabteilung (R-plane replacement unit, German air force)

RLA Reichsluftamt (German Air Office)

RMA Reichsmarineamt (Imperial Naval Office, Germany)

SFL Seeflugleitung (Naval Aviation Command, Austria-Hungary)

SGK Stellvertretende Generalkommandos (deputy general commands, German Army)

SSdI Staatssekretär des Innern (secretary of state of the interior, Germany)

SSdRMA Staatssekretär des Reichsmarineamts (secretary of state of the Imperial Naval Office, Germany)

SSW Siemens-Schuckert Werke

Ufag Ungarische Flugzeugwerke AG (Hungarian Aircraft
       Works)
USSdRLA Unterstaatssekretär des Reichsluftamts (undersecretary of
       state of the German Air Office)
VdMI Verein deutscher Motorfahrzeug-industrieller (Asso-
       ciation of German Motor Vehicle Industrialists)
VO Verbindungsoffizier (liaison officer, Austro-Hungarian
       Army)
VPK Verkehrstechnische Prüfungskommission (Transport
       Technology Test Commission, Prussian Army)
VTBK Verkehrstruppen Brigadekommando (Transport Troops
       Brigade Command, Austro-Hungarian Army)
WKF Wiener Karosserie Fabrik (Vienna Chassis Factory)
ZAK Zentralabnahmekommission (Central Acceptance
       Commission, Prussian Inspectorate of Flying Troops)

NOTES

Introduction

1. In the first category, see as examples: Oswald Bölcke, *Hauptmann Bölckes Feldberichte;* Max Immelmann, *Immelmann; der Adler von Lille;* Manfred von Richthofen, *Der rote Kampfflieger;* A.H.G. Fokker and Bruce Gould, *Flying Dutchman: The Life of Anthony Fokker;* Ernst Heinkel, *Stürmisches Leben.*

In the second category see as examples: Peter Gray and Owen Thetford, *German Aircraft of the First World War;* G. W. Haddow and Peter M. Grosz, *The German Giants: The Story of the R-Planes, 1914–1919.*

In the third category of aviation histories see as examples: Hilmer von Bülow, *Geschichte der Luftwaffe: eine kurze Darstellung der fünften Waffe;* Hans Ritter, *Der Luftkrieg.*

2. There is little in English on German and Austro-Hungarian industrial mobilization. On Germany see Gerald D. Feldman's excellent study, *Army, Industry, and Labor in Germany, 1914–1918;* and Robert B. Armeson's work, *Total Warfare and Compulsory Labor: A Study of the Military-Industrial Complex in Germany during World War I.* On Austria see Richard Riedl, *Die Industrie Österreichs während des Krieges* (Vienna: Hölder-Pichler-Tempsky, 1931); and Josef Redlich, *Austrian War Government.*

3. See as examples, Edward L. Homze, *Arming the Luftwaffe: The Reich Air Ministry and the German Aircraft Industry, 1919–39;* Herbert Molloy Mason, Jr., *The Rise of the Luftwaffe: Forging the Secret German Air Weapon, 1918–1940;* Karl-Heinz Völker, *Die Entwicklung der militärischen Luftfahrt in Deutschland, 1920–1933.*

4. Robert A. Kann, *The Habsburg Empire: A Study in Integration and Disintegration,* pp. 61–63. Oskar Regele, *Feldmarschall Conrad: Auftrag und Erfüllung, 1906–1918,* pp. 1–226 passim.

5. "Jahresbericht über die Tätigkeit des Deutschen Luftflottenvereins im Jahre 1909," *Die Luftflotte* 2, no. 5 (May 1910): 4–5. Memorandum, 1919 "Die

Förderung der Luftfahrt vor dem Kriege innerhalb des Rahmens der Betätigung des Deutschen Luftfahrer-Verbandes," IL 2/45, MA.

6. KAdL, *Die Militärluftfahrt bis zum Beginn des Weltkrieges 1914*, 1:1–73. *Die Wegbereiter der österreichisch-ungarischen Luftfahrt*, pp. 6–8, fol. no. 50, LA, OK.

7. Lt. Gen. Alfred von Lyncker, "Bericht über den Stand der Flugmaschinenfrage . . . ," IL 26/2, MA. *Wegbereiter*, p. 7, fol. no. 50; *Stand der Luftfahrtindustrie in Österreich-Ungarn vor Kriegsbeginn 1914*, pp. 2–3, fol. no. 36; LA, OK.

8. Ritter, *Luftkrieg*, p. 25. Bülow, *Luftwaffe*, p. 3.

9. KAdL, *Militärluftfahrt*, 1:117, 121; 2:118–35; 3:18–20. Peter Supf, *Das Buch der deutschen Fluggeschichte*, 1:266, 363. Correspondence between Euler and commander of Eighteenth Army Corps and Nassau Pioneer Battalion, fol. no. 238, NE, BA. IdV IIc no. 549.09, 26 January 1909, IL 26/6, MA.

10. *Wegbereiter*, p. 7, fol. no. 50; *Luftfahrtindustrie*, pp. 2–3, fol. no. 36; LA, OK.

11. KAdL, *Militärluftfahrt*, 2:125–35.

12. Ibid., 2:264; 2: chart no. 106; 3:310–20. See John Howard Morrow, Jr. *Building German Airpower, 1909–1914* (Knoxville: University of Tennessee Press, 1976), pp. 57–71.

13. KAdl, *Militärluftfahrt*, 3:172, 316–20. *Die Rumpler Werke AG, 1909–1918*, pp. 55–56, 65, 67.

14. Ibid.

15. David Landes, *The Unbound Prometheus: Technological Change and Industrial Development in Western Europe from 1750 to the Present*, p. 306.

16. KAdL, *Militärluftfahrt*, 3:239–47.

17. Ibid.

18. Idflieg no. Ia 91/14, "Entwurf, Mobilmachungsinstruktion d. GIdMV," 2 January 1914, IL 97/17, MA. KAdL, *Militärluftfahrt*, 1:184–85. KbKM no. 3979, 12 March 1913, MKr 1381, BKA. KAdL, *Militärluftfahrt*, 3:103, 107.

19. KbKM nos. 452 and 949, 25 January 1913, Mkr 1381; KbKM no. 20981, 18 September 1912, Mkr 1380; KbKM nos. 9789, 16 May 1913, 18118, 18 September 1913, Mkr 1382; Gen. Karl von Brug (II) memorandum, 26 July 1911, Mkr 1385; BKA.

20. CdAS no. A3157 I/13 to RMA, 23 February 1914, fol. no. 1200, AM, MA.

21. MLG to VTBK, 29 February 1912, 2 April 1912, KM, OK.

22. KuK KM nos. 720, 15 April 1913, 2475, 30 October 1913; Österreichischer Aero-Club to KuK KM, 18 April 1913; KuK KM nos. 866, 5 June 1913, 1633, 10 July 1914; KM, OK.

23. "Ungunstiger Stand der Militärluftfahrt in Österreich-Ungarn," *Neue freie Presse*, 6 June 1914; "Krise in unserer Militäraviatik," *Wiener Sonn- und Montagszeitung*, 8 June 1914; in KuK KM no. 1633, KM, OK.

24. KuK KM, 1 August 1914, *Das Luftfahrwesen*, fol. no. 19a, LA, OK.

25. KuK KM nos. 217, 10 February 1914, 2089, 22 July 1914, KM, OK.

26. On French aviation, see Albert Étévé, *La victoire des cocardes*, pp. 109–24. On England, see Harold Penrose, *British Aviation: The Pioneer Years, 1903–1914*, p. 543; and *British Aviation: The Great War and Armistice, 1915–1919*, p. 9.

27. J. A. Gilles, *Flugmotoren, 1910 bis 1918*, pp. 22, 32, 58. On French motors, see James M. Laux, "Gnome et Rhone: une firme de moteurs d'avion durant la grande guerre," in *Dix-neuf cent quatorze–dix-neuf cent dix-huit: l'autre front*, ed. Patrick Fridenson with J. J. Becker (Paris: les éditions ouvrières, 1975).

28. Penrose, *Aviation: 1915–1919*, pp. 18–19.

29. KAdL, *Militärluftfahrt*, 3:239–47.

Chapter 1

1. Alex Imrie, *Pictorial History of the German Army Air Service, 1914–1918*, pp. 21–22.

2. John R. Cuneo, *Winged Mars*, 2:92–94.

3. Ibid., 2:162.

4. Gen. Ernst von Höppner, *Deutschlands Krieg in der Luft: ein Ruckblick auf die Entwicklung und die Leistungen unserer Heeres-Luftstreitkräfte im Weltkrieg*, pp. 17, 22. Karl Köhler, "Auf dem Wege zur Luftwaffe," *Wehrwissenschaftliche Rundschau* 16, no. 1 (January 1966): 554–55. Cuneo, *Mars*, 2:165.

5. KAdL, *Beiträge zur Entwicklungsgeschichte des Flugzeugwesens und des Flugzeugbaues im Heer und in der Industrie*, no. 30, p. 46, IIL 234/32, MA. Telegram 20 October 1914 and following correspondence, MKr 1385, BKA. *Die Marineflugwaffe im Weltkriege Jahr 1914*, pp. 52–56, IIL 234/16, MA.

6. Idflieg no. 643, fol. no. 262, NE, BA. KAdL, *Entwicklungsgeschichte*, p. 46, IIL 234/32, MA.

7. Cuneo, *Mars*, 2:147.

8. Ibid.

9. Hans von Schiller, *Zeppelin: Wegbereiter des Weltluftverkehrs*, pp. 62–63. Peter M. Grosz and Egon Krüger, "Siemens-Schuckert Aircraft, 1909–1919." GC.

10. Euler to Idflieg, 4 August 1914, fol. no. 262, NE, BA. KAdL, *Entwicklungsgeschichte*, pp. 46–47, IIL 234/32, MA. Kommission zur Prüfung von Verträgen über Kriegslieferungen (hereinafter referred to as Commission on War Deliveries), stenographic reports, no. 3. Meeting on 11 August, 1917, p. 10, K10–4/2540, AM, MA.

11. Protocols of first and second meetings of the Commission of Parliamentary Deputies, six, 7 August 1914, fol. nos. 59, 267, NE, BA.

12. Ibid.

13. Fritz Blaich, *Kartell - und Monopolpolitik im Kaiserlichen Deutschland: das Problem der Marktmacht im deutschen Reichstag zwischen 1879–1914*, pp. 114, 117, 230.

14. Fritz Fischer, *Germany's Aims in the First World War*, pp. 280–82.
15. KM no. 785.8.14A1, K10-4/2532, AM, MA.
16. *Fünfundzwanzig Jahre DVL, 1912–1937*, p. 23, GC.
17. KM no. 2089/9.14.A7L to SGK, in KbKM no. 41685, 5 October 1914, MKr 1385, BKA.
18. Euler to Idflieg, 9 September 1914, fol. no. 253, NE, BA.
19. Protocol of KM meeting on aircraft industry, 2 September 1914, fol. no. 59, NE, BA.
20. Commission on War Deliveries, first meeting, 19 December 1916, p. 12, K10-4/2540, AM, MA.
21. Imrie, *Air Service*, p. 26.
22. Flugplatz Berlin-Johannisthal to RdI, no. 5983, 9 September 1914; no. 6000, 11 September 1914; no. 6032, 14 September 1914; no. 6293, 13 October 1914; no. 6477, 3 October 1914; IL2/35, MA. Cuneo, *Mars*, 2:147.
23. Cuneo, *Mars*, 2:157. Peter Supf, *Das Buch der deutschen Fluggeschichte*, 2:251–52.
24. A. R. Weyl, *Fokker: The Creative Years*, pp. 90–92. On Euler's difficulty, see Euler-Idflieg correspondence November 1914–March 1915, fol. no. 254, NE, BA.
25. Oswald Bölcke, Hauptmann Bölckes *Feldberichte*, pp. 25–26.
26. Fröbus (LFG) to Euler, 2 December 1914, fol. no. 257, NE, BA.
27. Ibid. Commission on War Deliveries, third session, p. 63, app. 15, pp. 51–52, apps. 4, 5, K10-4/2540, AM, MA. Euler to Sperling, 6 November 1915, fol. no. 20, NE, BA. Industry correspondence with VdMI, 14–15 January 1915, fol. no. 19, NE, BA. Weyl, *Fokker*, p. 131.
28. Commission on War Deliveries, first session, 19 December 1916, pp. 9–13, K10-4/2540, AM, MA. Correspondence with VdMI, 14–15 January 1915, fol. no. 19, NE, BA.
29. Cuneo, *Mars*, 2:162.
30. Rittmeister a.D. Hubert von Hösslin, *Die Organisation der K.B. Fliegertruppe, 1912–1919*, pp. 11–17, 27. KbKM no. 26225 to SGK, 16 August 1914 and apps.; II to KbKM, August 1914; Albatros to KbKM, 18 August 1914; II to Albatros, 24 August 1914; MKr 1385, BKA.
31. KbKM nos. 52452, 63843, 26 December 1914, and apps., MKr 1385, BKA. LVG telegram, 20 October 1914 and following Iluft—II correspondence; KMAD no. 2258/10.14. A7L to Idflieg, 31 October 1914; KbKM no. 50074, 9 November 1914, and apps.; MKr 1385, BKA.
32. Ibid.
33. KbKM no. 52456, 27 December 1914, and apps., MKr 1385, BKA.
34. KbKM nos. 52452, 63843, 26 December 1914, and apps., MKr 1385, BKA.
35. FEA no. 1139 to Iluft, 18 September 1914; KbKM no. 56011, 1 December 1914; MKr 1385, BKA.
36. KbKM no. 4616 to II and SGK, 24 January 1915, MKr 1385, BKA.

37. A. H. G. Fokker and Bruce Gould, *Flying Dutchman: The Life of Anthony Fokker,* pp. 117–18.

38. Kmdo der MLA no. GB1121 to KKdH, 15 October 1914; BdMLA no. GB78 to KKdH, 16 October 1914; SSdRMA no. BX 4352 to KKdH, 18 October 1914; stock no. 804 D215, AM, MA. Report of Commission on War Deliveries (tenth, eleventh, and twelfth meetings), February 1918, p. 34, stock no. K10-4/2540, AM, MA.

39. Hermann Moll, "Das Deutsche Marine- und Seeflugzeug von 1909 bis 1918," *MR* 55 (1958): 170. Cuneo, *Mars,* 2:445.

40. Budget Commission, volume 1915, no. 46, February 1915, stock no. 7631, vol. 2, AM, MA.

41. KAdM, *Atlas deutscher und Ausländischer Seeflugzeuge,* vol. 2, statistical sheets.

42. Kaiserliche Werft Wilhelmshaven no. K3459 to KKdH Marinesektion, 12 December 1914, stock no. 804 D215, AM, MA.

43. RMA Memorandum no. I on T-planes, October 1914, stock no. 805 D216, AM, MA.

44. Otto Göbel, *Deutsche Rohstoffwirtschaft im Weltkrieg, einschliesslich des Hindenburg Programms.* Alfred Müller, *Die Kriegsrohstoffbewirtschaftung 1914–1918 im Dienste des deutschen Monopolkapitals.*

Chapter 2

1. General Ernst von Höppner, *Deutschlands Krieg in der Luft: ein Ruckblick auf die Entwicklung und die Leistungen unserer Heeres-Luftstreitkräfte im Weltkrieg,* p. 37. Maj. a.D. Hilmer Freiherr von Bülow, *Geschichte der Luftwaffe: eine kurze Darstellung der fünften Waffe,* p. 58.

2. Idflieg Abt. Ia no. 656 Kr to GIdMV, 16 April 1915, IL26/134, MA.

3. KMAD, 3 May 1915 in KbKM nos. 53818, 43623, 7–8 June 1915, MKr 1386, BKA.

4. For example, see Peter Supf, *Das Buch der deutschen Fluggeschichte;* and Archivrat Maj. a.D. Hans Arndt, "Die Fliegerwaffe," in *Der Stellungkrieg, 1914–1918,* ed. Friedrich Seesselberg, pp. 310–69.

5. Dorner to Captain Wagenführ, 17 August 1915, ND, DM.

6. A. R. Weyl, *Fokker: The Creative Years,* pp. 106, 131–32.

7. Hans von Schiller, *Zeppelin: Wegbereiter des Luftverkehrs,* p. 63.

8. Peter M. Grosz and Egon Krüger, "Siemens-Schuckert," GC.

9. Richard Blunck, *Hugo Junkers: ein Leben für Technik und Luftfahrt,* pp. 90–102. Junkers File, GC.

10. A. H. G. Fokker and Bruce Gould, *Flying Dutchman: The Life of Anthony Fokker,* pp. 122–27.

11. Ibid.

12. Franz Immelmann, *Immelmann: Der Adler von Lille,* p. 93.

13. Quentin Reynolds, *They Fought for the Sky,* pp. 56–57.

14. Weyl, *Fokker,* p. 129.

15. There were only approximately 110 E3s at the front in April 1916 (Peter Gray and Owen Thetford, *German Aircraft of The First World War,* p. 82), far too few to prevent enemy air activity.

16. Grosz and Krüger, *Siemens-Schuckert,* GC. Gray and Thetford, *Aircraft,* pp. 183–85.

17. Commission on War Deliveries, first session, pp. 9–13, 48–49, K10–4/ 2540, AM, MA.

18. Figures for the industry as a whole are found in Euler to Sperling, 6 November 1915, fol. no. 20, NE, BA. For Berlin, see Commission on War Deliveries, third session, pp. 51–52, apps. 4, 5, K10–4/2540, AM, MA. Also see Appendix 3.

19. "Die Lohnbewegung in den Betrieben der Flugzeugindustrie Berlins," *Stuttgarter Metallarbeiter-Zeitung,* 22 May 1915, MKr 1386, BKA.

20. Generalmajor a.D. Ernst von Wrisberg, *Heer und Heimat, 1914–1918: Erinnerungen an die Kriegsjahre in Königlich preussische Kriegsministerium,* 2:213–29.

21. "Teuerungszuschlag in den Johannisthaler Flugzeugbetrieben," *Vorwärts,* 2 October 1915, MKr 1386, BKA. See Appendix 3, and Gerhard Bry, *Wages in Germany, 1871–1945,* p. 211, table 53.

22. Correspondence on Berlin association, fol. no. 20, NE, BA.

23. *Entwicklungsgeschichte: Statistik der Flugzeugfabriken, 1914–1918,* pp. 80–148, charts, IIL 234/32, MA. Idflieg, ZAK, Draft, *"Geschichte der deutschen Flugzeugindustrie,"* vol. 2a, GC.

24. *Ibid.* Albatros to KbKM, 18 August 1914, MKr 1385, BKA.

25. Figures are estimates based on Sir Walter Raleigh and H. A. Jones, *War in the Air: Being the Story of the Part Played in the the Great War by the Royal Air Force;* Abert Étévé, *La victorie des cocardes;* and Walter Jost and Friedrich Felger, *Was wir vom Weltkrieg nicht wissen.*

26. The dispersal occurred because the German army made no distinctions among its armed aircraft, so armed two-seaters and single-seaters were used together.

27. Feldflugchef no. 400, 5 June 1915, IL 42/14, MA.

28. Peter Grosz, "Hannover Aircraft, 1915–1919," *Air Pictorial,* July 1971, p. 252. Dr. Alfred Hildebrandt, "Die schwarzen Hannoverana," (*Flugzeug,* special issue, 3, no. 3 December 1920); 37–47.

29. Feldflugchef no. 7610, IIL 234/37, MA.

30. Ibid.

31. KbKM nos. 43623, 53818, 7–8 June 1915, MKr 1386, BKA. KbKM no. 51452 to II and SGK, 15 June 1915, MKr 1386. BKA. Rittmeister a.D. Hübert von Hösslin, *Die Organisation der K. B. Fliegertruppe, 1912–1919,* p. 28.

32. Feldflugchef no. 306 to II, 17 April 1915; II no. 147000 to KbKM, 14 June 1915; IL 42/10, MA. Feldflugchef no. 1323 fl to KbKM and II, 27 May 1915, MKr 1386, BKA. FEA no. 14029 to Flugzeug Depot Otto, 6 July 1915,

MKr 1386; Otto to K.b. Innenministerium, 9 July 1915, MKr 1387; BKA. Idflieg IIIc no. 31464 Kr to II, 2 September 1915; Idflieg IIIa no. 34475 Kr to II, 27 September 1915; MKr 1386, BKA.

33. Otto to K.b. Ministerium des königlichen Hauses und des Äussern, 14 April 1915, and following correspondence, MKr 1386, BKA. Otto to Kb. Inneniministerium, 9 July 1915, MKr 1387, BKA.

On labor problems at Otto, see KbKM nos. 95675, 101217, 25 November 1915, MKr 1386, BKA. On Otto's financial problems, see KbKM nos. 85149, 90572, 28 September 1915; KbKM no. 96804, 17 October 1915; KbKM 82003, 111748; MKr 1386; KbKM no. 99694/15, 21 February 1916, MKr 1387; BKA.

34. IMLuK no. 16386 to II, 17 December 1915 in KbKM 5811, 20 January 1916, and apps., MKr 1386, BKA.

35. Labor commission report of 11 October 1915 in KbKM 99694/15, 21 February 1916, and apps., MKr 1387, BKA.

36. FEA No. 14601 to Iluft, 13 July 1915, IL 42/10, MA. Idflieg IIIc no. 31464 Kr to II, 2 September 1915, MKr 1386, BKA.

37. Budget Commission, volumes February, December 1915, AM, MA. Herrmann Moll, "Das deutsche Marine- und Seeflugzeug von 1909 bis 1918," *MR* 55 (1958):170. MGFA, *Handbuch zur deutschen Militärgeschichte*, 5:301.

38. Raleigh and Jones, *War in the Air*, 2:377. Budget Commission, volume February 1915, no. 46, stock no. 7631, vol. 2, AM, MA.

39. Budget Commission, volume December 1915, stock no. 7633, vol. 3, AM, MA. KAdM, *Atlas*, vol. 2 *Statistische Blätter*. Gray and Thetford, *Aircraft*.

40. Ibid. RMA Memorandum no. II on T-planes, October 1915; SSdRMA no. BXc 12170 to KKdH, 29 October 1915, stock no. 805 D216, AM, MA. Moll, "Seeflugzeug," pp. 174–75.

41. Budget Commission, volume February 1915, AM, MA.

42. Georg Paul Neumann, *Die deutschen Luftstreitkräfte im Weltkrieg,* pp. 305–9.

43. For examples, see Helmut Otto, Karl Schmiedel, Helmut Schnitter, *Der erste Weltkrieg;* and Peter Graf Kielmansegg, *Deutschland und der erste Weltkrieg.*

Chapter 3

1. Euler to Kp Rüstabteilung für Fliegerwaffen, 22 March 1918, fol. no. 271, NE, BA.

2. Euler memorandum "Der Fall Garros," 21 October 1941, fol. no. 52, NE, BA. Idflieg BLV 1915, 1916. Euler to KMAD, 14 August 1915, to Idflieg, 13 August 1915, fol. nos. 59, 243, NE, BA. Sperling to Euler, 5, 11 November 1915, fol. no. 20, NE, BA. Conference in KpKM, 19 November 1915, summary fol. no. 63, NE, BA. Fol. no. 254, NE, BA.

3. Proceedings of conference in Reichstag, 20 January 1916, fol. no. 267, NE, BA.

4. Fröbus to Euler, 21 January 1916, fol. no. 20, NE, BA.

5. Note, 21 January 1916, fol. no. 20; note, 25 January 1916, fol. no. 59; NE, BA.

6. Fol. no. 267, NE, BA. Circular, KMAD no. 1484/6.16.A7L, 13 July 1916, fol. no. 62, NE, BA.

7. Note, 24, 29 May 1916, fol. no. 51, NE, BA.

8. Oberleutnant Behl, news report, 28 March 1916, Idflieg reports, GC.

9. Peter M. Grosz, "The Albatros Fighters D1 to D5a," manuscript, p. 1, GC. Peter Gray and Owen Thetford, *German Aircraft of The First World War*, p. 84. Johannes Werner, *Knight of Germany: Oswald Bölcke, German Ace*, pp. 159–60.

10. Grosz, "Albatros," p. 3.

11. A. H. G. Fokker and Bruce Gould, *Flying Dutchman: The Life of Anthony Fokker*, pp. 155–58.

12. Ibid., pp. 192–93. Oswald Bölcke, *Hauptmann Bölckes Feldberichte*, pp. 84–85.

13. John R. Cuneo, *Winged Mars*, 2:245–54.

14. CdGS no. 33825 to KM, 31 August 1916 in Erich Ludendorff, ed., *Urkunden der obersten Heeresleitung über ihre Tätigkeit*, 1916/1918, pp. 63–65.

15. Cuneo, *Mars*, 2:260.

16. Commission on War Deliveries, third session, 11 January 1917, p. 55, app. 9, K10–4/2540, AM, MA.

17. Kmdo des III Geschwaders GB no. 1917 Al to KKdH, 16 August 1916; collected sheets, "Facharbeiter der Flugzeugindustrie," 24 August 1916; fol. no. 805, Pq 77710, AM, MA.

18. Oberleutnant Behl, news report, 1 September 1916, Idflieg reports, GC.

19. Siegert, "Organisation der Bauüberwachung und Abnahme von Militärflugzeugen," 19 September 1916, fol. no. 236, NE, BA.

20. Gen. Ernst von Höppner, *Deutschlands Krieg in der Luft: ein Ruckblick auf die Entwicklung und die Leistungen unserer Heeres-Luftstreitkräfte im Weltkrieg*, p. 90.

21. Rittmeister a.D. Hubert von Hösslin, *Die Organisation der K. B. Fliegertruppe*, p. 29.

22. KMAD no. 1776/4.16.A7L to Euler, 1 May 1916; Euler to KMAD, 4 May 1916; KMAD No. 1221/5.16.A7L to Euler, 3 June 1916; Euler to KMAD, 4 November 1916; notes, 26 September–7 October 1916; fol. no. 263, NE, BA.

23. A. R. Weyl, *Fokker: The Creative Years*, pp. 194–96.

24. Idflieg Fzm III B no. 901 Kr16, 16 October 1916, fol. no. 236, NE, BA.

25. Ibid.

26. Feldflugchef no. 548, 31 August 1916, Mkr 1405, BKA.

27. KbKM nos. 15566, 13 February 1916, and apps., 6557 and apps., MKr 1386, BKA. KbKM no. 5811, 20 January 1916, and apps., MKr 1386, BKA. KbKM no. 20910, 28 March 1916, MKr 1387, BKA.

28. BB Idflieg reports, 25 March 1916, 8 September 1916; MKr 1387, BKA. Gray and Thetford, *Aircraft*, pp. 163, 177.

29. KbKM no. 45711 to II, 30 July 1916, IL 41/1, MA.

30. Max Spindler, ed., *Handbuch der Bayerischen Geschichte,* 4, pt. 2:820–23.

31. Hösslin, *K. B. Fliegertruppe,* p. 28.

32. Georg Paul Neumann, *Die deutschen Luftstreitkräfte in Weltkrieg,* pp. 313–14.

33. Ibid., pp. 305–11.

34. Ibid.

35. Ibid., p. 308.

36. Ibid., pp. 306–7.

37. Ibid., pp. 306–13.

38. Karl Köhler, "Auf dem Wege zur Luftwaffe," *Wehrwissenschaftliche Rundschau* 16, no. 1 (January 1966): 553.

39. Ibid.

40. Cuneo, *Mars,* 2:278.

41. Ibid., 2:278–80.

42. See, for example, Alistair Horne, *Death of a Generation* (New York: American Heritage, 1970).

Chapter 4

1. John G. Williamson, *Karl Helfferich, 1872–1924: Economist, Financier, Politician,* p. 175.

2. Gerald D. Feldman, *Army, Industry, and Labor in Germany, 1914–18,* p. 154.

3. Generalmajor Ludwig Wurtzbacher, "Die Versorgung des Heeres mit Waffen und Munition," in *Der Weltkampf um Ehre und Recht,* ed. Generalleutnant Max Schwartze, 6:115.

4. Major a.D. Hilmer Freiherr von Bülow, *Geschichte der Luftwaffe: eine kurze Darstellung der fünften Waffe,* p. 80. Archivat Maj. a.D. Hans Arndt, "Der Luftkrieg," in *Der Weltkampf um Ehre und Recht,* ed. Generalleutnant Max Schwartze, 4:585.

5. KMAD no. 2407/11.16. A7L to Idflieg, 30 November 1916, fol. no. 263, NE, BA.

6. BB Idflieg, report no. 16, February 1917, Mkr 1388, BKA.

7. *Flugsport,* October–December 1917.

8. Rumpler to Iluft, 20 October 1916; Idflieg Fzm IIIa no. 205–166 Kr16 to Iluft, 18 October 1916; Rumpler to Iluft, 4 November 1916; IL 41/17, MA.

9. BB Idflieg, report no. 16, 9 February 1917, MKr 1388, BKA.

10. *Flug–amtliches Organ des deutschen Flieger-Bundes* for year 1917.

11. Information on Idflieg in Ing. Karl Tindl, Flars Technische Auskunftei, no. 126, "Bericht über die Studienreise zur Idflieg," 12–22 October 1917, fol. no. 325, LA, OK.

12. Idflieg REA Kmdo. to R-plane factories, 22 January 1917, GC.

13. Idflieg no. 210/17 to aircraft factories, 31 July 1917, IL 41/1, MA. SSW, second aircraft conference, 14 February 1917, SS File, GC. Otto Göbel, *Rohstoffwirtschaft, einschliesslich des Hindenburg–Programms,* pp. 111, 117. Some of the aircraft factories also formed an Association of German Aircraft Industrialists Limited Liability Co. (Verband Deutscher Flugzeug-Industrieller GmbH) in 1917 that was attached to the Central Association of German Industrialists (Zentralverband Deutscher Industrieller). The role of this association during the war is not clear, although it emerged after the war as the aircraft industry's trade association, superseding the industry's prewar organization, the convention of Aircraft Industrialists, which had been attached to the Association of Motor Vehicle Industrialists.

14. Idflieg Fzm Al no. 390238 Kr to Euler, 12 January 1917; Idflieg Fzm B1 to Euler, 3 January 1917; Idflieg Fzm B1 no. 495597 Kr 17 to Euler, 25 January 1917; fol. no. 274, NE, BA.

15. Idflieg no. 139535 Kr17 to Euler, fol. no. 274, NE, BA.

16. Idflieg Fzm Al no. 370769 Kr17 to Hofmarschallamt, 9 February 1917; Idflieg Fzm ZAK No. 417372/17 to BAs, 24 March 1917; Idflieg Fzm no. 296651/17 to aircraft firms, 5 April 1917; fol. no. 274, NE, BA.

17. Idflieg Fzm ZAK No. 417372/17 to BAs, 24 March 1917, fol. no. 274, NE, BA.

18. Idflieg Fzm A no. 350901 to aircraft factories, 25 February 1917; Idflieg Fzm Al no. 371351 Krl7 to Euler, 28 February 1917; fol. no. 274, NE, BA.

19. Bau Programm 1917, fol. no. 274, NE, BA.

20. "Haftet der Lieferant eines Flugzeugs für Reparaturkosten des Bestellers," *Flugsport* 9 (1917): 109–12. "Sind die Betriebserfahrungen usw. des Flugzeugfirmen vogelfrei?," *Flugsport* 10 (1918): 634–35.

After the war, patent secrets were to be returned to the firms with the reinstatement of protection, but in December 1918 individuals were illegally publishing patent information despite the efforts of Wumba and the inspectorate to return such material to the rightful owners.

21. Idflieg Fzm Abt. A.I.B. no. 370522 Krl7 to Euler, 15, 24 May 1917; Euler to Idflieg and KpKM, 4 June 1917; fol. no. 63, NE, BA.

22. *Beiträge zur Entwicklungsgeschichte des Flugzeugwesens und des Flugzeugbaues im Heer und in der Marine,* no. 30, KAdL, IL 234/32, MA.

23. Feldman, *Army,* p. 126.

24. Commission on War Deliveries, ninth meeting, pp. 51–2, apps. 4, 5. Gerhard Bry, *Wages in Germany, 1871–1945,* p. 200, Table 49. See Appendix 3.

25. CdGS II no. 2452 to KpKM and Bethmann Hollweg, 9 March 1917, in *Urkunden der obersten Heeresleitung über ihre Tätigkeit, 1916 /18,* ed. Erich Ludendorff, pp. 136–37.

26. Heinrich Scheel, "Der Aprilstreik 1917 in Berlin," in *Revolutionäre Ereignisse und Probleme in Deutschland . . . 1917 /1918 während der Periode der grossen sozialisten Oktoberrevolution,* by Akademie der Wissenschaften, Berlin, Institut für Geschichte, pp. 51, 56, 57, 69.

27. CdGS II nos. 46581, 46582 to KpKM, KRA, 16 February 1917, in *Urkunden*, ed. Ludendorff, pp. 158–61.

28. On raw material prices see Euler to Idflieg, 23 July 1917, and apps., fol. no. 265, NE, BA. On G-plane prices, see unsigned Idflieg-KpKM correspondence, February 1917, GC.

29. Georg Paul Neumann, *Die deutschen Luftstreitkräfte im Weltkriege*, pp. 313–14.

30. Iluft no. 9772 to FEA, 20 November 1916, IL 41/10, MA. Idflieg Fzm ZAK no. 437260/17 UR to BA at BFW, 2 February 1917, MKr 1388, BKA.

31. Iluft no. 4008 to Fluba München I, II, Speyer, 10 February 1917; Selzer to Iluft, 20 February 1917; IL 41/17, MA.

32. Iluft no. 5148 to Selzer, 28 February 1917, IL 41/17, MA.

33. Kogenluft no. 78140 F1 III to KbKM, 3 March 1917, MKr 1388, BKA.

34. In general on BFW case, see KbKM nos. 37856, 38784, 39543, 42249, 17 March 1917, MKr 1388, BKA. Reports are Fluba no. 1110, 9903 to Iluft, 6, 7 March 1917; Iluft no. 6553 to II, 7 March 1917; MKr 1388, BKA. II no. 9799 IVa to KbKM, 10 March 1917, MKr 1388, BKA.

35. KbMB no. 10094 to KbKM, 8 March 1917, MKr 1388, BKA.

36. KbKM 42249 to Kogenluft, 17 March 1917, MKr 1388, BKA.

37. Protocol of R-plane conference, 14 December 1917, fol. no. 806, AM, MA.

38. SSdRMA no. BXe 8655 to CdAS, 29 July 1916; CdAS no. A24208I, 8 August 1916; fol. no. 1005; SSdRMA no. BXc 12936, 7 September 1917; fol. no. 805; AM, MA. Peter Gray and Owen Thetford, *German Aircraft of the First World War*, pp. 56–58, 64–67. *Fighter Aircraft of the 1914–1918 War*, pp. 164–65.

39. Gray and Thetford, *Aircraft*, pp. 68–71.

40. CdAS No. A22716I, July 1916; Kmdo. des III. Geschwaders no. 1917 Al, 16 August 1916; Kmdo. des II. Seefliegerabt. GB no. 8611, 4 December 1916; BdMFA GB no. F8408 to RMA, 26 December 1916; SSdRMA BXc no. 15843 to KKdH, 28 December 1916; fol. no. 805, AM, MA.

41. Gray and Thetford, *Aircraft*, pp. 133–35. Kmdo. der Seeflieger des Marinekorps GB nos. 630, 735 to SVK, 13, 30 June 1917, fol. no. 6468; SSd RMA no. M2390 to KKdH, 19 April 1918, fol. no. 806; Kmdo. des I. Seefliegerabt. B no. G91, to SVK, 16 May 1917, fol. no. 6469; AM, MA. Kommandeur bei den Hochseestreitkräften B no. 744 to SVK, 30 December 1917; II Seefliegerabt. memorandum, 22 February 1918; fol. no. 6469; AM, MA.

42. Gray and Thetford, *Aircraft*, pp. 578–84. G. W. Haddow & Peter M. Grosz, *The German Giants: The Story of the R-Planes*. SSdRMA no. M2390 to KKdH, 19 April 1918, fol. no. 806, AM, MA. Neumann, *Luftstreitkräfte*, p. 309.

43. Peter M. Grosz, "The Albatros Fighters D1 to DVa," p. 9, GC.

44. Grosz, "Albatros," pp. 12–13, GC. Gray and Thetford, *Aircraft*, pp. 209–12.

45. Grosz, "Albatros," p. 15, GC.

46. Ibid., pp. 1–4. Gray and Thetford, *Aircraft*, pp. 87–97. BB Idflieg Report no. 18, 15 March 1917, MKr 1388, BKA.

47. Gray and Thetford, *Aircraft*, p. 50. On Bloody April, see *Warplanes and Air Battles of World War I*, pp. 92–99.

48. Aaron Norman, *The Great Air War*, pp. 187–88.

49. Grosz, "Albatros," pp. 21–26. BB Idflieg Report no. 21, 1 May 1917, MKr 1388, BKA.

50. Alex Imrie, *Pictorial History of the German Army Air Service, 1914–1918*, p. 42.

51. Bülow, *Luftwaffe*, pp. 81–82.

52. Helmut Otto, Karl Schmiedel, and Helmut Schnitter, *Der erste Weltkrieg*, p. 74.

53. J. A. Gilles, *Flugmotoren, 1910 bis 1918*, p. 91.

54. KAdL, *Kurzer Überblick über die Entwicklung der deutschen Luftstreitkräfte bis zum 7 Aug. 1918*, p. 14, KAdL, vol. IIL 234/47, MA.

Chapter 5

1. Alex Imrie, *Pictorial History of the German Air Service, 1914–1918*, p. 43.

2. CdGS no. 58034 to KM, 25 June 1917 in II no. 31576, 13 July 1917, IL 41/1, MA.

3. Ibid.

4. CdGS no. 60050 to KMKA, 23 June 1917 in *Urkunden der obersten Heeresleitung*, ed. Erich Ludendorff, p. 162.

5. Idflieg Z1 no. 41, 3 July 1917, IL 41/1, MA.

6. J. A. Gilles, *Flugmotoren, 1910 bis 1918*, p. 101. KAdL, *Kurzer Überblick über die Entwicklung der deutschen Luftstreitkräfte bis zum 7 August 1918*, p. 4, IIL 234/47, MA.

7. Oberleutnant Krug, report no. 48, 24 July 1917, IL 43/41, MA.

8. Oberleutnant Reichelt, *Berechnung der Arbeiterzahlen bei Erhöhung der Produktion*, 21 August 1917, fol. no. 324, LA, OK. See also Ing. Karl Tindl, Flars Technische Auskunftei no. 126, *"Bericht über die Studienreise zur Idflieg,"* 12–22 October 1917, fol. no. 325, LA, OK.

9. Idflieg Z1 no. 210/17, 31 July 1917, IL41/1, MA.

10. Euler-Siegert correspondence, July–December 1917, fol. nos. 66, 265, 272, 273, NE, BA.

11. CdGS no. 69986 to KA, 12 November 1917 in *Urkunden*, ed. Ludendorff, pp. 166–67.

12. Wumba, 18 December 1917, K10-4/2543, AM, MA.

13. KA no. HF 103/9, 11 December 1917, fol. no. 269, NE, BA.

14. Euler to Idflieg, 23 July 1917, and app., fol. no. 265, NE, BA.

15. Commission on War Deliveries, thirteenth session, 15 February 1918, p. 35, K10-4/2540, AM, MA.

16. *Nachrichtenblatt* 1, no. 3 (18 November 1917), IL43/41, MA.

17. Ibid., no. 4 (3 December 1917), IL43/31, MA.

18. Gen. Ernst von Höppner, *Deutschlands Krieg in der Luft: ein Rückblick auf die Entwicklung und die Leistungen unserer Heeres-Luftstreitkräfte im Weltkrieg*, pp. 141–42.

19. Captain Stabl BB Idflieg monthly reports, December 1917–February 1918, IL41/1, MA.

20. LVG and SSW to Idflieg Fzm, 22 March 1918, Gotha File, GC. Höppner, *Krieg*, p. 142.

21. Georg Paul Neumann, *Die deutschen Luftstreitkräfte im Weltkrieg*, p. 71.

22. BB Idflieg no. 347/18, monthly report, January 1918, IL41/1, MA.

23. *Deutschland im ersten Weltkrieg*, 3:148.

24. Oberkmdo. in den Marken no. 339, 28 January 1918 and KM no. 930/18g A1 to Kaiser, in Wilhelm Deist, ed., *Militär und Innenpolitik im Weltkrieg, 1914–1918*, 2:1139, 1163. Walter Bartel, "Der Januarstreik 1918 in Berlin," in *Revolutionääre Ereignisse und Probleme in Deutschland während der Periode der grosser sozialistischen Oktoberrevolution, 1917 /1918*, by Akademie der Wissenschaften, Berlin, Institut für Geschichte, p. 64. BB Idflieg no. 526/18, 23 March 1918, IL 41/1, MA. Gilles, *Flugmotoren*, p. 117.

25. KbKM no. 82002 to II, SGK, IL42/43, MA. BB Idflieg no. 734/18, 24 April 1918, MKr 1389, BKA.

26. Excerpt from protocol of ZAK conference on 4 October 1917, *Nachrichtenblatt 1*, no. 1 (10 October 1917); excerpt from ZAK conference on 6 December 1917, apps., *Nachrichtenblatt* 2, no. 1 (12 January 1918); IL43/31, MA.

27. ZAK Kmdo. Stat. B no. 298/18, 26 March 1918, GC.

28. Junkers File, GC. Richard Blunck, *Hugo Junkers: ein Leben für Technik und Luftfahrt*, pp. 105–10. A. H. G. Fokker and Bruce Gould, *Flying Dutchman: The Life of Anthony Fokker*, pp. 147–48.

29. KbKM no. 110438A to SGK and II, 8 July 1917; II nos. 29810, 11 July 1917, 31576, 13 July 1917; IL41/1; Kogenluft to KbKM, 12 July 1917; IL43/33; MA.

30. II no. 31515 IVa to KbKM, 21 July 1917, IL 43/33, MA.

31. Iluft no. 22828 to II, 9 August 1917, IL 43/33, MA.

32. Reports of Kommission zur Regelung der Arbeiterfrage no. 19, June, 5 July 1917, FEA 1770/III to Iluft; no. 20, July, 27 August 1917, FEA 32351/III to Iluft; no. 21, September–October, 13 October 1917, FEA 49916/IV to Iluft; GC.

33. Rittmeister a.D. Hubert von Hösslin, *Die Organisation der K. B. Fliegertruppe, 1912–1919*, pp. 38–40, app. 3.

34. KbKM no. 176513A, 22 October 1917; KA Nürnberg to KbKM and KA, 17 October 1917; MKr 1388, BKA.

35. Gilles, *Flugmotoren*, p. 102. Oberleutnant Krug, no. 48, 24 July 1917, IL 43/31, MA.

36. Richthofen to Falkenhayn, 18 July 1917, GC.

37. Peter M. Grosz, "The Albatros Fighters D1 to DVa," pp. 21, 25, GC.

38. Ibid., p. 26.

39. Peter M. Grosz and Egon Krüger, *Pfalz: First Detailed Story of the Company and Its Famous Planes.* Peter Gray and Owen Thetford, *German Aircraft of the First World War*, pp. 187–90.

40. J. M. Bruce, *The Fokker DrI* (Profile Publications No. 55). Gray and Thetford, *Aircraft*, pp. 98–101.

41. Richthofen to Falkenhayn, 27 February, 2 April 1918, GC.

42. Hans Herlin, *Udet-eines Mannes Leben und die Geschichte seiner Zeit*, pp. 39–40.

43. Gray and Thetford, *Aircraft*, p. 225. Fokker and Gould, *Dutchman*, pp. 164–71.

44. Gray and Thetford, *Aircraft*, p. 107.

45. Alfred Everbusch to A. R. Weyl, 10 January 1958, Pfalz File, GC. On Richthofen's visit to Pfalz, see Karl Bodenschatz, *Jagd in Flanders Himmel: aus den sechzehn Kampfmonaten des Jagdgeschwaders Freiherr von Richthofen*, p. 166.

46. Peter Grosz, "Hannover Aircraft, 1915–19," *Air Pictorial*, July 1971, pp. 252–56; August 1971, pp. 290–93. Gray and Thetford, *Aircraft*, pp. xv–xxvii.

47. G. W. Haddow and Peter M. Grosz, *The German Giants: The Story of the R-planes, 1914–19.* Gray and Thetford, *Aircraft*, pp. 125–32, 218–21. Raymond H. Fredette, *Sky on Fire: The First Battle of Britain.*

48. Gray and Thetford, *Aircraft*, pp. 133–35, Kmdo. der Seeflieger des Marinekorps GB nos. 630, 735 to SVK, 13, 30 June 1917, fol. no. 6468; SSdRMA no. M2390 to KKdH, 19 April 1918, fol. no. 806; Kmdo. des I. Seefliegerabt. B no. G91 to SVK, 16 May 1917, fol. no. 6469; AM, MA.

49. Kmdo. des II. Seefliegerabt. GB no. 9424 to SVK, 9 October 1917, fol. no. 6490; SSdRMA BX no. 227 to KKdH, 16 October 1917, fol. no. 805.

50. Protocol of R-plane conference, 14 December 1917, fol. no. 806, AM, MA. Fliegerkommandeur bei den Hochseestreitkräften, position paper, 20 December 1917, fol. no. 806, AM, MA. SSdRMA BX no. 43 to KKdH, 5 January 1918; CdAS no. 669 D VI to KKdH, 21 January 1918; fol. no. 806, AM, MA.

51. SSdRMA no. 2390 to KKdH, 19 April 1918, fol. no. 806, AM, MA.

52. Imrie, *Air Service*, pp. 51–52. KAdL, *Die Luftstreitkräfte in der Abwehrschlacht zwischen Somme und Oise vom 8. bis 12. August 1918 und Rückblicke auf ihre vorangegangene Entwicklung*, p. 2.

53. KAdL, *Luftstreitkräfte*, pp. 14–15, II 1234/47, MA.

54. Ibid.

55. Idflieg to KM, 13 March 1918; KM to Idflieg, 26 March 918, GC.

56. Imrie, *Air Service*, pp. 54–56.

Chapter 6

1. MVO des MFC no. 42309f1 to MFC, 14 April 1918, fol. no. 6458, AM, MA. CdGS II/Ic no. 82986op to KM, 11 April 1918, in *Urkunden der obersten*

Heeresleitung über ihre Tätigkeit, 1916/1918, ed. Erich Ludendorff, p. 62.

2. BB bei IdFleig nos. 830/18, 29 May 1918; 963/18, 28 June 1918; 1018/18, 5 August 1918, MKr 1389, BKA.

3. BB bei Idflieg no. 1018/18, 5 August 1918, MKr 1389, BKA.

4. Ibid. SGK II AK no. 173941 to Bezirkskmdo. Kaiserslautern, 18 May 1918, IL 43/37, MA.

5. See *Flug* for year 1918.

6. MVO des MFC no. 42309 f1 to MFC, 14 April 1918, fol. no. 6458, AM, MA.

7. Ibid.

8. On Fokker D7, see the following: A. R. Weyl, *Fokker: The Creative Years,* pp. 267, 270, 275, 284, 310. MVO des MFC nos. 43190 f1, 15 May 1918, 44030 f1, 5 June 1918, to MFC; fol. no. 6458, AM, MA. Peter Gray and Owen Thetford, *German Aircraft of the First World War,* pp. 106–7. Quote from Sir Walter Raleigh and H. A. Jones, *The War in the Air: Being the Story of the Part Played in the Great War by the Royal Air Force,* 6:445.

9. MVO des MFC nos. 228, 28 July 1918, 289, 17 August 1918, 304, 19 August 1918, to SVK; fol. no. 6470 LuIV 28, AM, MA. Alex Imrie, *Pictorial History of the German Air Service, 1914–1918,* pp. 55–56.

10. Imrie, *Air Service,* pp. 55–56.

11. Ibid.

12. Archivrat Maj. a.d. Hans Arndt, "Die Fliegerwaffe," in *Der Stellungkrieg, 1914–1918,* ed. Friedrich Seesselberg, pp. 361–62.

13. The best evidence of Siegert's exhaustion is a long letter from Siegert to Euler upon the inspector's retirement (Siegert to Euler), 13 December 1918, fol. no. 265, NE, BA.

14. Siegert to Junkers, June 1918, Junkers file, GC.

15. MVO des MFC no. 350 MVO to SVK, 8 September 1918, fol. no. 6470 LuIV 28, AM, MA.

16. A. H. G. Fokker and Bruce Gould, *Flying Dutchman: The Life of Anthony Fokker,* pp. 206–8.

17. A. R. Weyl, *Fokker: The Creative Years,* p. 321.

18. Peter M. Grosz and Egon Krüger, *SSW Aircraft, 1909–1919,* GC.

19. Weyl, *Fokker,* p. 345.

20. Gray and Thetford, *Aircraft,* pp. 213–17.

21. Ibid., pp. 108, 216–17.

22. MVO des MFC no. 452 to SVK, 16 October 1918, fol. no. 6470 LuIV 28, AM, MA.

23. Weyl, *Fokker,* pp. 331–45.

24. Fokker and Gould, *Dutchman,* pp. 173–78.

25. Ibid., p. 178. H. J. Nowarra and K. S. Brown, *Von Richthofen and the Flying Circus,* 3d ed. (Letchworth: Harleyford, 1964), p. 188. Aaron Norman, *The Great Air War,* pp. 470–71.

26. Weyl, *Fokker,* p. 346. Gray and Thetford, *Aircraft,* p. xxxii. Hans Herlin,

Udet-eines Mannes Leben und die Geschichte seiner Zeit, pp. 81–88.

27. CdAS no. 5942 D II to KKdH, 30 September 1918, fol. no. 806, AM, MA.

28. Ernst Heinkel, *Stürmisches Leben*, pp. 79–85.

29. Gray and Thetford, *Aircraft*, pp. 72–74. Kdflieg FG no. 1259, 2 April 1918, fol. no. 6470; "Bericht über die Tätigkeit der Nordseeflugstationen," 21 May–5 June 1918, fol. no. 6458; AM, MA.

30. Gray and Thetford, *Aircraft*, pp. 75–78, 291–301. Heinkel, *Leben*, pp. 85–87.

31. Raleigh and Jones, *War*, 6:385–59, 376, 380. Befehlshaber der Aufklärungsschiffe G no. 5514 N to KKdH, 11 July 1918: Hochseekmdo. no. 6025A to SSdRMA, 23 July 1918; RMA telegram to KKdH, 31 July 1918; SSd RMA no. Lu 14702 to KKdH, 1 October 1918; SSdRMA no. Lul6750 to MFC, 7 November 1918; fol. no. 806, AM, MA. Marinebaumeister a.D. Gotth. Baatz, "Die Entwicklung des Seeflugzeugbaues im Kriege," pts. 2, 3, *IFW* 1, no. 12 (3 December 1919): 376–82; no. 13 (17 December 1919), 403–7.

32. BB bei Idflieg no. 1414/18, 8 November 1918, MKr 1389, BKA.

33. Ibid.

34. *Flug*, August, October 1918.

35. Rittmeister a.D. Hubert von Hösslin, *Die Organisation der K. B. Fliegertruppe*, pp. 38–40.

36. J. A. Gilles, *Flugmotoren, 1910 bis 1918*, pp. 186–87.

37. Raleigh and Jones, *War*, 6:435–36, 442–44, 491.

38. Imrie, *Air Service*, p. 58.

39. Hauptmann Hermann [pseud.], *The Luftwaffe: Its Rise and Fall* (New York: Putnam, 1943), pp. 3–7.

40. Heinz Hürten and Georg Meyer, *Adjutant im preussischen Kriegsministerium, Juni 1918 bis Oktober 1919: Aufzeichnungen des Hauptmanns Gustav Böhm*, p. 54.

41. Ulrich Kluge, *Soldatenräte und Revolution: Studien zur Militärpolitik in Deutschland, 1918–1919*, p. 49.

42. Ibid., pp. 71–73, 78, 110–12.

43. Alfred Müller, *Die Kriegsrohstoffbewirtschaftung 1914–1918 im Dienste des deutschen Monopolkapitals*, pp. 21–22.

44. Imrie, *Air Service*, p. 59.

45. Generalmajor Hermann Franke, ed., "Die Luftwaffe," *Handbuch der neuzeitlichen Wehrwissenschaften*, 2:177. *Atlas deutscher und ausländischer Seeflugzeuge*, statistical sheets. Raleigh and Jones, *War*, vol. 6, app. 7.

Chapter 7

1. Excerpt from Siegert's diary in fol. no. 265, NE, BA.

2. KbKM Armee-Abt. no. 148901A to II, 11 October 1917; II no. 10505

IVa to KbKM, 10 March 1918; Iluft no. 22495 F1 to II, 6 May 1918; KbKM no. 62964A to II, 10 May 1918; IL 43/37, MA.

3. Iluft no. 30290 F1 to II, 1 June 1918; IL43/37, MA.

4. Hans Radandt, "Hugo Junkers—Ein Monopolkapitalist und korrespondierendes Mitgleid der preussischen Akademie der Wissenschaften," *JFW, 1960,* pt. 1, pp. 94–95.

5. Ibid., p. 95.

6. CdGS Ic no. 64539 to Kogenluft, 8 October 1917; Kogenluft no. 61 G1 of 10 September 1917; fol. no. 270, NE, BA.

7. Radandt, "Junkers," p. 95. SVK to MFC, 17 May 1918, stock no. LuIV 28, AM, MA.

8. RdI II no. 1519 to AEG, 18 March 1918; AEG to Abt. Lu. RMA, 2 April 1918; SSdRMA no. BX 4974, 11 April 1918; stock no. 4369, AM, MA. SSdRMA no. Lu.13211, 1 October 1918; stock no. 5714, set III. 5.1, AM, MA.

9. Cited in protocol of RLA conference, 20 December 1918, fol. no. 281; and in protocol of RLA conference, 17 May 1919, fol. no. 289; NE, BA.

10. Among the pertinent sources on the revolutionary period, see the following works. Charles B. Burdick and Ralph H. Lutz, eds., *The Political Institutions of the German Revolution, 1918–1919;* Heinz Hürten and Georg Meyer, *Adjutant im preussischen Kriegsministerium, Juni 1918 bis October 1919: Aufzeichnungen des Hauptmanns Gustav Böhm;* Ulrich Kluge, *Soldatenräte und Revolution: Studien zur Militärpolitik in Deutschland, 1918–1919;* Eberhard Kolb, *Die Arbeiterräte in der deutschen Innenpolitik, 1918–1919* (Düsseldorf: Droste Verlag, 1962); Ralph H. Lutz, *The German Revolution, 1918–1919;* Susanne Miller, ed., *Die Regierung der Volksbeauftragten, 1918 /19,* 2 vols.; Gerhard W. Rakenius, *Wilhelm Gröner als erster Generalquartiermeister: die Politik der obersten Heeresleitung, 1918 /19.*

11. Miller, *Regierung,* 1:51.

12. *Der Waffenstillstand: das Dokumenten-Material der Waffenstillstands-Verhandlungen von Compiègne, Spa, Trier, und Brüssel, 1918–1919,* 1:25, 59, 97.

13. RLA (Flörke) to Euler, 2 March 1919, fol. no. 295a, NE, BA.

14. Wilhelm Siegert, *Funken aus der Luftwaffen-Schmiede,* pp. 130–34. See also Siegert documents, 10–15 November 1918, in fol. no. 283, NE, BA.

15. Bevoll des KbMFMA no. 13489 to KbMFMA, 20 November 1918, fol. no. MKr 1389, BKA.

16. Ibid. KbMFMA no. 295003, 21 November 1918, IL 43/104, MA.

17. Dornier to Student, 22 November 1918, ND, DM.

18. Siegert, *Luftwaffen-Schmiede,* p. 138.

19. Addendum to telegram from SSdI (Preuss) to Euler, 28 November 1918, fol. no. 283, NE, BA.

20. Euler to Siegert, 25 November 1918, fol. no. 283, NE, BA.

21. Siegert, *Luftwaffen-Schmiede,* p. 138.

22. Siegert to Euler, 13 December 1918, fol. no. 265, NE, BA.

23. Protocol of conference in RdI, 19 December 1918, fol. no. 281, NE, BA.

24. Protocol of conference in RLA, 20 December 1918, fol. no. 281, NE, BA.

25. KbMFMA no. 308455, app. (BFW to MfAA, 6 December 1918), fol. no. Mkr 1390, BKA.

26. Peter Grosz, "Hannover Aircraft, 1915–1919," *Air Pictorial,* August 1971, p. 293. A. H. G. Fokker and Bruce Gould, *Flying Dutchman: The Life of Anthony Fokker,* p. 217.

27. SSW Factory report, November 1918, GC.

28. Richard Blunck, *Hugo Junkers: ein Leben für Technik und Luftfahrt,* pp. 109–10. Radandt, "Junkers," p. 71.

29. Idflieg no. 294/119 to KMAD A7L, 24 January 1919, fol. no. 289; USS der Reichskanzlei no. 2213.19 to KM, 6 February 1919, fol. no. 288; NE, BA.

30. USSdRLA note, 31 January 1919, fol. no. 295a, NE, BA.

31. USSdRLA nos. 1072–81.19 to civil ministries, 24 February 1919, fol. no. 289; USSdRLA telegram, 25 February 1919, fol. no. 288; NE, BA.

32. Euler to Reichskommission für Luftfahrt, 28 February 1919, fol. no. 288; Euler to government agencies, 28 February 1919, fol. no. 289; NE, BA.

33. KMZD to chancellor, central government, and Prussian ministries, Berlin command, 28 February 1919, fol. no. 289, NE, BA. Finanzministerium I no. WA 5907 to KM, 3 March 1919; Reichswirtschaftsministerium I no. 2.3343 to USSdRLA, 11 March 1919; fol. no. 288, NE, BA. Protocol of RLA conference, 15 March 1919, fol. no. 388, NE, BA.

34. Huerten and Meyer, *Böhm,* p. 148.

35. KM no. 4499/19.A7L IV C, 23 April 1919, fol. no. 288, NE, BA.

36. USSdRLA to Gustav Scheidemann, fol. no. 288, NE, BA.

37. DMA Ic no. 54/19, 8 February 1919; DMA no. VI E 2737/19 to RdI, 15 March 1919; DMA Ic no. 115.19, 29 March 1919; IL 2/45, MA. Bevoll des KbMFMA at KpKM no. 1465, fol. no. MKr 1389, BKA.

38. Protocol of RLA conference, 17 May 1919, fol. no. 289, NE, BA. App. 3 of KbMFMA no. 98262 A of 18 July 1919, IL 43/114, MA. Staatskommissar Munich to KbMFMA, 16 May 1919, fol. no. MKr 1390, BKA. Idflieg to DMA, January 1919, R-plane file; AEG notice, 28 May, AEG file; GC.

39. Junkers file, GC. Derek Wood and Derek Dempster, *The Narrow Margin: The Battle of Britain and the Rise of Air Power, 1930–1940,* p. 36.

40. Peter Supf, *Das Buch der deutschen Fluggeschichte,* 2:455–56.

41. *Fs* 22 (30 April 1919), commercial register. Protocol of RLA conference, 17 May 1919, fol. no. 289, NE, BA.

42. Gerald D. Feldman, *Iron and Steel in the German Inflation, 1916–1923,* p. 70.

43. RLA, 7 May 1919, fol. no. 288, NE, BA.

44. Protocol of RLA conference, 17 May 1919, fol. no. 289, NE, BA.

45. Auswärtiges Amt, *Die Friedensbedingungen von Deutschlands Gegnern,* vol. 3, pt. 5, *Bestimmungen über Landheer, Seemacht, und Luftfahrt* (Charlotten-

burg: Deutsche Verlagsgesellschaft für Politik und Geschichte, 1919), pp. 78–80, 210.

46. USSdRLA no. 3801.19, 12 May 1919, protocol of RLA conference, 10 May 1919, fol. no. 288; protocols of RLA conferences, 13, 17 May, fol. no. 289; USSdRLA nos. 4100/19, 4111/19, protocols of RLA conferences, 26, 27 May 1919, fol. no. 281; NE, BA.

47. David E. Barclay, "A Prussian Socialism? Wichard von Möllendorff and the Dilemma of Economic Planning in Germany, 1918–1919," *Central European History* 11, no. 1 (March 1978): 50–82.

48. RLA no. 4575.19, protocol of RLA conference, 18 June 1919, fol. no. 289, NE, BA.

49. Karl-Heinz Völker, *Die Entwicklung der Militärischen Luftfahrt in Deutschland, 1920–1933,* p. 128.

50. Ibid., pp. 128–29. See also Edward L. Homze, *Arming the Luftwaffe: The Reich Air Ministry and the German Aircraft Industry, 1919–39,* p. 2.

51. Homze, *Luftwaffe,* p. 2. See also "Translation of Regular Information Bulletin No. 19: A Confidential Document of the French Sub-Secretary of State for Aeronautics, 18 Jan. 1921," in *Germany: A Compilation of Information for the Period August 1914 to May 1920,* p. 6, Smithsonian Institution, U.S. Air and Space Museum.

52. Völker, *Luftfahrt,* p. 130. Homze, *Luftwaffe,* p. 11. Walter Zürl, *Deutsche Flugzeugkonstrukteure: Werdegang und Erfolge unserer Flugzeug- und Flugmotorenbauer,* p. 94. *DLZ* 10 (22 December 1918). David Irving, *The Rise and Fall of the Luftwaffe: The Life of Field Marshall Erhard Milch,* p. 13.

53. "Bulletin no. 19: French Sub-Secretary of State for Aeronautics," *Germany: A Compilation,* pp. 11–28.

54. *Fs* 32–35 (1919–21). *IFW,* 1919–22. See commercial register in both journals.

55. Commission Interalliée de Controle Aéronautique en Allemagne, *Rapport technique,* vol. 1, *Avions, hydravions, aérostations, moteurs, et hélices.*

56. Press clipping, 25 July 1922, fol. no. 225, NE, BA.

57. USSdRLA to RdI, 18 July 1919, fol. no. 301; Euler to Verkehrsministerium, 8 October 1920, fol. no. 332; NE, BA. Hptm. Hermann von Wilamowitz-Möllendorff, "Frische Luft im Reichsluftamt," fol. no. 301, NE, BA.

58. Homze, *Luftwaffe,* p. 12.

Chapter 8

1. Albatros to KM/5M, 7 August 1914; KM/5M nos. 2927, 3511, 5421, 6531, 7680, 7681, 10.067, 10 August–27 November 1914; LSA no. 836/TA to KM, 4 December 1914; Flars no. 2832/I of 1917; KM; OK. Dr. Nemetz, "Die Militärluftfahrt Österreich-Ungarns im Jahre 1914, manuscript, pp. 44–47, fol. no. 3a, LA, OK.

2. LSA No. 645/TA to KM, 3 November 1914, LA, OK. Erich Kahlen,

"Die Entwicklung der Österreich-Ungarischen Fliegertruppe von 1914 bis 1916," manuscript (1942), pp. 4, 11, fol. no. 8, LA, OK. Ladislaus Madarasz, "Die k.u.k. Luftfahrtruppen im Weltkriege," *Luftflotten* 54 (July–October 1928): 551. *Statistische Angaben,* p. 35, fol. no. 19a; Flars no. 2832/I of 1917, fol. no. 324; LA, OK.

3. LSA nos. 167, 258/TA, 6518MVK, 1066TA, 241TA, 1146TA, 4997MVK, 14 August 1914–2 April 1915; KM/5M nos. 3710, 9259, 20073, 24, 5775, 11.388, 22 August 1914–10 April 1915; KM, OK. Österreichisches Bundesministerium für Heereswesen und Kriegsarchiv, ed., *Österreich-Ungarns letzter Krieg, 1914–1918,* 1:32.

4. KM/5M nos. 1785, 9597, 1686, 6232, 4278, 8525, 28 January–4 June 1915; LSA nos. 433MVK, 2066MVK, 699TA, 15,331TA, 23 January–28 May 1915; Skoda and Öffag to KM, 10 February, 5 March 1915; KpKM no. 1860/3.15.A71, 6 April 1915; KM,OK. KM/5L no. 174/1916, 7 June 1916, LA, OK.

5. KM/5M nos. 22509–10, 22193, 10, 30 December 1915, KM, OK. LFT nos. 2534/29, 2584/4, 28 November, 13 December 1915; LSA no. 6784MVK to LFT, 25 November 1915; LA, OK.

6. AOK no. 10.826 to KM, 2 June 1915, KM, OK.

7. LFT no. 258 to KM, 7 September 1915, LA, OK.

8. LSA nos. 4407, 5669 to LFT, 19, 22 November 1915; LFT no. 2497 to AOK, 22 November 1915; LA, OK. Flkmdo no. 659T to AOK, 4 January 1916, MAF, OK.

9. AOK no. 20.784, 22 January 1916, and app., LA, OK.

10. *Statistische Angaben,* p. 35, fol. 19a, LA, OK. CdGS no. 210 to KM, 22 January 1914, KM, OK. Madarasz "Luftfahrtruppen," pp. 543–47, charts.

11. KM/OK-MS Flug no. 772; Lohner no. 3928 to KM/MS, 7 January 1916; KM, OK.

12. KM/Abt. 10 nos. 120671, 15771, 1588, 38774, 20 January 1916–10 January 1917; KM/OK-MS Flug nos. 415, 517, 907, 14 February–7 April 1916; Honvedministerium no. 51647/4a–1916, 19 February 1916; Flars nos. 1217, 1108, 270, 3 April–15 September 1916; KM/5L nos. 6605, 752, 1472, 14 April–5 August 1916; KM Präsidialbüro no. 968, 29 May 1916; KM, OK.

13. For 1917 figures, see Flars no. 200, January 1917, KM, OK.

14. Ufag and Albatros to KM/MS, 17 July 1916; Albatros to Flars, 20 July 1916; KM Abt. 12MS no. 20386, 28 July 1916; Theodor Weichmann, report, 29 December 1916; KM/Abt. 10MS no. 422, 8 January 1917; MBA No. 1014/16 to KM/MS, 29 December 1916; KM, OK. Flars no. 1406/1916 to KM and app., 9 February 1917, LA, OK.

15. Information, 19 November 1916; Vertreter des KuK KM für Sicherstellung der Armeebedürfnisse, no. 1537 to KM/5L; AOK nos. 34.109 and app., 35.278, 10 December 1916; KM, OK. Protocol, 9 November 1916 conference, LA, OK.

16. Flars nos. 11952, 1406/1916, 223, 1330 and app., 2 January–11 October 1917; KM/5L no. 10193, 26 November 1917; KM, OK. Öffag, Phönix,

Ufag to KM/5L, 19 March–20 June 1917, LA, OK. Ufag 9701 to KM/MS, 15 October 1917; BA no. 989/17 to KM/MS, 16 October 1917; GIDL no. 204/s to KM/MS, 29 October 1917; Hansa-Brandenburg to KM/MS, 24, 29 November 1917; KM/Abt. 12 MS nos. 46501, 15 December 1917, 49695, 31 December 1917; MAF, OK.

17. LFT no. 2187 to KM, 17 July 1917; GIdL no. 3b to KM, 29 July 1917; KM/5L no. 6125, 2 August 1917; KM, OK.

18. LFT no. 883, 10 August 1917; KM/Abt. 10 no. 210398, 17 August 1917; KM/5L no. 6799, 13 September 1917; KM, OK.

19. Ernst Peter, "Die Entwicklung der Österreichischen Militarluftfahrt," pt. 2, "Von den ersten Flugparks zu den Luftstreitkräften 1918," *OMZ* 6 (1968): 421. Gerald D. Feldman, *Army, Industry, and Labor in Germany, 1914–1918,* pp. 190–94, 269.

20. *Statistische Angaben,* p. 35, fol. no. 19a, LA, OK.

21. Ibid., p. 30. Flars no. 326, 29 August 1917, LA, OK.

22. Oberleutnant Reichelt (Flars representative in Berlin), *Berechnung d. Arbeiterzahlen bei Erhöhung der Produktion,* 21 August 1917, fol. no. 324, LA, OK.

23. KM/5L No. 8260/17, 23 October 1917, KM, OK.

24. Ing. Karl Tindl, Flars Technische Auskunftei no. 126, "Bericht über die Studienreise zur Idflieg," 12–22 October 1917, fol. no. 325, LA, OK. Flars Technische Auskunftei no. 65, 26 October 1917, LA, OK.

25. Flars nos. 541, 323, 803, 927, 12 July–17 November 1917; AOK no. 92.160, 1 December 1917; LA, OK. KM/5L no. 8591, 29 October 1917; Ufag to KM/MS, 31 December 1917; KM, OK. Peter, "Militärluftfahrt," pt. 2, p. 421.

26. Flars Fzm No. 2884, meeting protocol of 11 December 1917, LA, OK.

27. Flars no. 21 to GIdL, 6 January 1918, fol. no. 324; GIdL no. 82, 23 January 1918; AOK no. 80.553 to GIdL, 2 March 1918, LA, OK.

28. Flars nos. 979 to KM, 18 February 1918, 274/18 to LFT, 4 March 1918; Ufag to LFT and KM/5L, 15 February 1918; LA, OK. KM/Abt. 12MS no. 39898, 21 October 1917, KM, OK.

29. KM/5L no. 384/int/1918 to Flars, 27 February 1918; Flars no. 265 to LFT, 1 March 1918; LFT no. 3667 to KM/5L, 27 February 1918; KM/Abt. 10 no. 56627 to LFT, 11 March 1918; LA, OK.

30. KM/Abt. 10 nos. 2200, 18 January 1918, 21.000/1918 to Flars, 18 February 1918; AOK nos. 97.561 to CdE, 29 April 1918, 250/1428 to LFT, 11 May 1918, 250/1428/II to CdE, 19 June 1918; LA, OK. KM/5L no. 5105, 1 May 1918; AOK nos. 97.713 to KM/5L, 193.615, 8 September 1918; KM, OK.

31. KM/Abt. 10MS no. 21635 to Flkmdo, 17 June 1918; Flkmdo no. 3677/F1 to KM/MS; KM, OK. CdAS no. 8061 DVI, 4 June 1918, stock no. 806, AM, MA.

32. MK no. 1370 to AOK, 2 March 1918; LFT no. 4355 to KM/5L and GIdL, 7 March 1918; GIdL no. 504/I, 13 March 1918; LA, OK.

33. Ernst von Wrisberg, *Wehr und Waffen* (Leipzig: Köhler, 1922), pp. 215, 230. Flars no. 541 to KM, 12 July 1917, KM, OK.

34. LFT nos. 1830, 9291, 10.386, 10385, 8 February–5 June 1918; Bevoll nos. 7359/23, 7359/Rei/P, 280 Lu/ZI, 15 June–2 August 1918; Flars no. 2596/2 to KM/5L, 18 May 1918; KM/5L no. 6450/1918 to LFT, 25 May 1918; LA, OK.

35. VO no. 116 to GIdL, 27 May 1918; KM/5L nos. 7900/1918, 1395, 6965, 5086/1918, 9541/1/1918, 13 June–30 August 1918; Bevoll nos. 7359/25Lu/Hi, 7634/2 Rei/P, 7634/2Ka/Le, 19 April–31 December 1918; LFT nos. 8091, 30 April 1918, 11963; LA, OK. MFB no. 1371, 2 July 1918; KM/Abt. 10MA no. 27172, 18 July 1918, MAF, OK.

36. Bevoll no. 7104/1 Lu/De to LFT, 19 February 1918; AOK nos. 99.645, 99.932, 194.292, 194.398, 30 July–6 September 1918; GIdL no. 1497/3, 10 August 1918; KM/5L no. 12113/18 to LFT, 9 September 1918; KM, OK.

37. Flars no. 4550 to LFT, 13 August 1918, KM, OK.

38. Bevoll nos. 6359, 7334 Rei/De, 8361 Rei/P, 8 December 1917–24 June 1918; Flars no. 5571/17 to LFT, 11 January 1918; KM/5L no. 10753/1917 to LFT, 31 January 1918; LA, OK.

39. "Denkschrift über den derzeitigen Stand und die Leistungsfähigkeit der Österreichischen Flugzeugindustrie," August 1918, app. to KM/5L no. 12113/18, 9 September 1918, KM, OK.

40. Einkaufskommission, reports April, May 1918; Metlitzky to LFT, 5 April 1918; AOK no. 98.940 to GIdL, 26 June 1918; LA, OK. KM/5L nos. 4886, 8492, 13514, 3 May–26 October 1918; Koluft der Ostarmee to GIdL in KM/5L no. 8492, 7 July 1918, KM, OK.

41. AOK no. 98.627, 7 June 1918; GIdL no. 1505; KM/5L no. 10.299, 24 August 1918; KM, OK.

42. *Angaben der Firmen,* KM/5L no. 1273/I; *Kommissionelle Besichtigung der Flugzeug u. Motoren-Firmen,* 29 July–3 August 1918; fol. no. 324, LA, OK.

43. KM/5L nos. 11.587, 12.000, 14286/1918, 28 August–11 October 1918, KM, OK.

44. *Statistische Angaben,* p. 35, fol. no. 19a, LA, OK.

45. *Mitteilungen des KK Österreichischen Aero-Klubs,* 1 January, 1 March 1919.

Conclusion

1. Georges Huisman, *Dans les coulisses de l'aviation, 1914–1918.* J. M. Spaight, *The Beginnings of Organized Air Power: A Historical Study.*

2. Rolf Dumke, "Comment," *JEH* 37, no. 1 (March 1977): 56–58.

3. Gerald D. Feldman, *Army, Industry, and Labor in Germany, 1914–1918,* p. 38.

4. M. H. Bauer, "Aus dem deutschen Flugzeugbau, 1914–1918," *Der Flieger,* 1953, p. 117.

5. Albert Étévé, *La victoire des cocardes*, pp. 147–48.

6. Harald Penrose, *British Aviation: The Great War and Armistice, 1915–1919*, p. 92.

7. See Appendix 1. On the French effort see Étévé, *Cocardes*, p. 150. On England, see Sir Walter Raleigh and H. A. Jones, *The War in the Air: Being the Story of the Part Played in the Great War by the Royal Air Force*, vol. 6, app. 1.

8. J. A. Gilles, *Flugmotoren, 1910 bis 1918*, pp. 60–72, 185–86.

9. Statistics on England are from Raleigh and Jones, *War*, vol. 6, app. 7. On France see Étévé, *Cocardes*, pp. 254, 305. On American production, see G. W. Mixter & H. H. Emmons, *U.S. Army Aircraft Production Facts*.

10. Raleigh and Jones, *War*, 6:28 nn. 2, 85. Étévé, *Cocardes*, p. 254.

11. BFW in October 1918 reported a labor force of 24.8 percent women and youth. II no. 55251, 17 October 1918, IL41/10, MA.

12. James M. Laux, "Gnome et Rhone: une firme de moteurs d'avion durant la grande guerre," in *Dix-neuf cent quatorze–dix-neuf cent dix-huit: l'autre front*, ed. Patrick Fridenson with J. J. Becker, p. 186. Étévé, *Cocardes* pp. 254, 276–77. Mixter and Emmons, *Production*, pp. 16–27. Raleigh and Jones, *War*, 6:28–51.

13. Gilles, *Flugmotoren*, p. 125. On Daimler, see Parliamentary Commission on War Deliveries, ninth session, 31 October 1917, pp. 44–46; thirteenth session, 15 February 1918, p. 35; K10–4/2540, AM, MA.

14. See Appendix 1.

15. *Atlas deutscher und ausländische Seeflugzeuge* (Warnemünde, 1918), statistical sheets, pp. 1–10. The English produced 2,578 seaplanes.

16. Alfred Müller, *Die Kriegsrohstoffbewirtschaftung 1914–1918 im Dienste des deutschen Monopolkapitals*, p. 22. Karl D. Seifert, *Geschäft mit dem Flugzeug: vom Weg der deutschen Luftfahrt*, pp. 23, 37.

17. Oberst Max Bauer, *Der Grosse Krieg in Feld und Heimat*, p. 231.

18. Ulrich Nocken, "Corporatism and Pluralism in Modern German History," in *Industrielle Gesellschaft und politisches System: beiträge zur politischen Sozialgeschichte*, ed. Dirk Stegman, B. J. Wendt, and P. C. Witt, pp. 37–56.

19. Robert A. Brady, *The Rationalization Movement in German Industry: A Study in the Evolution of Economic Planning*.

20. Edward L. Homze, *Arming the Luftwaffe*.

21. G. W. F. Hallgarten, *Das Wettrüsten: seine Geschichte zur Gegenwart*, pp. 119, 122.

22. Based on statistics in Gen. Ottokar Pflug's manuscript in the OK on weapons and munitions supply during the war.

23. Étévé, *Cocardes*, pp. 243–45.

24. Penrose, *Aviation: 1915–1919*, p. 467.

25. Gerhard Wissmann, "Imperialistische Krieg und technischwissenschaftlicher Fortschritt," *JFW 1962*, pt. 2, pp. 145–58.

26. Ernst Heinkel, *Stürmisches Leben*, p. 69.

27. Richard Blunck, *Hugo Junkers: ein Leben Für Technik und Luftfahrt*, p. 89.

28. On England, see Peter Fearon's articles, "The Formative Years of the British Aircraft Industry, 1913–1924," *Business History Review* 43, no. 4 (Winter 1969): 476–95; "The Vicissitudes of a British Aircraft Company: Handley Page Ltd. between the Wars," *Business History* 20, no. 1 January 1978): 63–86. See also Great Britain, Ministry of Munitions, *History of the Ministry of Munitions*, vol. 3, *Finance and Contracts*, pp. 121–22, 189–91.

Appendix 1

1. *Entwicklungsgeschichte des Flugzeugwesens: Statistik der Flugzeugfabriken, 1914–1918*, p. 150, IIL 234/32, MA. See also Walter Jost and Friedrich Felger, eds., *Was wir vom Weltkrieg nicht wissen*, p. 183. Commission Interalliée de Controle Aéronautique en Allemagne, *Rapport technique* (Chalais Meudon, 1922), 1:7.

2. Idflieg Akte 415 cited in KAdL, *Die Luftwaffe in der Abwehrschlacht zwischen Somme und Oise*, p. 4 n.4.

3. *Entwicklungsgeschichte*, pp. 80–148, IL 234/32, MA.

4. M. H. Bauer, "Aus dem deutschen Flugzeugbau, 1914–1918," *Der Flieger*, 1953, p. 117.

5. See note 2. Unfortunately, no figures were presented on August through November.

6. Commission Interalliée, *Rapport Technique*, vol. 1, pts. 2, 6. *Illustrierte Flug-Welt* 1, no. 12 (3 December 1919): 360. Peter Supf, *Das Buch der deutschen Fluggeschichte*, 2:450. Major a.D. Hilmer Freiherr von Bülow, *Geschichte der Luftwaffe: eine kurze Darstellung der fünften Waffe*, p. 128.

Bibliography

Unpublished Documents

Bayerisches Hauptstaatsarchiv, Department IV, Kriegsarchiv (BKA), Munich (Königlich bayerisches Kriegsministerium (KbKM): stock nos. MKr 1359–64, 1367, 1369–71, 1373–96.

Bundesarchiv (BA), Coblenz

(Nachlass August Euler (NE): vols. 1, 10, 11, 13, 15a, 16, 19–21, 23, 26–35, 45–52, 54–56, 59–67, 78–81, 220–28, 233, 235–81, 283, 288, 289, 293–301, 303, 311, 317, 331, 332, 338.

Bundesarchiv-Militärarchiv (MA), Freiburg

(Stock nos.: (Archiv der Marine [AM]) 804–06, 818, 861, 866, 867, 950, 1005, 1200, 3201, 4369, 4414, 4415, 4911, 5656, 5714, 6080, 6458, 6468–71, 7378, 7379, 7411, 7430–32, 7440, 7441, 7631–33, 7635.

Stock nos. IIL: (Reichsluftfahrtministerium, Kriegswissenschaftliche Abteilung der Luftwaffe [KAdL]) 234/1, /3, /5, /16, /24, /26, /32, /35, /37, /47, /48.

Stock nos. IL: (Reichsamt des Innern [RdI], Reichsverkehrsministerium) 2/26, /30, /35, /38, /41, /43, /45; (Grosser Generalstab [GG] 11–2/11, /12, /19, /21; (Königlich preussische Inspektion der Verkehrstruppen [IdV]) 25/32, /35, /36; (Königlich preussische General-Inspektion des Militär-Verkehrswesens [GIdMV]) 26/2, /6–9, /11, /12, /16, /18, /19, /24, /28, /29, /33, /34, /37, /39, /45, /46, /49, /50, /52, /58, /60, /65, /68, /75, /82, /83, /85, /87, /91, /93, /94, /108, /118, /131, /134; Königlich preussische Inspektion des Militär-Luft- und Kraftfahrwesens [IluK]) 27/1, /2, /11, /14, /17, /28, /37, /40, /51, /57, /68, /71, /82, /98; (Königlich preussische Inspektion der Fliegertruppen [IdFlieg]) 29/11, 30/1; (Königlich preussische Versuchs-Abteilung der Verkehrstruppen [VAdV]); 34/10, /13, /15, /17, /23, /26, /29, /31; (Königlich preussische Abteilung von der Verkehrstechnischen Pruefungskommission [VPK]) 35/4, /7–9, /13, /14; (Königlich bayerische Inspektion des Ingenieurkorps [II]) 41/1, /10, /14, /17, /30, /32, /33; (Königlich bayerische Inspektion des

Militär-Luft und Kraftfahrwesens [IMLuK]) 42/3, /6, /10, /14, /17, /28, /35, /43, /47, /50–52; (Königlich Inspektion des Militärluftfahrwesens [Iluft]) 43/3, /17, /24, /26, /31, /33, /37, /41, /42, /47, /48, /58, /59, /63, /67–69, /72, /75, /80, /84, /96, /98, /100, /102–4, /108, /109, /111, /112, /114, /115, /117; (Reichsarchiv, Luftstreitkräfte) 76/11, 91/1–4, /8, 92/3, 93/6, 96/1, 97/17–20.

Stock no. K10–4 (Archiv der Marine [AM]); /2532, /2540, /2550, /2563.

Stock no. L (Sammlung Luftwesen vor 1918): 05–1/1.

Deutsches Museum (DM), Munich

Nachlass Hermann Dorner (ND).

Österreichisches Kriegsarchiv (OK), Vienna

Kaiserlich und Königlich Kriegsministerium (KuK KM): documents for the years 1909–18.

Luftfahrtarchiv (LA), Kriegswissenschaftliche Abteilung der Luftwaffe, Vienna branch: folio nos. 3a, 8, 10, 12a, 16, 17, 19a, 32, 32a, 36, 37, 48, 50, 51, 55, 58, 148, 149a, 150, 153, 155, 163, 169, 170, 177, 324, 325; also eight cartons of uncataloged documents.

Marine Archiv, 3d Geschäftsgruppe, Flugwesen (MAF).

Documents for the years 1915–18.

Peter Grosz Collection (GC), Princeton, N. J.

Files on German and Austro-Hungarian aviation and aircraft industries, 1914–18.

Official Publications and Published Documents

Bayerische Flieger im Weltkrieg: ein Buch der Taten und Erinnerungen. Munich: Inspektion des bayerischen Luftfahrwesens, 1919.

Deutschen Waffenstillstands-Kommission. *Der Waffenstillstand 1918–1919: das Dokumenten-Material der Waffenstillstands-Verhandlungen von Compiegne, Spa, Trier, und Brüssel,* 3 vols. Berlin: Deutsche Verlags Gesellschaft für Politik und Geschichte, 1928.

Great Britain, Ministry of Munitions. *History of the Ministry of Munitions.* 12 Vols. London: His Majesty's Stationery Office, 1920–24.

Höppner, General Ernst von. *Deutschlands Krieg in der Luft: ein Rückblick auf die Entwicklung und die Leistungen unserer Heeres-Luftstreitkräfte im Weltkrieg.* Leipzig: Von Hase und Köhler, 1921.

Hösslin, Rittmeister a.D. Hubert von. *Die Organisation der K.B. Fliegertruppe, 1912–1919.* Edited by Bayerisches Kriegsarchiv. Munich: Verlag des Bayerischen Kriegsarchivs, 1924.

Kriegswissenschaftliche Abteilung der Luftwaffe. *Die Luftstreitkräfte in der Abwehrschlacht zwischen Somme und Oise vom 8. bis 12. August 1918 und Rückblicke auf ihre vorangegangene Entwicklung.* Berlin: Mittler und Sohn, 1942.

———. *Die Militärluftfahrt bis zum Beginn des Weltkrieges 1914.* 3 vols. 2d rev.

ed. Edited by Militärgeschichtliches Forschungsamt. Frankfort on the Main: Mittler und Sohn, 1965–66.

———. *Mobilmachung, Aufmarsch, und erster Einsatz der deutschen Luftstreitkräfte im August 1914.* Kriegsgeschichtliche Einzelschriften der Luftwaffe no. 3. Berlin: Mittler und Sohn, 1939.

Kriegswissenschaftliche Abteilung der Marine. *Atlas deutscher und ausländischer Seeflugzeuge.* 2 vols. Warnemünde: 1917–18.

Mixter, G. W., and Emmons, H. H. *U.S. Army Aircraft Production Facts.* Washington, D.C.: Government Printing Office, 1919.

Österreichisches Bundesministerium für Heereswesen und Kriegsarchiv. *Österreich-Ungarns letzter Krieg, 1914–1918.* 8 vols. Vienna: Verlag der Militärwissenschaftlichen Mitteilungen, 1931–38.

Raleigh, Sir Walter, and Jones, H. A. *The War in the Air: Being the Story of the Part Played in the Great War by the Royal Air Force.* 6 vols. Oxford: Oxford University Press, Clarendon Press, 1922–37.

Rangliste der Kaiserlich Deutschen Marine, 1913–1914. Berlin: Mittler und Sohn.

Rangliste der Königlich Preussischen Armee, 1911–1914. Berlin: Mittler und Sohn.

Reichsarchiv. *Der Weltkrieg 1914 bis 1918.* 17 vols. Berlin: Mittler und Sohn, 1925–44.

Reichstag. *Stenographische Berichte.* Vols. 261–305.

Memoirs

Bauer, Oberst Max. *Der grosse Krieg in Feld und Heimat: Erinnerungen und Betrachtungen.* Tübingen: Osiander'sche Buchhandlung, 1922.

Bodenschatz, Karl. *Jagd in Flanders Himmel: aus den sechzehn Kampfmonaten des Jagdgeschwaders Freiherr von Richthofen.* Munich: Knorr und Hirth, 1935.

Bölcke, Oswald. *Hauptmann Bölckes Feldberichte.* Gotha: Perthas, 1917.

Delbrück, Clemens von. *Die wirtschaftliche Mobilmachung in Deutschland, 1914.* Edited by Joachim von Delbrück. Munich: Verlag für Kulturpolitik, 1924.

Fokker, A. H. G. and Gould, Bruce. *Flying Dutchman: The Life of Anthony Fokker.* New York: Holt, Rinehart, and Winston, 1931.

Heinkel, Ernst. *Stürmisches Leben.* Edited by Jürgen Thorwald. Stuttgart: Mundus-Verlag, 1953.

Helfferich, Karl. *Der Weltkrieg.* 3 vols. Berlin: Ullstein, 1919.

Hirth, Hellmuth. *Zwanzigtausend Kilometer in Luftmeer.* Berlin: Braunbeck, 1913.

Immelmann, Franz. *Immelmann Der Adler von Lille.* Leipzig: K. F. Köhler, 1934.

Karman, Theodor von. *Die Wirbelstrasse: mein Leben für die Luftfahrt.* Hamburg: Hoffmann und Campe, 1968.

Ludendorff, Erich. *Meine Kriegserinnerungen, 1914–1918.* Berlin: Mittler und Sohn, 1919.

————, ed. *Urkunden der obersten Heeresleitung über ihre Tätigkeit, 1916 /18.* Berlin: Mittler und Sohn, 1920.

Richthofen, Rittmeister Manfred Frhrr. von. *Der rote Kampfflieger.* Berlin: Ullstein, 1917.

Siegert, Wilhelm. *Funken aus der Luftwaffen-Schmiede.* Berlin: Preussische Verlagsanstalt, 1919.

Tschudi, Georg von. *Aus vierunddreissig Jahren Luftfahrt: persönliche Erinnerungen.* Berlin: Reimar Hobbing, 1928.

Udet, Ernst. *Mein Fliegerleben.* Berlin: Ullstein, 1935.

Wrisberg, Generalmajor a.D. Ernst von. *Erinnerungen an die Kriegsjahre in königlich preussischen Kriegsministerium.* Vol. 2, *Heer und Heimat, 1914–1918;* vol. 3, *Wehr und Waffen.* Leipzig: Verlag von K. F. Köhler, 1921–22.

Secondary Literature

Akademie der Wissenschaften, Berlin, Institut für Geschichte. *Revolutionäre Ereignisse und Probleme in Deutschland während der Periode der grossen sozialistischen Oktoberrevolution, 1917 /1918.* Shriften des Instituts für Geschichte, ser. 1., vol. 6. Berlin: Akademie-Verlag, 1957.

Akademie der Wissenschaften, Berlin, Institut für Geschichte, Arbeitsgruppe erster Weltkrieg. *Deutschland im ersten Weltkrieg.* 3 vols. Berlin: Akademie-Verlag, 1968–69.

Armeson, Robert B. *Total Warfare and Compulsory Labor: A Study of the Military-Industrial Complex in Germany during World War I.* The Hague: Nijhof, 1964.

Arndt, Archivrat Maj. a.D. Hans. "Die Fliegerwaffe." In *Der Stellungkrieg, 1914–1918,* edited by Friedrich Seesselberg, pp. 310–69. Berlin: Mittler und Sohn, 1926.

————. "Die Fliegerwaffe im Weltkrieg." In *Ehrendenkmal der deutschen Armee und Marine,* edited by General der Infanterie a.D. Ernst von Eisenart-Rothe, pp. 281–95. Berlin and Munich: Deutscher National-Verlag AG, 1928.

————. "Der Luftkrieg." In *Der Weltkampf um Ehre und Recht,* edited by Generalleutnant Max Schwarte, 4:529–651. Leipzig: Alleinvertrieb durch Ernst Finking d.F., 1922.

Arz von Straussenberg, Arthur. *Kampf und Sturz der Mittelmächte.* Vienna: Günther, 1935.

Aubin, Hermann, and Zorn, Wolfgang. *Handbuch der deutschen Wirtschafts- und Sozialgeschichte.* Vol. 2. Stuttgart: Ernst Klett, 1976.

Auffenberg-Komarow, Moritz von. *Aus Österreichs Höhe und Niedergang.* Munich: Drei Masken Verlag, 1921.

Barclay, David E. "A Prussian Socialism? Wichard von Möllendorff and the Dilemma of Economic Planning in Germany, 1918–19," *Central European History* 11, no. 1 (March 1978): 50–82.

Baritsch, Dipl.-Ing. Karl. *Deutsche Industrien und der Krieg*. Hamburg: Verlag von Boysen und Maasch, 1915, 1916.

Bartel, Walter. *Die Linken in der deutschen Sozialdemokratie im Kampf gegen Militarismus und Krieg*. Berlin: Dietz Verlag, 1958.

Bathe, Rolf. "Deutschlands Luftstreitkräfte in der Sommeschlacht." *Deutsche Luftwacht, Luftwelt* edition 3, no. 6 (June 1936): 244–47.

———. "Von der Sommeschlacht bis zur Aisne-Champagne Schlacht." *Deutsche Luftwacht, Luftwelt* edition 3, no. 9 (September 1936:) 368–70.

Baumbach, Werner. *Zu Spät? Aufstieg und Untergang der deutschen Luftwaffe*. Munich: Richard Pflaum Verlag, 1949.

Baur, Rittmeister a.D. Fritz. *Wir Flieger! 1914–1918: der Krieg im Fliegerlichtbild*. Vienna: Selbstverlag, 1930.

Béjeuhr, Paul, ed. *Unser Krieg*. Vol. 1, *Der Luftkrieg: Luftkrieg / Luftschiffahrt / Flugwesen*. Dachau: Der Gelbe Verlag, 1915.

Benedikt, Heinrich. *Die wirtschaftliche Entwicklung in der Franz-Joseph-Zeit*. Vienna and Munich: Verlag Herold, 1958.

Bernhard, Georg. *Übergangswirtschaft*. Berlin: Verlag von Karl Sigismund, 1918.

Blaich, Fritz. *Kartell- und Monopolitik im kaiserlichen Deutschland: das Problem der Marktmacht im deutschen Reichstag zwischen 1879 und 1914*. Vol. 50. Beiträge zur Geschichte des Parlamentarismus und der politischen Parteien. Düsseldorf: Droste Verlag, 1973.

Bley, Hauptmann a.D. Wulf, ed. *Deutschland zur Luft*. Stuttgart: Friedrich Bahnenberger Verlag, 1936.

———. *Sie waren die ersten: Erstleistungen bei der Eroberung des Luftraumes*. Biberach: Köhlers Verlagsgesellschaft, 1953.

Blunck, Richard. *Hugo Junkers: ein Leben für Technik und Luftfahrt*. Düsseldorf: Econ-Verlag, 1951.

Bongartz, Heinz, ed. *Luftmacht Deutschland: Luftwaffe–Industrie–Luftfahrt*. Essen: Essener Verlagsanstalt GmbH, 1939.

Born, Karl Erich, ed. *Moderne deutsche Wirtschaftsgeschichte*. Neue wissenschaftliche Bibliothek. Cologne and Berlin: Kiepenheuer und Witsch, 1966.

Bosl, Karl. *Bayern im Umbruch: die Revolution von 1918, ihre Voraussetzungen, ihr Verlauf, und ihre Folgen*. Munich: R. Oldenbourg, 1969.

Brady, Robert A. *The Rationalization Movement in German Industry: A Study in the Evolution of Economic Planning*. New York: Fertig, 1974 [1933].

Brembach, Hellmuth, ed. *Adler über See: fünfzig Jahre deutscher Marineflieger*. Oldenburg and Hamburg: Gerhard Stalling Verlag, 1962.

Bruce, J. M. *British Aeroplanes, 1914–1918*. London: Putnam, 1957.

Brusatti, Alois, ed. *Die wirtschaftliche Entwicklung*. Vol. 1 of *Die Habsburgermonarchie, 1848–1918*, edited by Adam Wandruszka and Peter Urbanitsch. Vienna: Verlag der österreichischen Akademie der Wissenschaften, 1973.

Bry, Gerhard. *Wages in Germany, 1871–1945*. Princeton, N. J.: Princeton University Press, 1960.

Bülow, Major a.D. Hilmer Freiherr von. *Geschichte der Luftwaffe: eine kurze Darstellung der fünften Waffe.* Frankfort on the Main: Verlag Moritz Diensterweg, 1934.

Burdick, Charles B., and Lutz, Ralph H., eds. *The Political Institutions of the German Revolution, 1918–1919.* New York: Praeger, 1966.

Cesar, Wolfgang. "Die Luftfahrt in Deutschland." *Reichszentrale für Heimatdienst,* February 1926, GC.

Clark, Alan. *Aces High.* New York: Putnam, 1973.

Color Profiles of World War I Combat Planes. New York: Crescent Books, 1974.

Cramon, August von. *Unser österreichisch-ungarischer Bundesgenosse im Weltkrieg.* 2d ed. Berlin: Mittler und Sohn, 1921.

Cron, Hermann. *Geschichte des deutschen Heeres im Weltkriege, 1914–1918.* Berlin: Militärverlag Karl Sigismund, 1937.

Cuneo, John R. *Winged Mars.* 2 vols. Harrisburg, Pa.: Military Service Publishing Co., 1942, 1947.

Deist, Wilhelm. ed. *Militär und Innenpolitik im Weltkrieg, 1914–1918.* 2 vols. Quellen zur Geschichte des Parlamentarismus und der politischen Parteien, 2d series, vol. 1, pts. 1, 2. Düsseldorff: Droste Verlag, 1970.

Demeter, Karl. *The German Officer Corps in Society and State.* Rev. ed. Translated by Angus Malcolm. London: Weidenfeld and Nicolson, 1965.

Deutsch, Julius. *Geschichte der österreichischen Gewerkschaftsbewegung.* Vol. 2, *Im Weltkrieg und in der Nachkriegszeit.* Vienna: Wiener Volksbuchhandlung, 1932.

Dieckman, W. *Die Behördenorganisation in der deutschen Kriegswirtschaft, 1914–1918.* Schriften für kriegswirtschaftlichen Forschung und Schulung. Hamburg: Hanseatische Verlagsanstalt, 1937.

Dix, Arthur. *Wirtschaftskrieg und Kriegswirtschaft: zur Geschichte des deutschen Zusammenbruchs.* Berlin: Mittler und Sohn, 1920.

Dominik, Hans. *Unsere Luftflotten und Flieger: ihre Bedeutung und Verwendung.* Leipzig: Verlag von J. J. Arndt, n.d.

Dokumente und Materialien zur Geschichte der deutschen Arbeiterbewegung, 1914–1918. 2d ser., vols. 1, 2. Berlin: 1957, 1958.

Dornier, Claudius. "Fünfundzwanzig Jahre Dornier." *Deutsche Luftwacht, Luftwelt* edition 6, no. 3 (March 1939); 72–76.

Eberhardt, Generalleutnant Walter von, ed. *Unsere Luftstreitkräfte, 1914–1918: ein Denkmal deutschen Heldentums.* Berlin: Vaterländischer Verlag Weller, 1930.

Eckardt, Günther. *Industrie und Politik in Bayern, 1900–1919: der Bayerische Industriellen-Verband als Model des Einflusses von Wirtschaftverbänden.* Berlin: Duncker und Humblot, 1976.

"Ekkehard der deutschen Luftstreitkräfte: zum siebzigsten Geburtstag von Generalmajor Hermann von der Lieth-Thomsen, Der." *Deutsche Luftwacht, Luftwelt* edition 4, no. 4 (April 1937): 123–27.

Elze, Walter. "General Von Höppner: seine Stellung und seine Persönlichkeit."

Wehrwissenschaftliche Rundschau 16, no. 1 (January 1966); 560–61.

———. "Thomsen: der Grunder der Luftstreitkräfte (persönliche Erinnerungen)." *Wehrwissenschaftliche Rundschau* 16, no. 1 (January 1966), 561–62.

Étévé, Albert. *La victoire des cocardes.* Paris: R. Laffont, 1970.

Euler, August. *Der Fall Daimler: Denkschrift für die Geschichte der Luftfahrt.* Frankfort on the Main, 1918.

Faber, Kapitänleutnant. "Entwicklung und Ende des deutschen Seeflug- and Luftschiffwesens." *Marine Rundschau* 25 (October 1921): 410–17.

Fearon, Peter. "The Formative Years of the British Aircraft Industry, 1913–1924." *Business History Review* 43, no. 4 (Winter 1969): 476–95.

———. "The Vicissitudes of a British Aircraft Company: Handley Page Ltd. between the Wars." *Business History* 20 no. 1 (January 1978): 63–86.

Feldman, Gerald D. *Army, Industry, and Labor in Germany, 1914–1918.* Princeton, N. J.: Princeton University Press, 1966.

———. *Iron and Steel in the German Inflation, 1916–1923.* Princeton, N. J.: Princeton University Press, 1977.

Feuchter, Georg W. *Geschichte des Luftkrieges: Entwicklung und Zukunft.* Bonn: Athenaeum-Verlag, 1954.

Fighter Aircraft of the 1914–1918 War. Letchworth: Harleyford, 1960.

Fink, Carl. "Die Entwicklung des militärischen deutschen Luftbildwesens, 1911–1918." *Wehrwissenschaftliche Rundschau* 10, no. 7 (1960): 390–99.

Fischer, Fritz. *Germany's Aims in the First World War.* New York: W. W. Norton, 1967.

———. *Krieg der Illusionen: die deutsche Politik von 1911 bis 1914.* Düsseldorf: Droste Verlag, 1969.

Franke, Hermann, ed. "Die Luftwaffe." In *Handbuch der neuzeitlichen Wehrwissenschaften,* 3:151–85. Berlin: Mittler und Sohn, 1937.

Fredette, Raymond H. *The Sky on Fire: The First Battle of Britain, 1917–1918.* New York: Harcourt, Brace, Jovanovich, 1966.

Gersdorff, Ursula von. *Frauen im Kriegsdienst, 1914–1945.* Militärgeschichtliches Forschungsamt, Beiträge zur Militär- und Kriegsgeschichte, vol. 9. Stuttgart: Deutsche Verlags-Anstalt, 1969.

Gilles, J. A. *Flugmotoren, 1910 bis 1918.* Frankfort on the Main: Mittler und Sohn, 1971.

Göbel, Otto. *Deutsche Rohstoffwirtschaft im Weltkrieg, einschliesslich des Hindenburg-Programms.* Wirtschafts- und Sozialgeschichte des Weltkrieges, Deutsche Serie. Stuttgart: Deutsche Verlags-Anstalt, 1930.

Görlitz, Walter. *History of the German General Staff, 1657–1945.* Translated by Brian Battershaw. New York: Praeger, 1953.

Goodspeed, D. J. *Ludendorff: Genius of World War I.* Boston: Houghton Mifflin, 1966.

Gordon, Arthur. *Die Fliegerei.* Translated and edited by Georg Hensel and Günther Lohrengel. Gütersloh: Bertelsmann Verlag, 1964.

Gray, Peter, and Thetford, Owen. *German Aircraft of the First World War.* London: Putnam, 1962.

Grosz, Peter M. "Hannover Aircraft, 1915–1919." *Air Pictorial,* July 1971, pp. 252–56; August 1971, 290–93.

Grosz, Peter M., and Krüger, Egon. *Pfalz: First Detailed Story of the Company and Its Famous Planes.* West Roxbury, N. Y.: World War I Aero Publishers, 1964.

Gsell, Robert. *Fünfundzwanzig Jahre Luftkutscher: vom Luftsprung zur Luftherrschung.* Leipzig: Eugen Rentsch Verlag, 1936.

Günter, Adolf. *Vom Gleitflieger Lilienthals zu den Luftflotten Görings.* Stuttgart: Alemannen Verlag Albert Jauss, 1941.

Hackenberger, Willi. *Die alten Adler: Pioniere der deutschen Luftfahrt.* Munich: Lehmanns Verlag, 1960.

———. *Deutschlands Eroberung der Luft: die Entwicklung deutschen Flugwesens.* Berlin: Verlag Hermann Montanus, 1915.

Haddow, G. W., and Grosz, Peter M. *The German Giants: The Story of the R-planes, 1914–1919.* London: Putnam, 1962, 1969.

Hallgarten, G. W. F. *Imperialismus vor 1914.* 2 vols. Munich: Beck'sche Verlagsbuchandlung, 1951.

———. *Das Wettrüsten: seine Geschichte bis zur Gegenwart.* Frankfort on the Main: Europäische Verlagsanstalt, 1967.

Handbuch wirtschaftlicher Verbände und Vereine des deutschen Reiches, Jahrgang 1919. Berlin: Industrieverlag Späth und Linde, 1919.

Hardach, Karl. *Wirtschaftsgeschichte Deutschlands im zwanzigsten Jahrhundert.* Göttingen: Vanderhoeck und Ruprecht, 1976.

Hegener, Henri. *Fokker–The Man and the Aircraft.* Letchworth: Harleyford, 1961.

Henning, Friedrich-Wilhelm. *Das industrialisierte Deutschland, 1914 bis 1972.* Paderborn: Schöningh, 1974.

Herlin, Hans. *Udet–eines Mannes Leben und die Geschichte seiner Zeit.* Hamburg: Henri Nannen Verlag, 1958.

Herzfeld, Hans. *Die deutsche Rüstungspolitik vor dem Weltkriege.* Bonn and Leipzig: Kurt Schröder Verlag, 1923.

———. *Der erste Weltkrieg.* Munich: DTV, 1968.

Higham, Robin. *Air Power: A Concise History.* New York: St. Martin's Press, 1972.

———. *The British Rigid Airship, 1908–1931: A Study in Weapons Policy.* London: Foulis, 1961.

———. "Government, Companies, and National Defense: British Aeronautical Experience 1918–1945 as the Basis for a Broad Hypothesis." *Business History Review* 39 (1965): 323–47.

Higham, Robin, and Kipp, Jacob W. *Soviet Aviation and Air Power: A Historical View.* Boulder, Colo.: Westview Press, 1977.

Hillmann, Wilhelm. *Der Flugzeugbau Schütte-Lanz.* Berlin: Deutsche Verlagswerke Strauss, Vetter und Co., n.d.

Hinterstoisser, Franz. *Fünfundzwanzig Jahre Luftfahrt.* Vienna: Verlag von Strefflewis Militärische Zeitschrift, 1915.

Hinterthür, Theodor, ed. *Kriegsstellen und Kriegsgesellschaften für das deutsche Reich und für Bayern sowie die Kommunalen Kriegsorganisationen für München.* Munich: Verlag Chr. Kaiser, 1917.

Holley, I. B., Jr. *Ideas and Weapons.* New Haven, Conn.: Yale University Press, 1953.

Homze, Edward L. *Arming the Luftwaffe: The Reich Air Ministry and the German Aircraft Industry, 1919–39.* Lincoln: University of Nebraska Press, 1976.

Hoppe, Hermann. *Die Notwendigkeit und Bedeutung der kriegswirtschaftlichen Massnahmen.* Wirstiz: Verlag von A. Spieker, 1918.

Hubatsch, Walter. *Deutschland im Weltkrieg, 1914–1918.* Frankfort on the Main and Berlin: Ullstein, 1966.

Huisman, Georges. *Dans les coulisses de l'aviation, 1914–1918.* Paris: Renaissance du Livre, 1921.

Hürten, Heinz, and Meyer, Georg. *Adjutant im preussischen Kriegsministerium, Juni 1918 bis Oktober 1919: Aufzeichnungen des Hauptmanns Gustav Böhm.* Militärgeschichtliches Forschungsamt, Beiträge zur Militär- und Kriegsgeschichte, vol. 19. Stuttgart: Deutsche Verlagsanstalt, 1977.

Illustrierter Beobachter: Flugzeug macht Geschichte. Munich: Verlag Franz Eher Nachfolger, 1939.

Imrie, Alex. *Pictorial History of the German Army Air Service, 1914–1918.* Chicago: Henry Regnery Co., 1973.

Institut für Konjunkturforschung, Berlin. *Industrielle Mobilmachung: Statistische Untersuchungen.* Edited by Maj. Privat Dozent Kurt Hesse. Schriften zur Kriegswissenschaftlichen Forschung und Schulung. Hamburg: Hanseatische Verlagsanstalt, 1936.

Irving, David. *The Rise and Fall of the Luftwaffe: The Life of Field Marshall Erhard Milch.* Boston: Little, Brown and Co., 1973.

Italiaander, Rolf. *Spiel und Lebensziel: der Lebensweg des ersten deutschen Motorfliegers, Hans Grade.* Berlin: Gustav Weise Verlag, 1939.

Jablonski, Edward. *The Knighted Skies: A Pictorial History of World War I in the Air.* New York: Putnam, 1964.

Jäger, Hans. *Unternehmer in der deutschen Politik, 1890–1918.* Bonner historische Forschungen, vol. 30. Bonn: Ludwig Röhrscheid Verlag, 1967.

Jahn, Arthur, ed. *Die Luftwaffe, 1918.* Berlin: Verlag Gustav Braunbeck, 1918.

Jahrbuch der Luft-Fahrzeug-Gesellschaft. Vol. 6, *1912–1913.* Berlin: Verlag von Julius Springer, 1913.

Joachimczyk, Alfred Marcel. *Moderne Flugmaschinen.* Berlin: Verlag Klasing und Co., 1914.

Jones, Neville. *The Origins of Strategic Bombing: A Study of the Development of*

British Air Strategic Thought up to 1918. London: Kimber, 1973.

Jost, Walter, and Felger, Friedrich, eds. *War wir vom Weltkrieg nicht wissen.* 2d ed. Leipzig: Fikentscher Verlag, 1938.

Kälble, Harmut. *Industrielle Interessenpolitik in der Wilhelminischen Gesellschaft: Centralverband deutscher Industrieller, 1895–1914.* Veröffentlichungen der historischen Kommission zu Berlin beim Friedrich-Meinecke-Institut der freien Universität Berlin, vol. 27. Berlin: de Gruyter, 1967.

Kameradschaft der Luft: Festschrift anlässlich des fünfzigsten Geburtstages von Dr.-Ing. E. H. Dr. Phil. Ernst Heinkel. Berlin: Wiking Verlag, n.d.

Kann, Robert A. . *The Habsburg Empire: A Study in Integration and Disintegration.* New York: Praeger, 1957.

Király, Béla K.; and Fichtner, Paula S. *The Habsburg Empire in World War I: Essays on the Intellectual, Military, Political, and Economic Aspects of the Habsburg War Effort.* New York: Columbia University Press, 1977.

Kempe, Erich, and Brosek, Hugo. *Geschichte und Technik des Luftfahrwesens.* Stuttgart: Verlag von H. D. Sperling, 1919.

Kerchnave, Generalmajor a.D. Hugo. *Die unzureichende Kriegsrüstung der Mittelmächte als Hauptursache ihrer Niederlage.* Supplementary vol. 4 to *Österreich-Ungarns letzter Krieg.* Vienna: Verlag der Militärischen Mitteilungen, 1932.

Kessler, Harry Graf. *Walther Rathenau: sein Leben und sein Werk.* Wiesbaden: Rheinische Verlags-Anstalt, 1963.

Kessler, Oberlt. zur See Ulrich, "Ist die Organisation der Luftwaffe als dritter selbständige Streitkraft berechtigt?" *Marine Rundschau* 29 (July 1924): 189–208.

Kielmansegg, Peter Graf. *Deutschland und der erste Weltkrieg.* Frankfort on the Main: Akademische Verlagsgesellschaft Athenaion, 1968.

Killen, John. *The Luftwaffe: A History.* London: Frederick Mueller, 1967.

Kilmarx, Robert A. *A History of Soviet Air Power.* New York: Praeger, 1962.

Kitchen, Martin. *The Silent Dictatorship: The Politics of the German High Command under Hindenburg and Ludendorff, 1916–1918.* London: Croom/ Helm, 1976.

Kluge, Ulrich. *Soldatenräte und Revolution: Studien zur Militärpolitik in Deutschland, 1918–1919.* Göttingen: Vanderhoeck und Ruprecht, 1975.

Kocka, Jürgen. *Klassengesellschaft im Krieg, 1914–1918: Deutsche Sozialgeschichte, 1914–1918.* Kritische Studien zur Geschichtswissenschaft, vol. 8. Göttingen: Vanderhoeck und Ruprecht, 1973.

Köhler, Karl, "Auf dem Wege zur Luftwaffe." *Wehrwissenschaftliche Rundschau* 16, no. 1 (January 1966): 553–59.

———, ed. *Die Bibliographie zur Luftkriegsgeschichte.* Compiled in Militärgeschichtliches Forschungsamt. Frankfort on the Main: Mittler und Sohn, 1966.

———. "Konventionelle Luftkriegführung, 1914." *Marine Rundschau* 65, no. 6 (1968): 440–43.

Krüger, Peter. *Deutschland und die Reparationen 1918 /19: die Genesis des Reparationsproblems in Deutschland zwischen Waffenstillstand und versailler Friedensschluss.* Stuttgart: Deutsche Verlags-Anstalt, 1973.

Kuhl, Gen. d. Infanterie a.D. Von. "Der Generalstab im Weltkriege," *Ehrendenkmal der deutschen Armee und Marine.* Berlin und Munich: Deutscher National-Verlag, 1928.

Landes, David S. *The Unbound Prometheus: Technological Change and Industrial Development in Western Europe from 1750 to the Present.* Cambridge: Cambridge University Press, 1969.

Langsdorff, Werner J. *Flieger am Feind: einundsiebzig deutscher Luftfahrer erzählen.* Gütersloh: Bertelsmann, n.d.

Laux, James M. "Gnome et Rhone: une firme de moteurs d'avion durant la grande guerre." In *Dix-neuf cent quatorze–dix-neuf cent dix-huit: l'autre front,* edited by Patrick Fridenson with J. J. Becker. Paris: Les éditions ouvrières, 1975.

———. "The Rise and Fall of Armand Deperdussin." *French Historical Studies* 8, no. 1 (Spring 1973); 95–104.

Lemmen, Kapitänleutnant a.D., and Nedden, Oberleutnant zur See a.D. "Das Marine Flugwesen." In *Unsere Marine im Weltkriege 1914–1918,* edited by Vizeadmiral a.D. Dr. ess. Eberhard von Montey, pp. 401–24. Berlin: Vaterländischer Verlag Weller, 1927.

Lloyd, John. *Aircraft of World War I.* London: Ian Allan Ltd., 1958.

Lorenz, Charlotte, *Die gewerbliche Frauenarbeit während des Krieges.* Stuttgart, Berlin, and Leipzig: Deutsche Verlags-Anstalt, 1928.

Lüders, Marie-Elisabeth. *Das unbekannte Heer: Frauen kämpfen für Deutschland, 1914–1918.* Berlin: Mittler und Sohn, 1936.

"Luftfahrzeug" GmbH. Berlin, 1913.

Der Luftschiffbau Zeppelin und seine Tochtergesellschaften. Berlin and Halensee: Verlag M. Schröder, ca. 1925.

Lutz, Ralph H. *The German Revolution, 1918–1919.* Stanford University Publications in History, Economics and Political Science, vol. 1, no. 1. Stanford, Calif.: Stanford University Press, 1922.

———, ed. *The Causes of the German Collapse in 1918.* Hoover War Library Publications, no. 4. Stanford, Calif.: Stanford University Press, 1954.

———, ed. *Fall of the German Empire, 1914–1918.* 2 vols. Hoover War Library Publications, nos. 1, 2. Stanford, Calif.: Stanford University Press, 1932.

Madarasz, Ladislaus. "Die Kuk Luftfahrtruppen im Weltkriege." Translated by Eugen Buttner. *Militärwissenschaftliche Mitteilungen,* special volume *Luftflotten,* 59 (1928): 543–47.

Marine Aircraft of the 1914–1918 War. Letchworth: Harleyford, 1966.

Mason, Herbert Molloy, Jr. *The Rise of the Luftwaffe: Forging the Secret German Air Weapon, 1918–1940.* New York: The Dial Press, 1973.

Mauersberg, Hans. *Deutsche Industrien im Zeitgeschehen eines Jahrhunderts.* Stuttgart: Gustav Fischer, 1966.

May, Arthur J. *The Habsburg Monarchy, 1867–1914.* New York: Norton, 1951, 1968.

———. *The Passing of the Habsburg Monarchy, 1914–1918.* 2 Vols. Philadelphia: University of Pennsylvania Press, 1966.

Meesman, Paul. *Der Kriegsausgang und die deutsche Industrie.* Mainz: Verlag des Mittelrheinischen Fabrikanten Vereins, 1917.

Meitens, Emil. *Die Flieger-Abteilung (A) 235 im Weltkriege.* Zeulenroda: Bernard Sporn, 1928.

Meyer, Willy. *Von Wright bis Junkers: das erste Vierteljahrhundert Menschenflug, 1903–1928.* Berlin: Deutsche Verlagsgesellschaft für Politik und Geschichte, 1928.

Militärgeschichtliches Forschungsamt, ed. "Organisationsgeschichte der Luftwaffe von den Anfängen bis 1918." In *Handbuch zur deutschen Militärgeschichte,* 1648–1939, 3d ed., pt. 5, pp. 281–311, 356–58. Frankfurt on the Main: Bernard und Gräfe Verlag für Wehrwesen, 1968.

Miller, Susanne. *Die Regierung der Volksbeauftragten, 1918/19.* Quellen zur Geschichte des Parlamentarismus und der politischen Parteien, vol. 6, pts. 1, 2. Düsseldorf: Droste, 1969.

Moll, Hermann. "Das deutsche Marineflugzeug von 1918 bis 1944." *Marine Rundschau* 54, no. 2, 48–59, 109–16.

———. "Das deutsche Marine- und Seeflugzeug von 1909 bis 1918," *Marine Rundschau* 55 (1958): 168–81.

Müllenbach, Herbert. *Eroberung der Luft: vom "Fliegenden Menschen" zum "Grossen Dessauer."* Munich: Zentral-Verlag der NSDAP, ca. 1941.

Müller, Alfred. *Die Kriegsrohstoffbewirtschaftung 1914–1918 im Dienste des deutschen Monopolkapitals.* Berlin: Akademie-Verlag, 1955.

Müller-Breslau, Professor Heinrich. *Die deutsche Technik im Weltkriege.* Leipzig: Verlag "Naturwissenschaften," 1916.

Musciano, Walter A. *Eagles of the Black Cross.* New York: Ivan Obolensky, 1965.

Neumann, Georg Paul. *Die deutschen Luftstreitkräfte im Weltkriege.* Berlin: Mittler und Sohn, 1920.

———. *Deutsches Kriegsflugwesen.* Leipzig: Velhagen und Klasing, 1917.

———. *Flugzeuge.* Leipzig: Velhagen und Klasing, 1912/13.

Nimführ, Dr. Raimund. *Die Luftfahrt: ihre wissenschaftlichen Grundlagen und technische Entwicklung.* Leipzig: Teubner, 1913.

Norman, Aaron. *The Great Air War.* New York: The Macmillan Co,. 1968.

Nowarra, Heinz J. "Die alten Adler: aus den Anfangstagen der deutschen Flieger." *Jahrbuch des Luftwaffe* 4 (1967): 108–14.

———. *Die Entwicklung der Flugzeuge, 1914–1918.* Munich: Lehmanns, 1959.

———. *Fünfzig Jahre deutsche Luftwaffe, 1910–1960.* Vol. 1., *1910–1918.* Berlin: Eigenverlag, 1961; Genoa; Interconair, 1964, 1967.

Nuss, Karl. *Militär und Wiederaufrüstung in der Weimarer Republik.* Berlin: VEB, 1977.

Nussbaum, Helga, and Zumpe, Lotte, eds. *Wirtschaft und Staat in Deutschland: eine Wirtschaftsgeschichte des staatsmonopolistischen Kapitalismus in Deutschland vom Ende des neunzehnten Jahrhunderts bis 1945.* Vols. 1, 2. Vaduz, Liechtenstein: Topos Verlag, 1978.

Olszewski und von Elgott, Helmrich. *Das Flugzeug in Heer und Marine: handbuch über das gesamte Gebiet des Militärflugwesens.* Berlin: Schmidt, 1912.

Opel, Fritz. *Der deutsche Metallarbeiter-Verband während des ersten Weltkrieges und der Revolution.* Hannover: Norddeutsche Verlagsanstalt Gödel, 1958.

Otto, Helmut, Schmiedel, Karl; and Schnitter, Helmut. *Der erste Weltkrieg.* Berlin: Deutscher Militär Verlag, 1968.

Peball, Kurt, ed. *Conrad von Hötzendorff: private Aufzeichnungen: erste Veröffentlichungen aus den Papieren des Kuk Generalstabs-Chefs.* Vienna and Munich: Amalthea Verlag, 1977.

Penrose, Harald. *British Aviation: The Great War and Armistice, 1915–1919.* London: Putnam, 1969.

———. *British Aviation: The Pioneer Years, 1903–1914.* London: Putnam, 1967.

Peter, Ernst. "Die Entwicklung der österreichischen Militärluftfahrt." Pt. 1, "Die Kuk Luftschiffertruppe bis 1911." *Österreichische Militär Zeitschrift,* special volume (1965) no. 1, pp. 47–56.

———. "Die Entwicklung der österreichischen Militärluftfahrt." Pt. 2, "Von den ersten Flugparks zu den Luftstreitkräften 1918." *Österreichische Militär Zeitschrift* 6 (1968): 415–23.

Peters, Klaus. "Zur Entwicklung der österreichisch-ungarischen Militärluftfahrt von den Anfängen bis 1915." Ph.D. diss., University of Vienna, 1971.

Philipp, Dr. G. "Deutschlands Flugzeugführer Nr. 1 siebzigsten Geburtstag." *Deutsche Luftwacht, Luftwelt* edition 5, No. 12 (December 1938): 407–10.

Pinner, Felix. *Deutsche Wirtschaftsführer.* Charlottenburg: Verlag der Weltbühne, 1925.

Poturzyn, Hptm. a.D. Fischer von, ed. *Junkers und die Weltluftfahrt: ein Beitrag zur Entstehungsgeschichte deutscher Luftgeltung, 1909–1934.* Munich: Pflaum Verlag, 1935.

Radandt, Hans. "Hugo Junkers—ein Monopolkapitalist und korrespondierendes Mitglied der preussischen Akademie der Wissenschaften." *Jahrbuch für Wirtschaftsgeschichte, 1960,* pt. 1, pp. 53–135.

Rakenius, Gerhard W. *Wilhelm Gröner als erster Generalquartiermeister: die Politik der obersten Heeresleitung, 1918/19.* Militärgeschichtliches Forschungsamt, Militärgeschichtliche Studien, vol. 23. Boppard on the Rhine: Harold Boldt Verlag, 1977.

Reconnaissance and Bomber Aircraft of the 1914–1918 War. Letchworth: Harleyford, 1962.

Redlich, Josef. *Austrian War Government.* New Haven, Conn.: Yale University Press, 1929.

Regele, Oskar. *Feldmarschall Conrad: Auftrag und Erfüllung, 1906–1918.* Vienna and Munich: Verlag Herold, 1955.

Reichert, Jakob Wilhelm. *Wirtschaftspolitische Industrieverbände.* Berlin: Staatspolitische Verlag, n.d.

Reyper, Julius. *Graf Zeppelin und sein Werk.* Leipzig: Verlag von Dr. Max Gehlen, 1919.

Reynolds, Quentin. *They Fought for the Sky.* New York: Holt, 1957.

Ritter, Gerhard. *The Sword and the Scepter: The Problem of Militarism in Germany.* Translated by Heinz Norden. 4 vols. Coral Gables, Fla.: University of Miami Press, 1969–73.

[Ritter, Hans]. *Kritik des Weltkrieges: das Erbe Moltkes und Schlieffens im grossen Kriege.* Leipzig: Verlag von Köhler, 1920.

Ritter, Hans. *Der Luftkrieg.* Berlin and Leipzig: Verlag von Köhler, 1926.

Robertson, Bruce. *Sopwith–The Man and His Aircraft.* Letchworth: Harleyford, 1970.

Robinson, Douglas H. *Giants in the Sky: A History of the Rigid Airship.* Seattle: University of Washington Press, 1973.

————. *The Zeppelin in Combat: A History of the German Naval Airship Division, 1912–1918.* London: Foulis, 1962.

Rothenberg, Gunther E. *The Army of Francis Joseph.* West Lafayette, Ind.: Purdue University Press, 1976.

Rotth, August. *Wilhelm von Siemens: ein Lebensbild.* Berlin and Leipzig: de Gruyter, 1922.

Rumpler-Werke AG, 1908–1918, Die. Berlin: Ecksteins Biographischer Verlag, 1919.

Schiller, Hans von. *Zeppelin: Wegbereiter des Weltluftverkehrs.* Bad Godesberg: Kirschbaum, 1966.

Schmidt, Justus. *Kriegswichtige Industrie im System der Wirtschaftspolitik.* Berlin: Obelisk, 1937.

Schröter, Alfred. *Krieg-Staat-Monopol, 1914–1918.* Berlin: Akademie-Verlag, 1965.

Schutzinger, Heinrich. *Graf Zeppelin und der Bodensee.* Frauenfeld: Huber, 1918.

Schwerin von Krosigk, Lutz Graf. *Die grosse Zeit des Feuers: der Weg der deutschen Industrie.* Vols. 2, 3. Tübingen: Rainer Wunderich Verlag Hermann Lens, 1958, 1959.

Seifert, Karl Dieter. *Geschäft mit dem Flugzeug: vom Weg der deutschen Luftfahrt.* Berlin: VEB, 1960.

————. "Das grosse Geschäft: Anfang und Weg der imperialistischen deutschen Flugzeugindustrie." *Flügel der Heimat* 7, no. 11 (November 1958): 24–26.

Sieg der deutschen Technik, Der, Berlin: Kriegs-Presse-Amt, 1917.

Siemens, Georg. *Carl Friedrich von Siemens: ein grosser Unternehmer.* Munich: Karl Alber, 1960.

Silberstein, Gerard E. *The Troubled Alliance: German-Austrian Relations, 1914–1917.* Lexington: University Press of Kentucky, 1970.

Sokol, Hans, H. *Österreich-Ungarns Seekrieg, 1914–1918.* 2 vols. Vienna: Amalthea Verlag, 1933.

Solff, Oberleutnant a.d. K. *Motorluftschiffe und Flugmaschinen.* Berlin: Hillger, 1910.

Spaight, J.M. *The Beginnings of Organized Air Power: A Historical Study.* London: Longmans, Green, 1927.

Spindler, Max, ed. *Handbuch der bayerischen Geschichte.* Vol. 3, pt. 2, *Das neue Bayern, 1800–1970.* Munich: Beck'sche Verlagsbuchhandlung, 1975.

Stegmann, Dirk; Wendt, B.-J.; and Witt, P. C., eds. *Industrielle Gesellschaft und politisches System: Beiträge zur politischen Sozialgeschichte.* Bonn: Neue Gesellschaft, 1978.

Stenkewitz, Kurt. *Gegen Bajonett und Dividende: die Politische Krise in Deutschland am Vorabend des ersten Weltkrieges.* Schriftenreihe des Instituts für deutsche Geschichte an der Karl-Marx-Universität Leipzig. Berlin: Rütten und Löning, 1960.

Supf, Peter. *Das Buch der deutschen Fluggeschichte.* 2d ed. 2 Vols. Stuttgart: Drei Brunnen Verlag, 1956, 1958.

———. "Der Schöpfer der Blitzflugzeuge: Professor Dr. Ernst Heinkel: Fünfzig Jahre." *Deutsche Luftwacht, Luftwelt* edition 5, no. 1 (February 1938): 36–38.

Swoboda, Erich. *Igo Etrich und seine "Taube."* Vienna: Zweigstelle Wien der kriegswissenschaftlichen Abteilung der Luftwaffe, 1942.

Thomsen, Hermann von der Lieth-. "Die Luftwaffe vor und im Weltkriege." In *Die Deutsche Wehrmacht, 1914–1939: Rückblick und Ausblick,* edited by George Wetzell, pp. 487–527. Berlin: Mittler und Sohn, 1939.

Umbreit, Paul. *Die deutschen Gewerkschaften im Kriege.* Berlin: Deutsche Verlags-Anstalt, 1928.

Unsere Luftstreitkräfte. Berlin: Kriegs-Presse-Amt, 1918.

Unsere Luftwaffe: Jahrbuch des Luftfahrerdank. e. V. 1917. Leipzig: Kunstverlag "Bild und Karte," 1917.

Ursachen und Folgen: vom deutschen Zusammenbruch 1918 und 1945. Vols. 1–4. Berlin: Dokumenten-Verlag Dr. Herbert Wendler, 1958–60.

Völker, Karl-Heinz. *Dokumente und Dokumentarfotos zur Geschichte der deutschen Luftwaffe.* Militärgeschichtliches Forschungsamt, Beiträge zur Militär- und Kriegsgeschichte, vol. 9. Stuttgart: Deutsche Verlags-Anstalt, 1968.

———. *Die Entwicklung der militärischen Luftfahrt in Deutschland, 1920–1933.* Militärgeschichtliches Forschungsamt, Beiträge zur Militär- und Kriegsgeschichte, vol. 3. Stuttgart: Deutsche Verlags-Anstalt, 1962.

———. "Die Generalstabchefs der deutschen Luftwaffe, 1916–1945." *Jahrbuch der Luftwaffe* 5 (1968): 124–29.

———. "Zur fünfzig jährigen Geschichte der Führungsorganisation deutscher Luftwaffe." *Jahrbuch der Luftwaffe* 3 (1966): 118–23.

Vogelsang, C. Walther. *Die deutschen Flugzeuge im Wort und Bild*. Pt. 2. 2d ed. Berlin-Charlottenburg: Volckmann, 1914.

Voisin, A. P. *La doctrine de l'aviation française de combat au cours de la guerre (1915–1918)*. Paris: Berger-Levrault, 1932.

Wagner, Walter. *Die obersten Behörden der Kuk Kriegsmarine, 1856–1918*. Vienna: Ferdinand Berger, 1961.

Warplanes and Air Battles of World War I. New York: Beekman House, 1973.

Weber, Fritz. *Das Ende der alten Armee*. Salzburg: Bergland, 1955.

Wentscher, Bruno, ed. *Deutsche Luftfahrt*. Berlin: Deutsche Wille, 1925.

Werner, Johannes. *Knight of Germany, Oswald Bölcke: German Ace*. Translated by Claude Sykes. London: Hamilton, 1933.

Weyl, A. R. *Fokker: The Creative Years*. Edited by J. M. Bruce. London: Putnam, 1965.

Wiedenfeldt, Kurt. *Die Organisation der Kriegrohstoffbewirtschaftung im Weltkrieg*. Vol. 1 of *Rohstoff- und Energie-Wirtschaft im Kriege*, pp. 7–62. Hamburg: Hanseatische Verlagsanstalt, 1936.

Wilamowitz-Möllendorff, Hptm. a.D. Herrmann von. "Die Luftwaffe." In *Das deutsche Wehrwesen in Vergangenheit und Gegenwart*, pp. 415–72. Stuttgart and Berlin: Konradin-Verlag, 1936.

Williamson, John G. *Karl Helfferich, 1872–1924: Economist, Financier, Politician*. Princeton, N. J.: Princeton University Press, 1971.

Wissmann, Gerhard. *Geschichte der Luftfahrt von Ikarus bis zur Gegenwart: eine Darstellung der Entwicklung des Fluggedankens und der Luftfahrttechnik*. Berlin: VEB, 1964.

———. "Imperialistische Krieg und technischwissenschaftlicher Fortschritt." *Jahrbuch für Wirtschaftsgeschichte, 1962*, pt. 2, pp. 145–58.

Wood, Derek, and Dempster, Derek. *The Narrow Margin: The Battle of Britain and The Rise of Air Power, 1930–1940*. New York: McGraw Hill, 1961.

Wrisberg, Gen. a.D. Ernst von. "Das Kriegsministerium im Weltkriege." In *Ehrendenkmal der deutschen Armee und Marine*, edited by General der Infanterie a.D. Ernst von Eisenart-Rothe, pp. 204–10. Berlin and Munich: Deutscher National-Verlag, 1928.

Wurtzbacher, Generalmajor Ludwig. "Die Versorgung des Heeres mit Waffen und Munition." In *Der Weltkampf um Ehre und Recht*, edited by Generalleutnant Max Schwartze, 6:69–146. Leipzig: Ernst Finking, 1922.

Zeman, Z. A. B. *Twilight of the Habsburgs: The Collapse of the Austro-Hungarian Empire*. New York: American Heritage, 1971.

Zimmermann, Waldemar. "Die Veränderungen der Einkommens- und Lebensverhältnisse der deutschen Arbeiter durch den Krieg." In *Die Einwirkung des Krieges auf Bevölkerungsbewegung, Einkommen, und Lebenshaltung in Deutschland*, by Waldemar Zimmermann, Rudolf Meerwarth, and Adolf Günther, pp. 281–474. Stuttgart, Berlin and Leipzig: Deutsche Verlags-Anstalt, 1932.

Zürl, Walter. *Deutsche Flugzeugkonstrukteure: Werdegang und Erfolge unserer Flugzeug- und Flugmotorenbauer.* 3d ed. Munich: Pechstein, 1942.

———. *Pour le mérite-Flieger.* Munich: Pechstein, 1938.

Periodicals

Deutsche Luftfahrer Zeitschrift 12–24 (1909–20).

Flug–Amtliches Organ des deutschen Fliegerbundes, 1917–18.

Flugsport 1–13 (1908–1921).

Illustrierte Flug Welt (Illustriere Flug Woche), 1–3 (1919–21).

Luftflotte 1–8 (1909–16).

Zeitschrift für Flugtechnik und Motorluftschiffahrt 8–10 (1917–19).

Index